D1480974

CHILDREN'S SIBLING RELATIONSHIPS

Developmental and Clinical Issues

CHILDREN'S SIBLING RELATIONSHIPS
Developmental and Clinical Issues

Edited by

Frits Boer
University of Leiden, The Netherlands

Judy Dunn
The Pennsylvania State University

IEA LAWRENCE ERLBAUM ASSOCIATES, PUBLISHERS
1992   Hillsdale, New Jersey   Hove and London

Lawrence Erlbaum Associates, Inc., Publishers
365 Broadway
Hillsdale, New Jersey 07642

Cover design by Rosalind Orland

Library of Congress Cataloging-in-Publication Data

Children's sibling relationships : developmental and clinical issues /
edited by Frits Boer, Judy Dunn.
    p.   cm.
    Based on the First International Symposium "Brothers and Sisters,"
Research on Sibling Relationships, Therapeutic Applications, held in
Leiden, Netherlands in December 1990. This symposium was organized
by the Netherlands Organization for Postacademic Studies in the
Social Sciences (PAOS), Academic Centre for Child and Adolescent
Psychiatry (Curium) and the Dept. of Child and Adolescent Psychiatry
at the University of Leiden.
    Includes bibliographical references and index.
    ISBN 0-8058-1107-9
    1. Brothers and sisters—Congresses. 2. Parent and child—
Congresses. 3. Child psychology—Congresses. I. Boer, Frits.
II. Dunn, Judy. III. Netherlands Organization for
Postacademic Studies in the Social Science. IV. Rijksuniversiteit
te Leiden. Kinderpsychiatrisch Centrum Curium. V. Rijksuniversiteit
te Leiden. Dept. of Child and Adolescent Psychiatry.
VI. International Symposium "Brothers and Sisters," Research on
Sibling Relationships, Therapeutic Applications (1st : 1990 :
Leiden, Netherlands)
    [DNLM: 1. Adolescent Psychiatry—congresses. 2. Child
Development—congresses. 3. Child Psychiatry—congresses.
4. Parent-Child Relations—congresses. 5. Sibling Relations—in
infancy & childhood. WS 105.5.F2 C5374]
BF723.S43C45 1992
155.44 '3—dc20
DNLM/DLC
for Library of Congress   91-34638
                                        CIP

Printed in the United States of America
10 9 8 7 6 5 4 3 2

Contents

Acknowledgments   ix

Foreword
Philip D. A. Treffers   xi

Introduction
Judy Dunn   xiii

PART I: DEVELOPMENTAL ISSUES

1 Sisters and Brothers: Current Issues in Developmental Research
   Judy Dunn   1

   The Nature and Development of Sibling Relationships   *1*
   Influences on Sibling Differences   *3*
   Links Between Sibling Relationships and Parent–Child
     Relationships   *4*
   Sibling and Peer Relationships   *7*
   Sibling Relationships and Individual Outcome   *8*
   Siblings in Special Populations   *11*
   Conclusion   *13*

v

2 The Developmental Courses of Sibling and Peer Relationships
Duane Buhrmester   **19**

Relationship Structure   *19*
The Roles of Siblings and Peers in Socioemotional Need
    Fulfillment   *23*
The Developmental Course of Need Fulfillment   *27*
The "Big Picture" of Sibling and Peer Relationships   *29*
Conclusions   *37*

3 Siblings and Their Parents
Frits Boer, Arnold W. Goedhart, and Philip D. A. Treffers   **41**

"Compensating Siblings"   *41*
"Favoritism Breeds Hostility"   *43*
Consistency of Maternal Treatment   *44*
Differential Treatment   *45*
Study 1   *46*
Study 2   *48*
Discussion   *50*

**4 Sibling Caretaking: Providing Emotional Support
During Middle Childhood**
Brenda K. Bryant   **55**

The Sibling Component of Complex Family Functioning:
    The Myth of Sibling Relationships as Simply Dyadic   *56*
Sibling Caretaking in Families Where a Child Does Not Find the
    Parent Approachable as a Confidant About Stressful Life
    Experiences: A Preliminary Empirical Analysis   *62*

**5 Social Norms and the One-Child Family: Clinical and Policy
Implications**
Toni Falbo   **71**

Western Literature   *71*
The Parent–Child Relationship   *75*
The Persistence of Beliefs   *76*
China's One-Child Policy   *78*

PART II: CLINICAL ISSUES

6 Children's Experiences With Disabled and Nondisabled Siblings:
   Links With Personal Adjustment and Relationship Evaluations
   Susan M. McHale and Vicki S. Harris   **83**

   Study   *85*
   Sibling Relationship Experiences in Families With Disabled and
       Nondisabled Children   *86*
   Summary and Conclusion   *96*

7 The Brothers and Sisters of Mentally Retarded Children
   Ann Gath   **101**

   The Initial Reaction   *101*
   The Distress and Disappointment of Parents   *102*
   The Preoccupation of Parents With a Very Dependent Child   *102*
   Sharing the Load   *103*
   Sibling Rivalry   *103*
   Fairness   *104*
   Bullying and Stigma   *105*
   Problems Affecting Brothers and Sisters   *105*
   Placements Away From Home   *105*
   Concerns for the Future   *106*
   Genetic Counseling   *106*
   Conclusions   *107*

8 Siblings as Co-Patients and Co-Therapists in Eating Disorders
   Walter Vandereycken and Ellie Van Vreckem   **109**

   Research on Siblings   *109*
   Siblings and their Therapeutic Significance   *115*
   Conclusion   *121*

9 Sibling Relationships in Disharmonious Homes: Potential
   Difficulties and Protective Effects
   Jennifer Jenkins   **125**

   Methods   *128*
   Results   *130*
   Discussion   *135*

10   **Remembering and Reinterpreting Sibling Bonds**
       Stephen Bank   **139**

           Traumatic Sibling Memories: Two Illustrations   *140*
           A Theory of Sibling Attachment   *144*
           Reinterpreting the Memories   *147*

       Epilogue
       Frits Boer   **153**

       Author Index   **157**

       Subject Index   **163**

Acknowledgments

The contributions to this volume are based on presentations held at the *First International Symposium "Brothers and Sisters, Research on Sibling Relationships, Therapeutic Applications,"* held in Leiden, The Netherlands in December 1990. This symposium was organized by the Netherlands Organization for Postacademic Studies in the Social Sciences (PAOS), Academic Centre for Child and Adolescent Psychiatry (Curium), and the Department of Child and Adolescent Psychiatry at the University of Leiden. We are particularly indebted to Paul G. M. Engelen from PAOS, for his continuous support.

Foreword: Sibling Studies and Sibling Lore

Philip D. A. Treffers
University of Leiden

Scientific interest in siblings is a recent development. This is surprising, because siblings have held an important place in numerous legends throughout history. The ancient Egyptian story of the love between Isis and her brother Osiris—from whom the Egyptian pharaohs are descended—is one of the oldest known. The theme returns later in Mozart's *Magic Flute* and in Robert Musil's greatest work, *The Man Without Qualities*.

At the beginning of the 17th century, in his essay, *Of Parents and Children*, Francis Bacon referred to the position of siblings in the family: "A man shall see, where there is a house full of children, one or two of the eldest respected, and the youngest made wantons; but in the midst some that are as it were forgotten, who many times nevertheless prove the best."

Brothers and sisters play a role in the work of almost all the great writers. In one of his touching letters to his wife, Italo Svevo wrote, "I agree with Tolstoy—and Tolstoy also was an old man when he came to this conclusion—that the simplest relationships are those between brother and sister." In Svevo's novel *Una Burla Riuscita* [A Successful Joke] the—anything but simple—relation between two old brothers stood central. And in *Confessions of Zeno* he wrote about the complicated interactions existing among three sisters. Svevo's three sisters lead us effortless to Chekhov . . . and one is tempted to associate further, because it is not difficult at all to call to mind other important books in which sibling relationships are described or even form a central theme. I cannot resist the temptation to quote once more from one of my favorite books, *Speak, Memory*, in which Vladimir Nabokov (1989) described his slightly younger brother:

He is a mere shadow in the background of my richest and most detailed recollec-
tions. I was the coddled one; he, the witness of coddling. (. . .) As a child, I
was rowdy, adventurous and something of a bully. He was quiet and listless,
and spent much more time with our mentors than I. At ten, began his interest
in music (. . .) and [he] spent hours on end playing snatches of operas, on a up-
stairs piano well within earshot. I would creep up behind and prod him in the
ribs—a miserable memory. (p 257)

If the study of siblings can teach us anything, it is how multifaceted and
fascinating the relationship between brothers and sisters is. Although researchers
in the past gave passing attention to this relationship, it is only during the last
decade that sibling research has emerged on a larger scale. The work of Judy
Dunn, professor of human development at The Pennsylvania State University
is well-known: She could be considered the godmother of research in the area
of siblings.

Frits Boer, lecturer at the University of Leiden, began research into siblings
in 1987. The findings of this research are reported in his doctoral thesis, *Sibling Relationships in Middle Childhood: An Empirical Study* (1990). His work can
be considered a sequel in a Leiden tradition: The founder of child psychiatry
in Leiden, Dirk Arnold van Krevelen, wrote his doctoral dissertation on *The
Only Child*. This book was published in 1946, so the time had come for a sibling!

It was at the time of Frits Boer's graduation that the first international symposium on siblings was held at Leiden University. Scientists from the whole
world presented the results of research in this field, including studies of the
relationships between siblings, and studies of only children. These contributions are collected in this book, which offers a unique overview of the state
of the art of sibling research.

REFERENCES

Boer, F. (1990). *Sibling relationships in middle childhood: An empirical study*. Leiden, The Netherlands:
DSWO Press, University of Leiden.
Nabokov, V. (1989). *Speak, memory: An autobiography revisited* (2nd ed.). New York: Vintage Books.
Van Krevelen, D. A. (1946). *Het Eenige Kind* [The only child]. Utrecht, The Netherlands: Erven
J. Bijleveld.

Introduction

Judy Dunn
The Pennsylvania State University

To many practicing clinicians, and indeed to most parents, it is obvious that the relationship between siblings is one characterized by distinctive emotion and intimacy from infancy onwards. It is a relationship that offers children unique opportunities for learning about self and other, and one that has considerable potential for affecting children's well-being, intimately linked as it is to the relationship each child has with the shared parents. Yet, the significance of siblings in children's development was, until the 1980s, a neglected topic in systematic research. This neglect seems particularly surprising given the interest that clinicians and family systems theorists have expressed in the part that siblings play in family relationships and in the adjustment of individuals (e.g., Levy, 1937; Minuchin, 1988; Petty, 1953; Winnicott, 1964), and given the importance that Piagetian theory attributes to children's interactions with other children. More recently there has been a welcome increase in research on siblings, and the contributions to this volume—originally presentations to the First International Symposium on Siblings held in Leiden, in December 1990—illustrate some of the exciting directions that this new interest is taking.

The first half of the book focuses on developmental issues. The first chapter (by Dunn) provides an overview of the issues in sibling research that are currently receiving particular attention: developmental changes in sibling relationships during early childhood and the nature of sibling relations in middle childhood; the links between sibling relationships and those with parents, peers, and friends; the influence of sibling relationships on individual outcome and adjustment; and the impact on children of growing up with disabled or sick siblings. Each of these issues is examined in detail in later chapters, and some topics—the connections between parent-child and sibling relationships, for instance—recur throughout the volume. A striking development in the last few years has been the growth of interest in siblings during middle childhood. In chapter 2, Buhrmester discusses the developmental changes that take place in their relationship as children move through middle childhood and adolescence, setting the developmental trajectory within the framework of children's other relationships—those with parents and those with peers. His focus makes clear that gender and age segregation are important issues for both peer *and* sibling relationships over this period, in contrast to the findings on siblings during the preschool period.

In chapters 3, by Boer, Goedhart, and Treffers, and 4, by Bryant, the connections between parent-child relationships and sibling relationships come center stage. The intriguing proposal that a poor relationship with a parent can be compensated for by the relationship with a sibling is seriously called into question in the chapter by Boer and his colleagues, which focuses on a study of a nonclinical population; specific differences in the emotional support provided by the two relationships are highlighted by Bryant. In view of the vast differences between the parent-child relationship and sibling relationships—differences in nature, in dynamics, in development, and in their developmental implications—it is difficult to see how one could possibly compensate for the other—if compensation implies substitution—except in a very global sense. The developmental issues raised in these chapters—for example, Bryant's focus on siblings as providers of support for unhappy siblings—have many implications for those concerned with the care of children.

The notion of compensation is seen in a different light in Falbo's discussion of only children (chapter 5). She succinctly shows that the widely held and damaging views of only children are strikingly inaccurate. Only children are in fact no different from those with siblings on a wide variety of personality and adjustment measures. Does this imply that siblings have no developmental impact? Not necessarily. Falbo argues that parents compensate for the absence of siblings with their especially close relations with their only children, and outlines a study of Chinese families that provides a striking comparison with the American and European data on only children. Such comparisons between cultures are very much needed: We slip too easily into generalizations about family relationships based only on our own cultures.

In the second half of the book we move to more explicitly clinical concerns, considered in the context of research findings (McHale & Harris, chapter 6; and Jenkins, chapter 9) and their practical implications for those in a clinical role (Gath, chapter 7; Vandereycken & Van Vreckem, chapter 8; and Bank, chapter 10). Three themes are prominent. The first is the possible vulnerability of children with disabled or sick siblings (discussed by McHale & Harris, Gath, and Vandereycken & Van Vreckem), or those in disharmonious homes (discussed by Jenkins). The second, in marked contrast, is the positive supportive role that children can play for their troubled or ill siblings, discussed in the chapters by Jenkins and Vandereycken and Van Vreckem. On this issue there is an encouraging accumulation of findings showing that *some* siblings can and do function in supportive and helpful ways. Siblings have been seen in the literature on many disorders as having only a marginal role, as Vandereycken and Van Vreckem demonstrate, but it is chiefly the *problems* caused to the non-sick sibling that have been studied. In contrast, Vandereycken and Van Vreckem show us that children can have a very positive role in helping their siblings. They make the important point that the patterns of impact on siblings may differ very much in families with different problems. More research that takes account of the variation in how families deal with disabled or sick members is badly needed.

The third theme is that recurring motif of the links between these different sibling roles and experiences, and the parents' differing relationships with their different children (Bank, Gath, McHale & Harris, and Vandereycken & Van Vreckem). The significance of children's *perceptions* of differential parental behavior is emphasized by McHale and Harris on the basis of their findings on children with disabled siblings, and this valuable point illustrates a more general matter: The lessons of the chapters that focus on clinical issues are useful, also, for those attempting to understand normal developmental principles. McHale and Harris draw our attention to the fact that it was children's interpretation of what was happening to them, and of the behavior of their disabled sibling, that was linked to their adjustment; the lesson here is surely not confined to children with disabled siblings.

The chapters throughout this book lead us to question some of the usual assumptions concerning family experiences—assumptions about only children, about the impact of a disabled sibling, and about the compensation that one relationship can provide for another. They bring to light important developmental principles in highlighting the significance of relative and nonshared experiences within the family, the role of perceptions and attributions, and the range of different processes that link different relationships. They remind us that, although the complexity of the questions we try to answer in studying children's development is daunting, careful systematic study can begin to shed light on those questions. If we are to understand children's development and gain insight into ways to help them, we have to include siblings—as part of their family world—in that study.

REFERENCES

Levy, D. M. (1937). Studies in sibling rivalry. *American Journal of Orthopsychiatry, Research Monograph 2.*

Minuchin, P. (1988). Relationships within the family: A systems perspective on development. In R. A. Hinde & J. Stevenson-Hinde (Eds.), *Relationships within families* (pp. 7–26). Oxford: Oxford University Press.

Petty, T. A. (1953). The tragedy of Humpty Dumpty. *Psychoanalytic Study of the Child, 8*, 404–422.

Winnicott, D. W. (1964). *The child, the family and the outside world*. London: Penguin.

Part I

Developmental Issues

Chapter 1

Sisters and Brothers: Current Issues in Developmental Research

Judy Dunn
The Pennsylvania State University

The idea that siblings can play an important role in children's development has a long history: brothers and sisters appear as significant figures in folk stories and in classical and biblical writing, and they are conspicuous in many biographical and autobiographical accounts of childhood and adolescence. Even though they figure prominently in our cultural stories and accounts of individual development, they have received scant attention from developmental psychologists until relatively recently. Since about the 1980s, the volume of research on siblings by both developmental psychologists and clinicians has grown rapidly, spanning a wide array of developmental issues. In this chapter I consider some of the chief themes in this work: the nature of sibling relationships and how they change with development, individual differences in sibling relationships, the links between sibling relationships and parent–child and peer relationships, sibling relationships and individual adjustment and outcome, and sibling relationships in special populations.

THE NATURE AND DEVELOPMENT OF SIBLING RELATIONSHIPS

Research into the nature of sibling relationships has made especially vigorous progress in two domains, namely, the study of developmental changes in the relationships of young siblings and the study of siblings' relationships in middle childhood. Before considering these, we should note that there has been much progress on the issue of how we can best measure the relationship of siblings of different ages (e.g., Buhrmester & Furman, 1987; Dunn, Stocker, & Plomin, 1990a), and a new awareness of the importance of obtaining assessments of the relationship from different family members and sources (e.g., Boer, 1990).

How does the relationship between siblings change as children develop greater powers of understanding and communicating with each other? It is clear that, during the early years, there are marked changes in the nature of the relationship. Younger siblings play an increasingly active role in the relationship during the preschool years (Munn & Dunn, 1988), and their older siblings begin to take an increasing interest in them some time between their third and fourth birthday (Brown & Dunn, in press). The nature of collaboration and cooperation with an older sibling change as children reach 4 years old, and these studies also strongly suggest that sibling relationships become more important in children's sociocognitive development by the time they are 4—and become both effective companions and effective antagonists. Furthermore, children's efforts become more efficacious as they intervene in mother–sibling interactions, making them more active participants in family life (Dunn & Shatz, 1989).

Particularly exciting is the increased interest in the sibling relationship in middle childhood. We have learned that sibling relationships become more egalitarian during middle childhood, though there is some disagreement about whether the change reflects a decrease in the dominance both siblings attempt to exert (Buhrmester, this volume; Burmester & Furman, 1987) or an increase in the power exerted by younger siblings on their older siblings (Vandell, Minnett, & Santrock, 1987). There is also some inconsistency in the reports on changes in closeness and conflict, with Vandell and her colleagues reporting an increase in positive emotional tone and conflict between 8 and 11 years, and Buhrmester and his colleagues finding little change in intimacy and affection but a decline in companionship between 8 and 17 years. The changes in age depend on whether it is the perceptions of older or younger siblings that are being documented; the argument put forward by Buhrmester, that the changes in warmth during adolescence parallel those found for perceptions of relationships with parents, and are likely to reflect increasing involvement with peers outside the family, is a convincing one.

On the issue of whether there is stability in the development of the way siblings relate to one another over the period when they move into middle childhood and adolescence, we remain in need of more information. In our own studies of children in Cambridge, England, the correlations over a 4-year period (from the preschool to middle childhood periods) were for the positive aspects of the relationship, $r(40) = .42$ and $r(40) = .60$, for the younger and older siblings, respectively, and for the negative aspects of the relationship, $r(40) = .28$ and $r(40) = .43$. Although these correlations are significant, and we could choose to stress the stability they represent, they are certainly not very high, and it is clear that for many sibling pairs, there are marked changes in their relationships as they progress from preschool to middle childhood. The question of what factors lead to changes in the relationship is clearly of interest, and we consider it in the next section.

INFLUENCES ON SIBLING DIFFERENCES

For clinicians, parents, and developmental researchers the striking differences between sibling pairs in closeness and hostility are of considerable interest. What factors influence these differences? We know more about what influences hostility and conflict between siblings than what leads to affection and closeness.

First, it is clear that the temperament of both siblings in a dyad is important in relation to the level of conflict between them, with children who are active, intense, or unadaptable in temperament having more conflicted relationships (Boer, 1990; Brody & Stoneman, 1987; Brody, Stoneman, & Burke, 1987; Stocker, Dunn, & Plomin, 1989). The match between the temperament of the two children is also important (Munn & Dunn, 1988).

Second, recent research on the impact of life events on family relationships is providing some useful leads for explaining individual differences in sibling relationships (see, e.g., Jenkins, this volume). Research on divorce, for instance, shows that after divorce the presence of a stepfather is associated with poor sibling relationships (Hetherington, 1988), and that the quality of the spouse-ex-spouse relationships contributes significantly to the quality of the sibling relationship (MacKinnon, 1989). Difficult relations between siblings after divorce are also reported to be more common in dyads with at least one boy (Hetherington, 1988; MacKinnon, 1989). The question of how normative life transitions affect siblings' relationships is an interesting one, on which we have, as yet, little systematic information; it seems likely, for example, that the transition to secondary school, and indeed school changes more generally, may affect the sibling relationship.

How the gender of the siblings and the age gap between them affect the quality of their relationship is less clear than is the impact of temperament and of divorce. Findings are inconsistent: The recent studies of siblings in middle childhood show, for example, that family constellation effects influence the relationship in complex ways (Buhrmester, this volume; Buhrmester & Furman, 1991). However, in the preschool and early childhood periods, the data reported show few relations with these variables or simply inconsistent results (Dunn, 1988b; Stoneman, Brody, & MacKinnon, 1984; Teti, Bond, & Gibbs, 1986; Teti, Gibbs, & Bond, 1989). Whether there is a developmental pattern, with birth position, gender, and age gap increasing in importance with development remains unknown.

The issue of the extent to which individual differences in sibling dyads' relationships are linked to differences in other family relationships is currently receiving much attention, especially the question of how the quality of the parent–child relationship is linked to that of the sibling relationship. Before turning to this issue, we should note that there is evidence that the emotional climate of the family, including marital conflict and satisfaction, is linked to the quality of the relationship between siblings (Brody & Stoneman, 1987). As Jenkins (this volume) describes, conflict is more common among siblings from disharmonious homes, but siblings also provide real support for one another in homes with unhappy marriages (Jenkins & Smith, 1990).

LINKS BETWEEN SIBLING RELATIONSHIPS AND PARENT–CHILD RELATIONSHIPS

That parent–child relationships are important influences on the relationships that develop between siblings is an idea that has had wide currency in clinical and developmental writing from Freud onward (Boer et al., this volume). Just how extensive the links between parent–child and sibling relationships in fact are, and what processes might mediate any associations between the two, are issues that are currently the focus of much debate.

One important question is whether the security of children's attachment to their parents is linked to the quality of their later sibling relationships. The prediction from attachment theory is that children who are insecurely attached to their parents will be more hostile to their siblings, as they "re-enact aspects of the non-nurturant caregiver role" in their interaction with one another (Teti & Ablard, 1989, p. 1520). The notion is that the child's "internal working model" of relationships, formed within the context of the mother–child relationship, will be carried forward to the sibling relationship. There is some evidence that when both the younger and the older sibling are securely attached to their mother, they are more likely to develop non-antagonistic relationships, whereas when both were insecurely attached, they were less likely to do so (Teti & Ablard, 1989). Still, it is not clear that attachment status, per se, played a causal role in mediating these connections; it is possible that, for example, the children's temperament might have been causally important, with each child eliciting similar reactions from the other individual in each of their dyadic relationships. Moreover, most aspects of sibling behavior in the Teti and Ablard study did not, in fact, show links to attachment status.

Compatible with the predictions of attachment theory are the findings on links between positive parental care and good sibling relationships in middle childhood, discussed by Boer, Goedhart, and Treffers (this volume). As Boer et al. note, such evidence does not fit with the argument that there is an inverse relation between parent–child and sibling relations, with intense relationships developing in sibling pairs who grow up in families in which parents are uninvolved, the "vacuum of parental care" discussed by Bank (this volume; see also Bank & Kahn, 1982). It is possible that this "compensatory" pattern is to be found chiefly in extreme groups, such as those studied by Bank, rather than in the nonclinical populations, such as those on whom Boer and his colleagues focused.

A second theme in the research on connections between parent–child and sibling relationships concerns differential parental treatment. As Boer et al. (this volume) comment, there is a notable consensus in recent research that maternal differential treatment is associated with more conflicted and hostile sibling relationships (Boer, 1990; Brody & Stoneman, 1987; Brody et al., 1987; Bryant & Crockenberg, 1980; Stocker, Dunn, & Plomin, 1987). These links appear to be especially strong in families under stress: They are reported in studies of siblings following divorce (Hetherington, 1988), in studies of siblings of cancer patients (Cairns, Clark, Smith, & Lansky, 1979), and in research on children whose siblings have disabilities (McHale & Gamble, 1987, 1989; McHale & Harris, this volume). The evidence for links between parental differential treatment and children's adjustment (discussed further on) suggests that this aspect of family life is of considerable importance in development.

The evidence for such associations is, of course, correlational, and as Boer and colleagues emphasize in their chapter (this volume), we have to be very cautious in making causal inferences about the direction of these links. The issue of causal influence is one that arises, too, in a third theme in the parent–child–sibling research, namely, the role of parental involvement in sibling conflict. It is usually assumed that parental involvement in such conflict increases the conflict because—it is presumed—children quarrel with their siblings to gain parental attention (Dreikurs, 1964), and because if parents intervene, their children do not have the opportunity to learn how to resolve conflict themselves (Brody & Stoneman, 1987). Schachter and Stone (1987) have argued that in extreme cases, the deprivation of opportunities to practice conflict resolution can lead to serious pathological consequences, in which individuals become bullying, anti-social, and self-seeking. We have two kinds of evidence related to this matter. First, correlational studies show that the frequency of sibling conflict is indeed related to the frequency of parental intervention in such conflict (Brody & Stoneman, 1987; Brody et al., 1987; Dunn & Munn, 1986a), but it is not clear that parents' involvement *led* to the frequent conflict in these data: It could well be that parents become involved in sibling quarrels when they are intense and frequent, *as a result* of the conflict. To answer these questions about direction of effects the second source of evidence, intervention studies, is of particular importance. However, to date such studies have been small in scale, and present some methodological problems (see Brody & Stoneman, 1983). In my view, the issue of how much parent intervention per se increases sibling conflict remains unresolved; further research that examines the impact of different kinds of parental intervention is required.

A fourth theme in the parent–sibling research concerns the effects of the birth of a sibling. The birth of a sibling is accompanied by sharp changes in the parent–child relationship, and these changes are linked to the quality of the relationship that develops between the siblings (Dunn & Kendrick, 1982). These links might be seen as one aspect of a more general increase in problems following the sibling's birth, associated with changes in parent–child interaction; a number of studies have now replicated and extended the studies of the early 1980s documenting the increase in such problems (discussed further on). The issue of what other kinds of process might mediate the connections between the relationships is considered next.

In summary, a number of general theoretical issues concerning the mechanisms linking the parent–child and sibling relationships, then, are raised by the research just outlined. The first is that there are a range of processes of very different sorts implicated in the connections between parent–child and sibling relationships. At one level, the general emotional disturbance found to accompany the sibling birth may be important as a link; then there are a range of other processes of increasing specificity and cognitive complexity that may also be implicated (Dunn, 1988a). For example, there is evidence from two independent studies for links between how mothers talk to their firstborn children about the newborn sibling, and the quality of the behavior shown by older and younger sibling to each other over time (Dunn & Kendrick, 1982; Howe & Ross, 1990). Such evidence indicates that even with young siblings, the connections between the parent–child and sibling relationships may involve processes of attribution and reflection.

A second issue is the one explored by Boer and colleagues (this volume), concerning the notion of *compensatory* versus *congruous* patterns of relationships. Clearly the issue of whether compensatory patterns are characteristic only of extreme groups merits further study.

Third, there may be interactive effects involving both attachment security and differential treatment by parents: Some results indicate that differential treatment is particularly influential for children who are insecurely attached (Volling & Belsky, 1991).

A fourth issue concerns the degree to which parent–child and sibling relationships are in fact *independent* of one another, rather than closely linked in either a compensatory or congruous fashion. For example, our recent research on the development of sociocognitive skills and family relationships indicates that there is no relation between the skills of conflict management children show in disputes with their mothers and those they use with their siblings (Slomkowski & Dunn, 1991). Not only are such findings difficult to assimilate with current views of social competence as an individual capacity, they are also difficult to reconcile with the widely held assumption that it is social competence that mediates links between relationships. This idea has been explored particularly extensively in relation to the research showing links between parent–child and troubled peer relationships (Asher & Coie, 1990). It is to peer relationships that we turn next.

SIBLING AND PEER RELATIONSHIPS

The question of whether there are connections between children's sibling relationships and those that they form with their friends and peers raises many of the same issues about mediating processes that arise in considering parents and siblings. A number of different theoretical approaches suggest we should expect such links: A social learning framework would predict that children learn particular interactional behaviors and attitudes within their family relationships that are then generalized to their relationships with children outside the family (Parke et al., 1989; Putallaz, 1987). Within an attachment framework, it is predicted that the internal working models of relationships that children form with their parents would be carried forward to affect their relationships outside the family (Bretherton, 1985; Sroufe & Fleeson, 1986). A third possibility is that children's personality characteristics elicit similar responses from different social partners (Caspi & Elder, 1988). Although the processes thought to underlie the links are different, each of these theoretical positions would lead us to expect sibling relationships and peer relationships to have similar patterns of individual differences.

One could also argue for predicting quite different types of relations between siblings and peers. For example, although friendships and sibling relationships are both close, intimate dyadic relationships, there are striking differences between them. Siblings do not choose each other, very often do not trust or even like each other, and may be competing strongly for parental affection and interest; the sources of conflict and hostility in this relationship are likely to be very different from those leading to tension in a friendship. Indeed, a recent study documents that conflicts with siblings and with friends in adolescence differ in onset, course, and aftermath, as well as in their significance within the particular relationship (Raffaelli, 1991). In contrast to children and their siblings, children within a friendship dyad have chosen each other as companions, and they trust and feel affection for one another.

The differences between sibling relationships and popularity within the peer group are even greater. The regard of the peer group as a whole—the most widely used measure of peer relations—clearly differs very much from the intimacy of the dyadic sibling relationship, and it could well be argued that we should not expect close links between the quality of sibling relationships and peer status.

What support is there for each of these two contrasting views? The little data we have do not tell a simple story. First, in the case of peer relations, there is little evidence for connections either in the preschool period (Berndt & Bulleit, 1985) or for 5- to 10-year-olds (Stocker & Dunn, 1991); however, positive links between aggression and activity with siblings were found to be related to similar behavior with peers among 7- to 8-year-olds (Vandell, Minnett, Johnson, & Santrock, 1990). There may, however, be differences in the associations for boys and girls in adolescence; girls who were neglected by peers were found, by East (1989), to have positive relationships with siblings.

In the case of friendship, more associations have been found with the quality of sibling relationships; yet the pattern of results does not suggest a simple ''carry-over'' from one relationship to the other, except in the case of very young siblings. Kramer (1990) found that 3- to 5-year-olds who were close to their friends were friendlier to their infant siblings than children who had less close friendships. However, beyond the first year of the sibling relationship, studies report either no links (Abramovitch, Corter, Pepler, & Stanhope, 1986) or indications that children who were competitive and controlling to their siblings were especially positive to their friends (Stocker & Dunn, 1991).

These results could be explained in terms of a range of different mediating processes. For example, one interpretation might be to suggest that compensatory mechanisms were important: that children who had difficulties with their siblings were especially likely to seek close intimacy with their friends. A very different account of the findings would be to propose that through the experience of the competitive sibling relationship, these children developed sociocognitive abilities that helped them to form close relationships with their friends. However these findings are interpreted, we should recognize that they call into question the theoretical models that predict simple links between children's relationships within their family, and their relationships with peers. We should also note that the mediating processes linking *close* relationships may differ from those connecting children's sibling relationships with the general regard and acceptance of their peer groups.

SIBLING RELATIONSHIPS
AND INDIVIDUAL OUTCOME

The question of whether children's interactions with their siblings influence their well-being and adjustment, and their sociocognitive development more generally, is one that has attracted much interest recently.

First, how far do siblings influence children's well-being and adjustment? Consider, as illustration, three outcome domains in which, according to recent developmental research, siblings may play a formative role, namely agressive behavior, self-esteem, and internalizing and externalizing problems.

Particular interest has been shown in the impact of hostile aggressive sibling interaction, and here, the research shows consistently for children from the second year through middle childhood that aggressive behavior from one sibling is correlated with aggression by the other (Beardsall, 1986; Brody et al., 1987; Dunn & Munn, 1986a). Detailed observational work by Patterson and his group (Patterson, 1984, 1986) shows the shaping role that siblings play in the development of aggressive behavior, in both clinic and nonclinic samples, and that children who are very aggressive with their siblings are likely to be rejected by their peers (Dishion 1990). In addition, poor sibling relationships are disproportionately found in children who are later assessed as clinically disturbed (Richman, Stevenson, & Graham, 1982). With the exception of the work of Patterson's group, the findings linking poor sibling relations and other behavior problems are all correlational, and thus we cannot assume that sibling interaction plays a causal role in the development of problems: Problems in the sibling relationship could well be an index of more general disturbance. Still, it is clear that the question of whether children's experiences with their siblings play a role independent of other family influences is one that deserves investigation.

A novel recent approach to the issue of sibling influence on children's adjustment considers the *differences* between the siblings' experiences within the family. Siblings, who share 50% of their segregating genes and the same family background, nevertheless differ markedly in adjustment and personality. This fact, documented in a wide range of studies, presents a serious challenge to the conventional studies of family influences on adjustment, because siblings share so many of the family variables assumed to be important, such as marital adjustment, maternal mental health, and child-rearing attitudes. The question then, of why they should be so different from one another has led to a new perspective on studying the family experiences that are *special to each sibling* (Dunn & Plomin, 1990). Thus, the question asked is whether relative differences in affection or discipline from parents, or in the friendly or hostile experiences within the sibling relationship itself, are systematically linked to individual outcome.

The initial results from studies of these differential experiences show that there are, indeed, links with adjustment. For example, internalizing and externalizing problems were found, in a sample of 90 children, to be associated with maternal differential treatment (Dunn, Stocker, & Plomin, 1990b). Differential experiences within the sibling relationship were also implicated in these outcomes, though at a level only approaching significance. In the case of self-esteem, results from our Cambridge study show that children feel better about themselves if they "deliver" more negative behavior to the sibling than they receive. It is likely, too, that evaluative social comparisons within the family, in which one child is explicitly compared with a sibling, are also important. Consider the following example (from Dunn, 1988c), in which a child of only

30 months witnesses and comments on his mother's evaluation of his younger sister. Andy is a cautious, anxious, and sensitive child, with an ebullient assertive younger sister, Susie, aged 14 months. He overhears his mother's proud comment on his sister and adds a muted comment on himself in comparison:

> Mother to Susie: Susie, you *are* a determined little devil!
>
> Andy to mother: *I'm* not a determined little devil.
>
> Mother to Andy (laughing): No you're not! What are you? A poor old boy!

Given the evidence that children are extremely sensitive to social comparison processes within the family from the preschool period onward (Dunn, 1988c), we should surely take seriously the potential of such exchanges in the development of children's sense of their own worth and competence, which we know to be linked to later indices of adjustment.

Finally, there are the indirect effects on children's adjustment of the arrival of a sibling. Studies in the 1980s reported that the birth of a sibling had immediate consequences for children's adjustment and behavior (Dunn & Kendrick, 1982). Recent studies have now confirmed and extended these findings (Gottlieb & Mendelson, 1990; Howe & Ross, 1990; Kramer, 1990; Stewart, Mobley, Van Tuyl, & Salvador, 1987; for reviews, see Teti, in press; Vandell, 1987). Increases in a wide range of problems are described: disturbances in bodily functions, withdrawal, aggressiveness, dependency, and anxiety. It is thought that these changes are related to parallel changes in the interaction between the firstborn sibling and the mother.

Siblings as Sources of Support

Siblings can have quite a different role in relation to children's adjustment: They can be an important source of support in times of stress. For example, Jenkins (this volume; Jenkins & Smith, 1990) has shown that children growing up in disharmonious homes have fewer problems if they have a good sibling relationship. They appear to benefit both from offering comfort to, and from receiving comfort from their siblings (Jenkins, Smith, & Graham, 1989): Confiding with a sibling was much more commonly reported as a coping mechanism than was confiding with a friend. An interesting line of clinical research that highlights the importance of sibling support is the study of siblings as therapists for children with eating disorders, reported by Vandereycken and Van Vreckem (this volume).

Siblings and Sociocognitive Development

The idea that child–child interaction plays a special part in the development of children's social and moral understanding is one that has had wide currency (e.g., Doise & Mugny, 1984; Hartup, 1983; Piaget, 1932; Sullivan, 1953).

If such an argument is plausible, then it seems likely that siblings, who are so familiar with one another and who spend—at least in early childhood—much time interacting with one another, may well be a potent source of influence in these domains. Recent work suggests there are indeed associations between the kinds of experiences children have had with their siblings, and various aspects of their sociocognitive development, at least during early childhood. For example, aspects of prosocial and cooperative behavior, pretend play, and conflict management in the preschool period have all been reported to be associated with sibling behavior (Dunn & Dale, 1984; Dunn & Munn, 1986b; Slomkowski & Dunn, 1991). Furthermore, performance on sociocognitive assessments in early childhood (Dunn, Brown, Slomkowski, Tesla, & Youngblade, in press) and in middle childhood (Beardsall, 1986) has also been linked to experiences with siblings. We found, for example, that children who had cooperated with their siblings in play at 33 months, and whose older siblings had been affectionate toward them, were more successful 7 months later in assessments of affective perspective taking and of the ability to understand links between beliefs and behavior. Of course, with all of these studies, the associations are essentially correlational, and the direction of effects is, therefore, by no means clear. It could well be that siblings who are good at affective perspective taking are more effective and interesting play companions, and that these sociocognitive skills *lead to* their extensive cooperative interactions with their siblings, rather than vice versa. In common sense terms it seems likely that both processes operate. It is also worth noting that studies of young siblings have reported that children benefit from observing and imitating their older siblings (Hesser & Azmitia, 1989; Wishart, 1986).

SIBLINGS IN SPECIAL POPULATIONS

The final issue we consider concerns the experiences of sibling pairs in which one child is disabled or suffers from some problem. How, for instance, does growing up with a disabled or sick sibling affect children's adjustment and well-being? Are there positive consequences from such experiences? Can children act as supports for their troubled siblings? These questions are often raised by clinicians caring for families with sick or disabled siblings, and some progress has recently been made toward answering them.

First, it is important to recognize that the research literature on sibling relationships of children with illnesses or disabilities is very heterogeneous with respect to the severity and types of disability or illness; it may well prove extremely important to distinguish different problems and disabilities if we are to understand their implications for the sibling relationship (see, e.g., Vandereycken and Van Vreckem, this volume). Moreover, few studies focus on the behavior, perceptions, and adjustment of *both* the handicapped or sick child and his or her sibling. With these caveats in mind, three general points can be made concerning the effects of growing up with a handicapped sibling.

The first is that most studies report that children with handicapped siblings suffer from more emotional and behavioral problems than children with non-handicapped siblings. The nature and extent of these problems are related to characteristics of the handicapped child, such as the severity of the handicap or illness, and his or her temperament. They are also related to characteristics of the nonhandicapped sibling—birth order, temperament, and gender—and of the parents, such as parental childrearing attitudes and the quality of the marriage (for reviews, see Crnic & Leconte, 1986; Ogle & Powell, 1985; Senapati & Hayes, 1988; Sourkes, 1987; see also special issue of the *Journal of Children in Contemporary Society*, edited by Schachter & Stone, 1987).

The second point concerning children's adjustment, however, is that these problems are often not severe. McHale and Gamble (1987) point out that children who have siblings with disabilities often fall within the normal range of scores for behavioral and psychological problems; although their scores are high, they are still below the clinical cut-off.

The third point is that there is much variability in the responses of children to the presence of a disabled or sick sibling in the family. This variability has led investigators to argue that research should be re-directed away from the preoccupation with negative outcomes for family members. Rather, it is proposed, research on siblings with a handicap or severe illness should follow the approaches used in research on nondisabled siblings: The adjustment and perceptions of both siblings should be studied, the links between their relationship and the other family relationships should be investigated, and a wide variety of methodological approaches, including observations, should be employed.

A study that illustrates the usefulness of examining not only the adjustment of the nonhandicapped sibling but other aspects of family relationships is the investigation of children with juvenile rheumatic disease by Daniels, Moos, Billings, and Miller (1987). In this study the adjustment of the children suffering from the disease was found to be linked to stress in the family, to parental behavior, and also to the quality of their relationships with their siblings. The evidence is growing from such studies that children can indeed act as supports and helpful influences for their disabled, sick, or troubled siblings. As Vandereycken and Van Vreckem (this volume) and others (Miller & Cantwell, 1986) have documented, children can, indeed, act as therapists for their siblings. The clinical and social value of research that will further our understanding of the potential of siblings as providers of support and help to troubled children is clear.

Perhaps we should not be surprised that the same issues shown to be important in research on nonhandicapped siblings stand out as key in the development of children with handicapped siblings. A second line of study that illustrates the importance of including the parent–child relationships in research on siblings and also highlights the value of examining the daily life experiences of the children, is that carried out by McHale and her colleagues on disabled siblings (McHale & Gamble, 1989; McHale & Harris, this volume). They showed that it was not the time that the nonhandicapped siblings spent in caregiving their disabled sibling that was linked to emotional problems—the usual assumption made—but rather, it was the behavior of the handicapped sibling, especially aggressive behavior, and the child's dissatisfaction with parental differential behavior, that were associated with the adjustment of the nonhandicapped child. The argument made by McHale and Harris that we should pay special attention to the attributions that children make concerning their siblings' problems—or, indeed, their parents' behavior—is one that is echoed in other studies of children with chronically sick siblings (Sourkes, 1987). It is probably equally relevant for children with nonhandicapped siblings.

CONCLUSION

A number of overarching issues are evident in this rapidly growing field of research on siblings. There is a new attention to children as family members, evident in the recognition of children's sensitivity to differential treatment and the salience of differential experiences within the family, and in the (sometimes controversial) discussion of the links between parent–child and sibling relationships. There is increasing attention to the perceptions and interpretations of children concerning their siblings and their family relationships. There is a new consciousness of the different dimensions of the sibling relationship, including the positive supporting role that siblings can play in each other's lives, and also of the developmental changes that take place in the sibling relationship as children grow up.

There is also a new awareness of how limited our research has been in the range of samples and cultures we have studied, a new concern about studying siblings later in the life span (Bedford & Gold, 1989), and a more critical attitude about the grounds for drawing inferences about the causal direction of influences within the family. The questions that need to be asked about siblings are becoming clearer as their importance to both developmental psychologists and clinicians is recognized.

ACKNOWLEDGMENTS

Preparation of this chapter was supported in part by grants from the National Institute of Child Health and Human Development (HD-23158), the National Institute of Mental Health (MH-46535), and the National Science Foundation (BNS-8806589).

REFERENCES .

Abramovitch, R., Corter, C., Pepler, D. J., & Stanhope, L. (1986). Sibling and peer interaction: A final follow-up and a comparison. *Child Development, 57,* 217–229.

Asher, S. R., & Coie, J. D. (1990). *Peer rejection in childhood.* Cambridge: Cambridge University Press.

Bank, S., & Kahn, M. D. (1982). *The sibling bond.* New York: Basic.

Beardsall, L. (1986). *Conflict between siblings in middle childhood.* Unpublished doctoral dissertation, University of Cambridge, Cambridge, England.

Bedford, V. H., & Gold, D. T. (1989). Siblings in later life: A neglected family relationship [Special issue]. *American Behavioral Scientist, 33,* 3–126.

Berndt, T. J., & Bulleit, T. N. (1985). Effects of sibling relationships on preschoolers' behavior at home and at school. *Developmental Psychology, 21,* 761–767.

Boer, F. (1990). *Sibling relationships in middle childhood.* Leiden: DSWO University of Leiden Press.

Bretherton, I. (1985). Attachment theory: Retrospect and prospect. In I. Bretherton & E. Waters (Eds.), *Growing points of attachment theory and research. Monographs of the Society for Research in Child Development* (pp. 3–35), *50*(Serial No. 209, Nos. 1–2).

Brody, G. H., & Stoneman, Z. (1983). Children with atypical siblings. In B. Lahey & A. Kazden (Eds.), *Advances in clinical child psychology* (Vol. 6, pp. 285–326). New York: Plenum.

Brody, G. H., & Stoneman, Z. (1987). Sibling conflict: Contributions of the siblings themselves, the parent-sibling relationship, and the broader family system. *Journal of Children in Contemporary Society, 19,* 39–53.

Brody, G. H., Stoneman, Z., & Burke, M. (1987). Child temperaments, maternal differential behavior, and sibling relationships. *Developmental Psychology, 23,* 354–362.

Brown, J., & Dunn, J. (in press). Talk with your mother or your sibling? Developmental changes in early family conversations about feelings. *Child Development.*

Bryant, B. K., & Crockenberg, S. B. (1980). Correlates and dimensions of prosocial behavior: A study of female siblings with their mothers. *Child Development, 51,* 529–544.

Buhrmester, D., & Furman, W. (1987). The development of companionship and intimacy. *Child Development, 58,* 1101–1113.

Cairns, N., Clark, G., Smith, S., & Lansky, S. (1979). Adaptation of siblings to childhood malignancy. *Journal of Pediatrics, 95,* 484–487.

Caspi, A., & Elder, G. H. (1988). Emergent family patterns: The intergenerational construction of problem behavior and relationships. In R. A. Hinde & J. Stevenson-Hinde (Eds.), *Relationships within families* (pp. 218–240). Oxford: Oxford University Press.

Crnic, K. A., & Leconte, J. M. (1986). Understanding sibling needs and influences. In R. R. Fewell & P. F. Vadasy (Eds.), *Families of handicapped children: Needs and supports across the life-span* (pp. 75–98). Austin, TX: PRO-ED, Inc.

Daniels, D., Moos, R. H., Billings, A. G., & Miller, J. J. (1987). Psychological risk and resistance factors among children with chronic illness, healthy siblings, and healthy controls. *Journal of Abnormal Child Psychology, 15,* 295–308.

Dishion, T. J. (1990). The peer context of troublesome child and adolescent behavior. In P. E. Leone (Ed.), *Understanding troubled and troubling youth.* Newbury, CA: Sage.

Doise, W., & Mugny, G. (1984). *The social development of the intellect.* Oxford: Pergamon.

Dreikurs, R. (1964). *Children, the challenge.* New York: Hawthorne Books.

Dunn, J. (1988a). Connections between relationships: Implications of research on mothers and siblings. In R. A. Hinde & J. Stevenson-Hinde (Eds.), *Relationships within families: Mutual influences* (pp. 168–180). Oxford: Oxford University Press.

Dunn, J. (1988b). Sibling influences on development in childhood. *Journal of Child Psychology and Psychiatry, 29,* 119–127.

Dunn, J. (1988c). *The beginnings of social understanding.* Cambridge, MA: Harvard University Press.

Dunn, J., Brown, J., Slomkowski, C., Tesla, C., & Youngblade, L. (in press). Young children's understanding of feelings and beliefs: Individual differences and their antecedents. *Child Development*.

Dunn, J., & Dale, N. (1984). I a daddy: 2-year-olds' collaboration in joint pretend play with sibling and with mother. In I. Bretherton (Ed.), *Symbolic play: The development of social understanding* (pp. 131-158). New York: Academic Press.

Dunn, J., & Kendrick, C. (1982). *Siblings: Love, envy, and understanding*. Cambridge, MA: Harvard University Press.

Dunn, J., & Munn, P. (1986a). Sibling quarrels and maternal intervention: Individual differences in understanding and aggression. *Journal of Child Psychology and Psychiatry*, *27*, 583-595.

Dunn, J., & Munn, P. (1986b). Siblings and the development of prosocial behaviour. *International Journal of Behavioral Development*, *9*, 265-284.

Dunn, J., & Plomin, R. (1990). *Separate lives: Why siblings are so different*. New York: Basic.

Dunn, J., & Shatz, M. (1989). Becoming a conversationalist despite (or because of) having a sibling. *Child Development*, *60*, 399-410.

Dunn, J., Stocker, C., & Plomin, R. (1990a). Assessing the relationship between young siblings. *Journal of Child Psychology and Psychiatry*, *31*, 983-991.

Dunn, J., Stocker, C., & Plomin, R. (1990b). Nonshared experiences within the family: Correlates of behavioral problems in middle childhood. *Development and Psychopathology*, *2*, 113-126.

East, P. L. (1989, April). *Missing provisions in peer-withdrawn and aggressive children's friendships: Do siblings compensate?* Paper presented at the biennial meeting of the Society for Research in Child Development, Kansas City, MO.

Gottlieb, L. N., & Mendelson, M. J. (1990). Parental support and firstborn girls' adaptation to the birth of a sibling. *Journal of Applied Developmental Psychology*, *11*, 29-48.

Hartup, W. W. (1983). Peer relations. In P. H. Mussen (Ed.), *Handbook of child psychology* (Vol. 4, pp. 103-196). New York: Wiley.

Hesser, J., & Azmitia, M. (1989, April). *The influence of siblings and non-siblings on children's observation and imitation*. Paper presented at the biennial meeting of the Society for Research in Child Development, Kansas City, MO.

Hetherington, E. M. (1988). Parents, children, and siblings: Six years after divorce. In R. A. Hinde & J. Stevenson-Hinde (Eds.), *Relationships within families: Mutual influences* (pp. 311-331). Oxford: Oxford University Press.

Howe, N., & Ross, H. S. (1990). Socialization, perspective-taking, and the sibling relationship. *Developmental Psychology*, *26*, 160-165.

Jenkins, J. M., & Smith, M. A. (1990). Factors protecting children living in disharmonious homes: Maternal reports. *Journal of American Academy of Child and Adolescent Psychiatry*, *29*, 60-69.

Jenkins, J. M., Smith, M. A., & Graham, P. J. (1989). Coping with parental quarrels. *Journal of American Academy of Child and Adolescent Psychiatry*, *28*, 182-189.

Kramer, L. (1990, April). Becoming a sibling: With a little help from my friends. In M. Mendelson (Chair), *Becoming a sibling: Adjustment, roles and relationships*. Symposium conducted at the Seventh International Conference on Infant Studies, Montreal.

McHale, S. M., & Gamble, W. C. (1987). Sibling relationships and adjustment of children with disabled brothers and sisters. *Journal of Children in Contemporary Society*, *19*, 131-158.

McHale, S. M., & Gamble, W. C. (1989). Sibling relationships of children with disabled and nondisabled brothers and sisters. *Developmental Psychology*, *25*, 421-429.

McKinnon, C. E. (1989). An observational investigation of sibling interactions in married and divorced families. *Developmental Psychology*, *25*, 36-44.

Miller, N. B., & Cantwell, D. (1986). Siblings as therapists: A behavioral approach. *American Journal of Psychiatry*, *133*, 447-450.

Munn, P., & Dunn, J. (1988). Temperament and the developing relationship between siblings. *International Journal of Behavioral Development*, *12*, 433-451.

Ogle, P. A., & Powell, T. P. (1985). *Brothers and sisters: A special part of exceptional families.* Baltimore, MD: Paul H. Brooks.

Parke, R. D., MacDonald, K. B., Burks, V. M., Carson, J., Bhavnagri, N., Barth, J. M., & Beitel, A. (1989). Family and peer systems: In search of the linkages. In K. Kreppner & R. M. Lerner (Eds.), *Family systems and life-span development* (pp. 65–92). Hillsdale, NJ: Lawrence Erlbaum Associates.

Patterson, G. R. (1984). Siblings: Fellow travellers in coercive family processes. *Advances in the Study of Aggression, 1,* 173–214.

Patterson, G. R. (1986). The contribution of siblings to training for fighting: A microsocial analysis. In D. Olweus, J. Block, & M. Radke-Yarrow (Eds.), *Development of antisocial and prosocial behavior: Research, theories, and issues* (pp. 235–261). New York: Academic.

Piaget, J. (1932). *The moral judgment of the child.* London: Routledge & Kegan Paul.

Putallaz, M. (1987). Maternal behavior and children's sociometric status. *Child Development, 54,* 1417–1426.

Raffaelli, M. (1991, April). *Conflict with siblings and friends in late childhood and adolescence.* Paper presented at the biennial meeting of the Society for Research in Child Development, Seattle, WA.

Richman, N., Stevenson, J. E., & Graham, P. (1982). *Preschool to school: A behavioral study.* London: Academic.

Schachter, F. F., & Stone, R. K. (1987). Sibling deidentification and split-parent identification. *Journal of Children in Contemporary Society, 19,* 55–75.

Senapati, R., & Hayes, A. (1988). Sibling relationships of handicapped children: A review of conceptual and methodological issues. *International Journal of Behavioral Development, 11,* 89–115.

Slomkowski, C., & Dunn, J. (1991). *Managing conflict in the family: Young children's disputes with mother and sibling.* Manuscript submitted for publication.

Sourkes, B. M. (1987). Siblings of the child with a life-threatening illness. *Journal of Children in Contemporary Society, 19,* 159–184.

Sroufe, L. A., & Fleeson, J. (1986). Attachment and the construction of relationships. In W. W. Hartup & Z. Rubin (Eds.), *Relationships and development* (pp. 51–72). Hillsdale, NJ: Lawrence Erlbaum Associates.

Stewart, R. B., Mobley, L. A., Van Tuyl, S. S., & Salvador, M. A. (1987). The firstborn's adjustment to the birth of a sibling: A longitudinal assessment. *Child Development, 55,* 1322–1332.

Stocker, C., & Dunn, J. (1991). Sibling relationships in childhood: Links with friendships and peer relationships. *British Journal of Developmental Psychology, 8,* 227–244.

Stocker, C., Dunn, J., & Plomin, R. (1989). Sibling relationships: Links with child temperament, maternal behavior, and family structure. *Child Development, 60,* 715–727.

Stoneman, Z., Brody, G. H., & McKinnon, C. E. (1984). Naturalistic observations of children's roles and activities while playing with their siblings and friends. *Child Development, 55,* 617–627.

Sullivan, H. S. (1953). *The interpersonal theory of psychology.* New York: Norton.

Teti, D. M. (in press). Sibling interaction. In V. B. Van Hesselt & M. Hersen (Eds.), *Handbook of social development: A lifespan perspective.* New York: Plenum.

Teti, D. M., & Ablard, K. E. (1989). Security of attachment and infant-sibling relationships: A laboratory study. *Child Development, 60,* 1519–1528.

Teti, D. M., Bond, L. A., & Gibbs, E. D. (1986). Sibling-created experiences: Relationships to birth-spacing and infant cognitive development. *Infant Behavior and Development, 9,* 27–42.

Teti, D. M., Gibbs, E. D., & Bond, L. A. (1989). Sibling interaction, birth spacing, and intellectual/linguistic development. In P. Zukow (Ed.), *Sibling relationships across cultures* (pp. 117–139). New York: Springer-Verlag.

Vandell, D. L. (1987). Baby sister/baby brother: Reactions to the birth of a sibling and patterns of early sibling relations. *Journal of Children in Contemporary Society, 19,* 13–37.

Vandell, D. L., Minnett, A. M., & Santrock, J. W. (1987). Age differences in sibling relationships during middle childhood. *Journal of Applied Developmental Psychology, 8,* 247–257

Volling, B., & Belsky, J. (1991). *The contributions of mother-child and father-child relationships to the quality of sibling interaction: A longitudinal study*. Manuscript submitted for publication.

Wishart, J. G. (1986). Siblings as models in early infant learning. *Child Development, 57*, 1232–1240.

Chapter 2

The Developmental Courses of Sibling and Peer Relationships

Duane Buhrmester
University of Texas at Dallas

Sibling relationships are not static, changing as children move through different developmental periods. Nor are they played out in a social vacuum, but they are embedded within the context of relationships with other family members and peers. These ecological realities make it difficult to understand fully the changing nature of sibling relationships without simultaneously considering developmental changes in other relationships. Accordingly, the purpose of this chapter is to examine the changing nature of sibling relationships vis-à-vis other relationships during middle childhood and adolescence, drawing on several studies that Wyndol Furman and I have conducted (Buhrmester & Furman, 1987, 1990; Furman & Buhrmester, 1985a, 1985b, in press; Furman, Jones, Buhrmester, & Adler, 1989). The primary point of reference is relationships with friends, although other relationships (particularly those with parents and romantic partners) are also considered as points of comparison. I begin by discussing a number of different dimensions along which children's relationships can be characterized.

RELATIONSHIP STRUCTURE

Children's relationships with siblings and peers can be described in terms of a number of structural characteristics (Furman & Buhrmester, 1983). Four aspects of relationship structure are considered in this chapter: biosocial structure, social-role structure, systemic structure, and socioemotional structure.

Although the empirical findings described in this chapter primarily deal with the socioemotional structures of relationships, it is difficult to interpret these findings without reference to other aspects of relationship structure.

Biosocial Structure

The term *biosocial structure* is used here to refer to the status of one child relative to another child in terms of certain biologically linked characteristics. Sibling researchers frequently call these family or sibship *constellation variables,* which include birth order, age-spacing between siblings, and child and sibling gender. The correlates of the biosocial structure of sibling relationships have been examined extensively and are discussed in greater detail further on.

These biologically linked characteristics also capture important structural features of peer relationships, although it is awkward to refer to them as "constellation variables" in that context. In fact, biosocial variables seem to exercise a pervasive influence on peer relationships. For example, children show a clear preference to interact with same-sex peers. This preference starts at a very young age and intensifies through middle childhood. In one longitudinal study, Maccoby and Jacklin (1987) found that preschoolers spent 3 times as much time playing with same-sex peers as they did with opposite-sex peers. By the time the children were 6½, they spent 11 times as much time with same-sex peers as with opposite-sex peers. Relative gender affects not only rates of peer interactions, but also the qualities of those interactions. Maccoby (1988) pointed out that play styles and modes of social influence are different in boy–boy and girl–girl interactions, with boy–boy interactions being rougher, more physical, and involving considerably more body contact than girl–girl interactions. Boy–boy interactions also seem to be geared toward individualistic enhancement, whereas girl–girl interactions are geared toward enhancing relationships. Because of the different orientations of boys and girls, then, boy–girl interactions often fail to be mutually satisfying (Maccoby, 1990).

Age differences among peers also exert a powerful influence on interactions, with mixed-aged peer relationships being far less frequent than same-aged relationships (Hartup, 1983). Although this is partially due to the age-graded structure of our educational systems, children often segregate themselves by age even in contexts that encourage mixed-aged relationships. For example, in multigrade classrooms, upward of 80%–90% of children's friendships are with same-grade peers. Observational data also show that mixed-age interactions are qualitatively different from same-aged interactions, with asymmetries in power and influence more evident in mixed-age dyads (Hartup, 1983).

In sibling research, the influence of biosocial structure on sibling relationships has sometimes been downplayed and overlooked (Furman & Buhrmester, 1985b; Stocker, Dunn, & Plomin, 1989). When considered in light of the peer data, it is puzzling why stronger links have not been found between biosocial status and the qualities of sibling relationships. As is seen here, there are already data revealing parallels between the effects of biosocial structure on sibling and on peer relationships.

Social-Role Structure

Social roles constitute another important aspect of relationship structure (Bigner, 1974; Brody, Stoneman, & R. MacKinnon, 1982). Siblings can occupy varying roles, including friend, competitor, caregiver/caregivee, teacher/learner, manager/managee, and so forth, each of which is accompanied by different norms for behavior. Similarly, peers can enact a variety of roles, including playmate, best friend, competitor, confidant, romantic partner, sexual partner, and so on. Sex roles also provide a pervasive type of role structure that prescribes norms for both same-sex and mixed-sex interactions (Maccoby, 1990). Any one relationship can comprise multiple roles, with partners slipping in and out of different roles depending on the context and flow of interaction. It is important, therefore, that our characterizations of relationships consider how frequently different role structures are enacted.

Although I have not directly assessed role structure in our sibling research, Brody and his colleagues have found developmental changes in the social-role structure of sibling relationships. In a study of preschool-aged and school-aged sibling pairs, they found that older school-aged female siblings took on a teacher role more often than any other sibling, and that younger school-aged females took on a learner role more often than any other younger sibling (Brody, Stoneman, C. E. MacKinnon, & R. MacKinnon, 1985). These findings illustrate the complex ways that social-role structure interacts with biosocial structure (and with sex-role structure) to shape the developmental course of sibling relationships. As is evident further on, some of the major developmental changes that take place in sibling relationships are probably best understood in terms of changes in role structures.

Systemic Structure

The term *systemic structure* denotes the nature of the larger relational units in which relationships are embedded. The most extensive theorizing about systemic structure comes from family systems theory (Minuchin, 1974). The systemic structure of sibling relationships involves the overall configuration of the sibship constellation. Many children have relationships with two or more siblings, with some holding the position of eldest, others holding the position of youngest, and still others holding the middle position where they simultaneously act as a younger and older sibling. Bossard and Boll (1956) described the interwoven systems and subsystems that exist in large families, often involving complex authority structures that shift depending on which siblings are present.

The nature of interactions can vary depending on whether interactions occur in dyads, triads, or larger systems. Just as the father's presence affects a mother's interaction with her child (e.g., Belsky, 1981), the presence of three versus two siblings is likely to influence the quality of sibling interactions. Although virtually no empirical studies have addressed this possibility, related studies have shown that the presence of the mother clearly affects siblings' interactions. For example, in a study of preschool-aged sibling pairs, Corter, Abramovitch, and Pepler (1983) found that the presence of the mother reduced the overall level of sibling interaction, and that interactions between siblings tended to be less antagonistic and more positive if the mother was absent. Similar effects are likely to be found in comparisons of dyadic versus triadic sibling interactions. To the extent that our assessments of sibling relationships are in exclusively dyadic (or triadic) contexts, researchers may be missing out on important systemic features of sibling life.

Peer relationships also have a complex and changing systemic structure. Several different interrelated peer system units can be identified (Brown, 1989; Dunphy, 1963). At a dyadic level, children have reasonably stable playmates and friends from a very young age (Howes, 1987). When children enter school or group settings, their dyadic relationships occur within the context of popularity and dominance hierarchies (Asher & Coie, 1990; Hartup, 1983). During preadolescence, stable same-sex peer groups begin to emerge and the importance of being in a group increases during early adolescence, tapering off during the late teen years (Brown, Eicher, & Petrie, 1986; Gavin & Furman, 1989; Savin-Williams, 1980). Dunphy's (1963) classic ethnographic study of Australian youth provides good examples of the systemic structure of adolescents' group lives. He described how the most popular members of cliques during adolescence venture out to form romantic relationships with members of cliques of the opposite sex. This hierarchical integration of cliques results in a more encompassing "crowd" structure, which provides a context for social mixing during later adolescence. Like most researchers, I have generally skirted the complexity of systemic structure of children's relationships by focusing on a few of the more important types of dyadic units, such as friendships and romantic relationships. It is increasingly evident, however, that researchers need to seriously consider systemic factors in both designing studies and interpreting findings.

Socioemotional Structure

The term *socioemotional structure* is used here to refer to the behavioral and affective interdependencies in children's personal relationships. Several aspects of socioemotional structure are identifiable (Kelley, 1979). One fundamental aspect concerns the nature of interdependence in relationships (U. Foa & E. B. Foa, 1975). In some cases, interdependencies are involuntary, such as when membership in a family or classroom creates forced interactions, for example, having to share a bedroom or play area. In other cases, interdependencies are voluntary, such as when two peers (or siblings) choose to be friends. In all cases, it is informative to identify the types of need fulfillment that create the basis of interdependence in relationships (Sullivan, 1953; Weiss, 1974). By characterizing relationships in terms of the needs they fulfill, we learn a great deal about the functional role they play in individual adjustment and development. Indeed, one overriding goal of much of Furman and my work has been to map developmental changes in the need-fulfilling functions of children's family and peer relationships.

Another aspect of socioemotional structure concerns the nature and extent of power and authority that are exercised in relationships, ranging from the egalitarian to the asymmetrical (Hartup, 1983). Peer relationships are generally considered to be more egalitarian than parent–child relationships (Piaget, 1932; Youniss & Smollar, 1985), whereas sibling relationships vary between these two extremes. Although the power structure of relationships is closely linked to their biosocial and role structures, power structure is not completely reducible to those factors. For example, asymmetries in influence emerge even within the highly egalitarian structure of friendships.

In summary, at least four different aspects of relationship structure can be identified. There is a dynamic interplay among the different facets of relationship structure, with biosocial structure influencing role structure, which in turn influences and is influenced by socioemotional structure. This dynamic interplay makes it hard, if not impossible, to study one aspect of relationship structure without considering others. Because sibling relationships vary considerably in terms of each of these aspects of structure, it is particularly difficult to study all forms of sibling relationships (and even more difficult to arrive at simple conclusions). Despite these challenges, the field has made steady progress over the past decade toward finding better ways to grapple with and understand this complexity. I now turn to consider findings from our research that shed light on the changing structures of sibling and peer relationships.

THE ROLES OF SIBLINGS AND PEERS
IN SOCIOEMOTIONAL NEED FULFILLMENT

What do children subjectively get out of their relationships with siblings and peers? In attempting to answer this question, I have found Weiss' (1974) and Sullivan's (1953) theorizing about social provisions and needs to be useful in characterizing the socioemotional functions of different types of relationships (Buhrmester & Furman, 1986).

As can be seen in Table 2.1, both Weiss and Sullivan contend that people have needs for "tender" attachments, playful involvement with others, vali-

TABLE 2.1
Two Theorists' Taxonomies of Social Provisions and Social Needs

Robert Weiss' (1974) Social Provisions	*Harry Stack Sullivan's (1953)* Social Needs
Attachment: Security and affection	Tender contact from the mothering one
Social integration: Companionship and the sharing of experience	Coparticipation in playful activities
Enhancement of worth: Affirmation of one's value and competence	Acceptance and status in peer society
Emotional intimacy: Close, intimate relationship	Intimacy and consensual validation
Reliable alliance: A lasting, dependable bond, though not necessarily an emotional one	
Guidance: Tangible aid, advice, and support	
Opportunity for nurturance: Responsibility for the well-being of a dependent other	
	Sexually arousing contact

dation of worth, and emotionally intimate exchanges. Weiss additionally discussed desires for permanence or alliance in relationships, advice and support, and the opportunity to nurture others, whereas Sullivan described how sexuality is a powerful desire in certain relationships.

Both Weiss and Sullivan further asserted that there is specialization in terms of the types of relationships that satisfy different social needs. For example, attachment needs are primarily fulfilled through parent–child relationships, whereas intimate disclosure and sexuality are primarily found in non-family relationships during adolescence. Moreover, this theoretical view encourages us to consider need fulfillment at the level of the *network* of personal relationships, rather than simply in terms of isolated dyadic relationships.

What roles do peers and siblings play in need fulfillment? Furman and I investigated this question by developing a self-report questionnaire, entitled Network of Relationships Inventory (NRI), to assess Robert Weiss' six social provisions (Furman & Buhrmester, 1985a). Each item asks children to rate how often or to what degree a need is met in a relationship. For example, an item tapping companionship reads: "How much free time do you spend doing interesting and enjoyable things with this person?" Children rate relationships this way with each member of their network. Subsequent research indicates that the scale scores are reliable and moderately to strongly correlated with independent ratings made by relationship partners. For instance, separate ratings made by parents and children of their relationships correlate .40 to .70 (Furman et al., 1989), and ratings made by reciprocal best friends correlate

.60 to .80 for the intimacy and companionship scales (Buhrmester, 1990). Although the relationship between these self-report ratings and observable behaviors have yet to be thoroughly examined, the available findings clearly indicate that the scales capture a subjective reality that is shared by the insiders of relationships (Olson, 1977).

Figure 2.1 presents preadolescent boys' and girls' (N = 198) ratings of four social needs as met through relationships with siblings, friends, parents, grandparents, and teachers. Ratings of the latter three relationships are included as useful points of comparisons. These data provide clear evidence of the specialized nature of the need-fulfilling roles of friends and siblings during preadolescence. As can be seen, both friends and siblings are important sources of companionship, with friends being reported as the most frequent source of playful companionship, followed closely by siblings.

The affection or attachment items ask how much the pair liked, loved, and really cared about each other. Consistent with expectations, both siblings and peers were perceived as less frequent sources of affection than parents. Siblings were, nonetheless, viewed as substantial providers of affection. For friendships, there was a noteworthy sex difference in the exchange of affection, with girls reporting more expression of sentiment than boys. This is a relatively common finding in the literature on friendship, which may reflect greater expressive and communal sex-role orientation in girl–girl relationships, or alternatively that it is considered socially undesirable for boys to admit to such sentimentality (Berndt, 1988).

Both friends and siblings were perceived as providing less instrumental assistance than parents and teachers, which is not surprising in light of the relatively egalitarian authority and competence structure of children's relationships with other children. The graph for siblings is misleading, however, because it masks a sizable sibling constellation effect: Children with older siblings reported that their siblings provided levels of instrumental assistance approaching that of parents, whereas children with younger siblings reported that their siblings provided little assistance.

Finally, the findings for intimate disclosure ratings indicated that siblings and, even more so, friends were important confidants for preadolescents. There was a noteworthy interaction involving sex of child and sex of partner. In general, girls reported more frequent intimate exchanges with other females, including mothers, sisters, and female friends. Boys, on the other hand, reported less consistent differences in intimacy with male and female partner. Although these differences were not large, they are consistent with research findings by social psychologists revealing that females may have a stronger need for, and may be more competent at, exchanges involving intimate disclosure (Reis, 1986; Wheeler, Reis, & Nezlek, 1983). As a result, females seem to be drawn toward other females to satisfy intimacy needs.

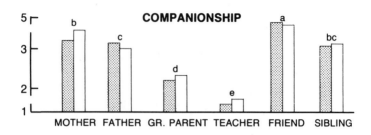

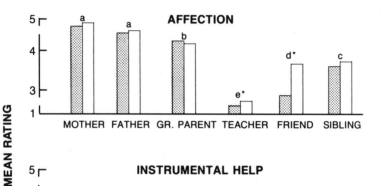

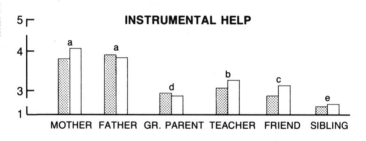

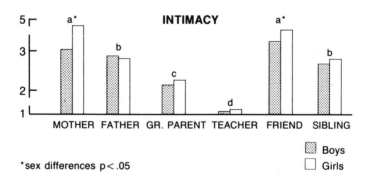

*sex differences p < .05

▨ Boys
☐ Girls

FIG. 2.1. Mean ratings of social provisions for relationships with mother, father, most important grandparent, closest friend, and most important sibling (adapted from Furman & Buhrmester, 1985a). Copyright 1985 by the American Psychological Association. Adapted by permission.

THE DEVELOPMENTAL COURSE
OF NEED FULFILLMENT

How do need-fulfilling roles change over the course of development? We have examined this issue in several different cross-sectional studies (Buhrmester, 1990; Buhrmester & Furman, 1987; Furman & Buhrmester, in press). As would be expected, the nature of the change depends on the particular need considered and the type of relationship involved. The findings for ratings of intimate disclosure reveal some of the most interesting and pronounced developmental changes across middle childhood and adolescence.

Figure 2.2 presents an overview of ratings for relationships with siblings, peers, and parents, and provides a broad view of age differences in reports of intimate disclosure. The data on relationships with parents provides an interesting basis for comparison. During preadolescence, parents were reported as youths' most frequent confidants, but starting in early adolescence, parents' roles as confidants diminished (although they remained important) to a low point in middle adolescence. This decline is probably a manifestation of the adolescent "separation and individuation" process (Blos, 1979), wherein youth strive to establish an autonomous identity by loosening their dependencies on their parents. As adolescents seek to exercise their emerging autonomy, they choose not to reveal all of their personal thoughts and feelings to their parents.

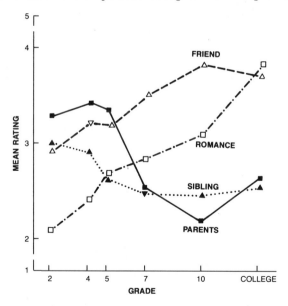

FIG. 2.2. Age differences in reports of intimate disclosure with most important sibling, same-sex friend, romantic partner, and parents (averaged ratings for mothers and fathers). Second graders rated "opposite-sex friends" in place of "romantic partners," as very few children reported having a romantic partner.

There were interesting sex differences in these age trends. The greatest declines occurred in girls' reports of disclosure with fathers, which dropped off precipitously during early adolescence (roughly coinciding with pubertal changes). Girls' ratings of disclosure with their mothers showed only a marginal drop during adolescence. Further attesting to the special nature of disclosure among females, high school and college females reported more disclosure with mothers than did high school and college males. Boys' reports of disclosure with parents also dropped off sharply beginning in early adolescence, with high school and college males reporting slightly higher levels of disclosure with mothers than fathers. These findings are largely consistent with those reported by other researchers (Blyth & Foster-Clark, 1987; Kandel & Lesser, 1972; Youniss & Smollar, 1985).

As suggested by Sullivan, same-sex friends were reported to be adolescents' primary confidants during early and middle adolescence (Parker & Gottman, 1989), and again, we found sex differences: Starting at about the fourth grade and continuing through the college years, females reported greater disclosure with same-sex friends than did males (also see Sharabany, Gershoni, & Hoffman, 1981). Even though reported disclosure with friends increased during adolescence for both sexes, the sharpest growth for girls occurred during the transition to junior high school, whereas the bulk of the increase for boys did not occur until high school.

Relationships with opposite-sex peers showed a steady rise in importance across adolescence, both in terms of the number of individuals reporting that they were involved in a "steady romantic" relationship, and in terms of the reported frequency of intimate exchanges. During the early elementary school years, reports of intimate conversations with opposite-sex peers were rare, which is not surprising in light of the already-described sex segregation that typifies this period. Reported disclosure with romantic partners began to rise during preadolescence, and then increased steadily across middle and late adolescence. It was not, however, until college that adolescents reported greater intimate disclosure with romantic partners than with same-sex friends. Here, again, there were interesting sex differences. Starting in middle adolescence, males reported confiding more with girlfriends than with male friends. Females, however, did not report a comparable move toward relatively greater reliance on male confidants; rather, even in our college sample, females reported about the same or slightly more disclosure with female friends as compared to boyfriends. Apparently, as studies of adult relationships have found, interactions with females provide an atmosphere that both males and females find to be conducive to intimate disclosure (Reis, 1986).

Finally, the developmental trend for sibling relationships was roughly similar to that of relationships with parents. There was a slight decrease from preadolescence to adolescence in reported disclosure with siblings. As in our earlier findings, the biosocial structure of relationships affected disclosure patterns, with subjects showing a clear preference for older rather than younger siblings as confidants. This preference was relatively constant across preadolescence and adolescence, amounting to more than one-half scale point (roughly one-half of a standard deviation). It would be incorrect, however, to interpret these data as indicating that siblings do not play an important role in need fulfillment during adolescence. Similar to the relationship with parents, disclosure and companionship with siblings remain moderately high in absolute terms. In addition, other ratings show that siblings remain important sources of affection and of a sense of reliable alliance throughout adolescence (Furman & Buhrmester, in press).

Although there was a modest trend toward girls' reporting greater intimacy with siblings than boys, there was also an interesting interaction between sex of siblings and whether siblings were older or younger than subjects. Older sisters were by far the most frequent sibling confidants, once again pointing to the uniqueness of interacting with females, particularly older females, who are themselves interested in, and probably good at, intimate exchanges.

Overall, these findings show that siblings and peers are important suppliers of companionship, affection, and intimacy. There are also clear parallels between sibling and peer relationships in the effects of biosocial variables on patterns of need fulfillment. Most notably, the gender composition of dyads influences the exchange of intimate disclosure: During middle childhood, intimate exchanges are most common in same-sex sibling and peer dyads, whereas during adolescence both males and females gravitate toward female peers and older female siblings as confidants. These effects of biosocial structure are obviously intertwined with the evolving gender-role structure of interpersonal relationships. There are also differences between the need-fulfilling roles of relationships with siblings and with peers. The developmental paths of sibling and peer relationships diverge during early adolescence when dependency on peers sharply rises and dependency on siblings wanes. This divergence comes during the time when youths are experiencing puberty and striving to construct autonomous identities outside the family. Friends become soulmates in this enterprise, whereas siblings are often left behind with the family.

THE "BIG PICTURE" OF SIBLING AND PEER RELATIONSHIPS

The need-fulfilling role of a relationship is embedded within, and interacts with, other features of relationship structure. Hence, different dimensions of dyadic relationships are considered next.

The Features of Sibling Relationships

When Furman and I began our work on sibling relationships, there were no systematic accounts of the qualitative features of sibling relationships. In fact, most of the literature on "sibling relationships" did not examine sibling *relationships* at all, but rather examined whether constellation variables like birth order and age-spacing were related to assessments of individual personality (Bryant, 1982; Dunn, 1983). To redress this situation, we interviewed preadolescent children in order to identify the features or dimensions that children naturally used to describe and evaluate their relationships. Based on their responses, we identified 12 different features of sibling relationship that comprise virtually all the qualities that investigators have discussed as important in sibling relationships (see Table 2.2).

Next, we developed a questionnaire—the Sibling Relationship Questionnaire (SRQ)—to assess each of these features. A factor analysis of preadolescents' SRQ ratings revealed three general dimensions tapping Warmth/Closeness, Relative Status/Power, and Conflict, along with a fourth weakly defined dimension tapping Rivalry. Subsequent research suggests that the SRQ is a reliable and valid measure of children's perceptions of their relationships and is able to assess relationship qualities at two different levels: (a) "feature" scores that provide a detailed picture that is readily translatable into interac-

TABLE 2.2
Factor Pattern Coefficients of Sibling Relationship Questionnaire Scales

	Factors			
Qualities	Warmth/ Closeness	Relative Status/Power	Conflict	Rivalry
Intimacy	70	—	—	—
Prosocial behavior	83	—	—	—
Companionship	78	—	—	—
Similarity	70	—	—	—
Nurturance by sibling	28	−77	—	—
Nurturance of sibling	26	85	—	—
Admiration by sibling	67	25	−29	—
Admiration of sibling	69	−28	—	—
Affection	69	—	−36	—
Dominance by sibling	—	−65	55	—
Dominance over sibling	—	80	41	—
Quarreling	—	—	88	—
Antagonism	—	—	92	—
Competition	—	—	63	36
Parental partiality	—	—	—	96

Note: Scores are factor loadings on a principal components analysis with a general pro-max rotation. Factor loadings below .25 are not presented. Factors are minimally correlated (−.20 > r < .20), except Conflict and Rivalry (r = .35).

tional behaviors, and (b) "factor" scores that provide a broader and more par-
simonious description of relationships (Furman et al., 1989).

Links Between the Biosocial Structure
and the Socioemotional Structure of Sibling Relationships

How does the biosocial structure of sibling dyads affect the socioemotional features of their relationships? The findings from several studies using the SRQ
can be summarized rather succinctly (Buhrmester & Furman, 1990; Furman
& Buhrmester, 1985b): First, biosocial status is modestly related to how warm
and close siblings report feeling toward one another (accounting for perhaps
10% of the variance). The most consistent finding is that same-sex siblings
report greater companionship, intimacy and affection than opposite-sex siblings.
There is also a trend, particularly evident during middle and late adolescence,
for individuals to feel closer to older rather than to younger siblings.

Second, biosocial status is modestly to moderately linked to reported conflict among siblings (accounting for perhaps 20% of the variance). Here, age-
spacing is the most consistently related factor, with greater quarreling and antagonism reported in narrow- as compared to wide-spaced sibling dyads (i.e.,
less vs. more than 4 years difference in age). In addition, youth report somewhat more conflict and rivalry with younger than with older siblings. Stocker
et al. (1989) recently completed more elegant analyses of the links between
constellation variables and relationship qualities in a sample of younger children, and found that temperamental differences and parental behaviors account for more of the variance in warmth and conflict than does the biosocial
structure of the relationship.

Finally, the findings for the Relative Power/Status provide a noteworthy
exception to the conclusion that biosocial structure has little influence on relationship quality. The relative age of the siblings has a sizable impact on whether
a child adopts a dominant/nurturant role or a dominated/nurtured role. In
this case, relative age accounts for upward of 60% of the variance in children's
perceptions of their relationship. This comes as no surprise, as the greater physical maturity of older siblings puts them in a position of greater competence
and power in dealing with younger siblings.

Comparing Developmental Changes in the Socioemotional
Structure of Sibling and Peer Relationships

How are the qualities of sibling relationships similar to, or different from, the
qualities of peer relationships? We have used the NRI (described earlier) to
address this question. The NRI contains separate scales assessing conflict and
relative power. By summing ratings across the six social provisions, a composite

index of perceived support or warmth can be derived. Figure 2.3 presents ratings for these three dimensions for relationships with same-sex friends, romantic partners, siblings, and parents.

The ratings for same-sex friendships clearly revealed the egalitarian and supportive nature of these relationships. Ratings of relative power indicate that children feel that they had "about the same" influence as their friend (also see Hunter, 1985; Hunter & Youniss, 1982). In addition, ratings of support were high across the four grade levels, reaching a peak in middle adolescence, confirming that support is one of the key defining features of friendship during adolescence (Berndt & Perry, 1986). Finally, conflict occurred infrequently in friendship and declined even further during late adolescence. Although youths certainly get in squabbles with friends, because of the voluntary basis of friendships they tend to break off their friendship if conflict rises above a moderate threshold (Berndt & Perry, 1986).

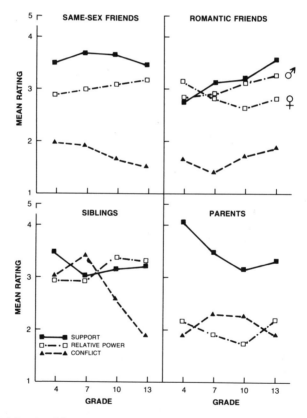

FIG. 2.3.   Age differences in mean ratings of support, conflict, and relative power for relationships with most important sibling, closest same-sex friend, romantic friend, and parents (averaged ratings for mother and father).

Ratings of romantic relationships revealed that there is considerable evolution over the course of adolescence in the socioemotional structure of romantic ties. In general, romantic relationships are similar to friendships in that they are voluntary relationships that are defined by a supportive and egalitarian power structure in which conflict is relatively infrequent. However, accompanying a developmental increase in dependence on romantic relationships for support we found changes in rates of reported conflict and in the balance of power. Among young romantic friends, conflict was reported infrequently, probably reflecting the idealized nature (i.e., a ''crush'') of these relationships (Ausubel, Montemayor, & Svajian, 1977). During late adolescence, however, conflict was on the rise, most likely due to the increased interdependency (and concomitant opportunities for conflict) that arises in ''going together'' relationships that are characteristic of this age period. These findings parallel those from studies of developing adult relationships, which find that accompanying increased commitment to a romantic relationship, there is also an increased frequency in, and tolerance for, conflict (Braiker & Kelley, 1979). Indeed, among adults, conflicts occur by far most frequently among spouses. Although the power structure of romantic relationships is fundamentally egalitarian, there was evidence of an increasing gender-related asymmetry in reported power, with both college males and females reporting that males had somewhat greater influence in the relationship (see Fig. 2.3). These findings for late adolescence are consistent with adult gender-role stereotypes and with the findings from other studies of adult romantic relationships (Peplau, 1979).

Before turning to the findings for sibling relationships, it is instructive first to describe parent–child relationships as a backdrop for understanding the developmental trajectory of family relationships during adolescence. Figure 2.3 shows that adolescence is a time of transition in parent–child relationships. Although the data indicate that Anna Freud (1958/1969) erred when she described adolescence as a period of ''storm and stress'' when pathology is ''normal,'' there is clear evidence of a moderate increase in parent–child conflict during this period. Other survey and observational studies indicate that the majority of parent–adolescent conflicts are not about profound differences in morals and values, but are more mundane squabbles over day-to-day privileges and responsibilities (Montemayor, 1983). Levels of conflict have been linked to puberty, with the apex of conflict coinciding with the apex of pubertal change (e.g., Steinberg, 1988).

Accompanying increased conflict is a change in the power balance in parent–child relationships (Youniss & Smollar, 1985). Subjects reported a decreased sense of influence and power during middle adolescence, which was recovered in later adolescence. Findings from observational studies suggest that this decrease in youths' sense of power is probably more perceived than real; by and large, there is a normative linear increase across adolescence in the observable influence and freedom parents give over to youth (Hill & Holmbeck,

1986). Our findings suggest that adolescents' desire for autonomy may out-
pace what parents are willing to concede, resulting in youths' reporting that
they are less empowered than they actually are.

Finally, there is a lessening of adolescents' dependency on their parents to
fulfill their social needs. This does not constitute "detachment" in most cases,
but does seem to reflect the shift toward greater interdependence with peers
(Hill & Holmbeck, 1986). The greatest declines occur in behaviorally linked
needs such as companionship and intimate disclosure, with less decline seen
in emotional needs, like affection. The general picture is one of a separation
and individuation process that results in a fundamental transformation of
parent–child relationships (Grotevant & Cooper, 1986). As adolescents strive
to establish individual identities outside the family, parents gradually loosen
their control. The findings from this and other studies suggest that, in the end,
a certain degree of rapprochement is usually reached, in which young adults
are attached to, but in many ways independent from, their parents (Shaver,
Furman, & Buhrmester, 1985).

The developmental course of sibling relationships is distinct from the courses
of peer and parent–child relationships. For example, one unique feature of sibling relationships is their relatively high level of conflict: During preadolescence and early adolescence, reports of conflicts with siblings averaged a full
standard deviation higher than that reported for any other type of relationship. This situation changed during middle and late adolescence, when there
was a rapid decline in reported conflict with siblings. In order to better understand this decline in conflict, it is necessary to take a more detailed look at
developmental changes occurring in other aspects of sibling relationships.

Furman and I recently completed a cross-sectional study in which we used
the SRQ to gather a relatively detailed account of normative courses of sibling
relationships during preadolescence and adolescence (Buhrmester & Furman,
1990). The findings from this study of over 350 Grade 3, 6, 9, and 12 students
can be summarized as follows:

First, significant transformations occurred in the Relative Status/Power structure of sibling relationships, with relationships becoming more egalitarian and
less asymmetrical as children enter adolescence. Figure 2.4 presents ratings
for the two SRQ nurturance scales—one assessing nurturance received from
the sibling and the other assessing nurturance given to the sibling—that are
broken down according to whether the sibling is older or younger than the subject. Scores are plotted according to the age of the younger child in the dyad.
As can be seen, during early and middle childhood there is a large asymmetry
between the amount of nurturance that younger siblings receive from older
siblings and the amount of nurturance directed from younger toward older siblings. When younger siblings reached about 11 or 12 years of age, the amount
of nurturance received from older siblings decreased markedly to a point where
relationships were more egalitarian in structure. Similar developmental trends

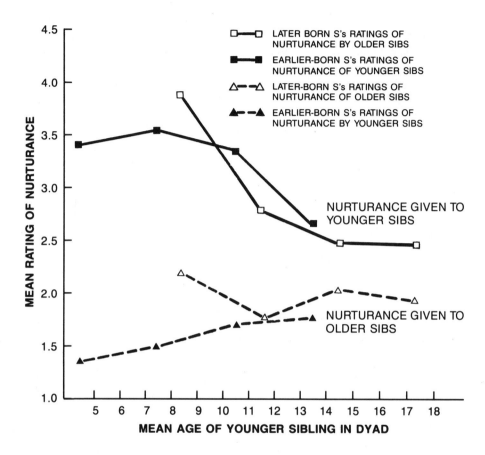

FIG. 2.4. Age differences in mean ratings of nurturance plotted according to the average ages of younger siblings in dyads (adapted from Buhrmester & Furman, 1990). Copyright 1991 by the Society for Research in Child Development, Inc. Adapted by permission.

were evident for ratings of dominance. These trends seem traceable to age-related differences in the developmental status of the individual children in the dyad. The bulk of this transformation was completed by the time the younger sibling was roughly 12 years old, the age at which children typically show a reasonable amount of self-sufficiency and can be trusted to be left alone without continuous supervision.

These changes seem to represent a basic shift in the role and power structure of the relationships, with older siblings giving up the explicit or implicit responsibility for caregiving duties. At first glance, this may seem like a trivial change in family responsibilities, but from the perspective of siblings, this is probably an important milestone in their relationship. The younger child in the dyad most certainly feels emancipated from the often oppressive authority that parents had given the older sibling in the form of a dictate to "look after" the younger child. The older sibling is also likely to feel liberated by not being required to let the younger sibling "hang out" with him or her. Thus, the shedding of caregiver/caregivee roles eliminates a role structure that was undoubtedly responsible for some domineering and conflicted interactions. This developmental trend parallels, to some degree, the changes in the authority structure observed in parent–child relationships.

Second, as children grew older, their sibling relationships typically became less intense. Ratings on every major dimension dropped off to some degree with age, including the exercise of power, the warmth of the relationship, and the extent of reported conflict. This trend can be traced to the decreasing quantity of interactions among siblings as they grew older. In fact, the most pronounced age-related decrements among the items loading heavily on Warmth/Closeness were for ratings of companionship. Data from home-based studies by other investigators corroborate our findings by showing that during the preschool years, siblings spend a vast majority of their time together (Ellis, Rogoff, & Cromer, 1981), but by adolescence, they spend a relatively small fraction of their time in direct interaction (Raffaelli & Larson, 1987). It is important, however, not to overstate the degree to which sibling relationships became more distant during late adolescence. Indeed, the decreases in ratings of intimate disclosure and affection across adolescence were relatively modest, suggesting that the emotional attachments between siblings remained moderately strong despite the decline in companionship. Cicirelli (1982) reported that many adults maintain strong attachments to their siblings across the life span even though they have infrequent contact.

Finally, there was preliminary evidence of a basic asymmetry in the affectional tone of older and younger siblings that increased somewhat during adolescence. For instance, Fig. 2.5 reveals that there was a discrepancy between older and younger siblings' perceptions of conflict: Children who were younger siblings reported that conflict with older siblings dropped off steadily with age, whereas children who were older siblings did not report a parallel decline in conflict with younger siblings. In addition to perceiving less conflict with older siblings, children who were younger siblings reported greater admiration for, and intimacy with, older siblings than vice versa. Younger siblings apparently looked up to and valued interactions with older brothers and sisters, whereas older siblings viewed younger siblings as an annoyance. This asymmetry in sentiments may be part of a separation and individuation process in which earlier-born adolescents try to distance themselves from the family, whereas the later-born children try to be "more grown up" by identifying with the greater autonomy of the older sibling.

Overall, it is clear that sibling relationships are not static during adolescence. There are identifiable normative developmental changes that parallel,

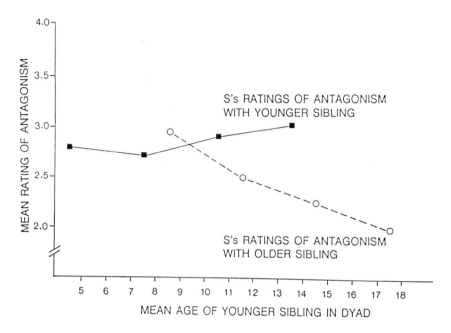

FIG. 2.5.   Age differences in mean ratings of antagonism plotted according to the average ages of younger siblings in dyads (adapted from Buhrmester & Furman, 1990). Copyright 1991 by the Society for Research in Child Development, Inc. Adapted by permission.

and are possibly causally linked to, changes occurring in other spheres of youths' social lives.

CONCLUSIONS

Three general observations seem warranted. First, the structure of sibling relationships changes in important ways during middle childhood and adolescence, and thus, there is good reason to think that the processes that are important in relationships at one age may not be so important at others. Because our cross-sectional studies yield only a series of still photos of how different aged youth construe their relationships, the next step is to gather longitudinal data that will examine more directly the processes involved in change and continuity.

Second, it is difficult to understand sibling relationships out of context; we must take account of the broader social contexts of peer and family relationships in which sibling relationships are embedded. This chapter has taken an initial step toward contextualizing sibling relationships by comparing and contrasting them with other types of personal relationships.

Finally, when the courses of sibling and peer relationships are mapped simultaneously, we see the unnecessary isolation of current work in these two domains of relationships. For example, the effects of relative sibling age and sex of sibling have seldom been linked together with findings about sex and age segregation in peer relationships, although the parallels are striking. The potential for cross-fertilization of fields is great. The larger body of literature on peer relationships can surely shed light on the nature and development of sibling relationships. Maccoby (1990), for example, has argued that the past focus on parent–child relationships as the primary determinant of sex-typing has been overly narrow and that considerable sex-role socialization occurs in relationships with same-sex and opposite-sex peers. It could be argued that siblings may be playing a similarly important role by either reinforcing or counteracting the sex-role socialization of peers. Clearly, we are just beginning the task of building an integrated understanding of the changing nature, causes, and consequences of children's relationships with siblings, peers, and parents.

REFERENCES

Asher, S. R., & Coie, J. D. (Eds.). (1990). *Peer rejection in childhood.* New York: Cambridge University Press.

Ausubel, D., Montemayor, R., & Svajian, N. (1977). *Theory and problems of adolescent development.* New York: Grune & Stratton.

Belsky, J. (1981). Early human experience: A family perspective. *Developmental Psychology, 17,* 1–23.

Berndt, T. J. (1988). The nature and significance of children's friendships. In R. Vasta (Ed.), *Annals of child development* (Vol. 5, pp. 155–186). Greenwich, CT: JAI.

Berndt, T. J., & Perry, T. B. (1986). Children's perceptions of friendships as supportive relationships. *Developmental Psychology, 22,* 640–648.

Bigner, J. A. (1974). Second-borns' discrimination of sibling role concepts. *Developmental Psychology, 10,* 564–573.

Blyth, D. A., & Foster-Clark, F. (1987). Gender differences in perceived intimacy with different members of adolescents' social networks. *Sex Roles, 17,* 687–718.

Bossard, J., & Boll, E. (1956). *The large family system.* Philadelphia: University of Pennsylvania Press.

Braiker, H. B., & Kelley, H. H. (1979). Conflict in the development of close relationships. In R. L. Burgess & T. L. Huston (Eds.), *Social exchange in developing relationships* (pp. 135–168). New York: Academic Press.

Brody, G. H., Stoneman, Z., & MacKinnon, R. (1982). Role asymmetries in interaction between school-aged children, their younger siblings, and their friends. *Child Development, 53,* 1364–1370.

Brody, G. H., Stoneman, Z., MacKinnon, C. E., & MacKinnon, R. (1985). Role relationships and behavior among preschool-aged sibling pairs. *Developmental Psychology, 21,* 124–129.

Brown, B. B. (1989). The role of peer groups in adolescents' adjustment to secondary school. In T. J. Berndt & G. W. Ladd (Eds.), *Peer relationships in child development* (pp. 188–215). New York: Wiley.

Brown, B. B., Eicher, S. A., & Petrie, S. (1986). The importance of peer group ("crowd") affiliation in adolescence. *Journal of Adolescence, 9,* 73–96.

Bryant, B. K. (1982). Sibling relationships in middle childhood. In M. E. Lamb & B. Sutton-Smith (Eds.), *Sibling relationships: Their nature and significance across the lifespan* (pp. 87–121). Hillsdale, NJ: Lawrence Erlbaum Associates.

Buhrmester, D. (1990). Friendship, interpersonal competence, and adjustment in preadolescence and adolescence. *Child Development, 61,* 1101–1111.

Buhrmester, D., & Furman, W. (1986). The changing functions of friendship in childhood: A neo-Sullivanian perspective. In V. J. Derlega & B. A. Winstead (Eds.), *Friendship and social interaction* (pp. 41–62). New York: Springer-Verlag.

Buhrmester, D., & Furman, W. (1987). The development of companionship and intimacy. *Child Development, 58,* 1101–1113.

Buhrmester, D., & Furman, W. (1990). Perceptions of sibling relationships during middle childhood and adolescence. *Child Development, 61,* 1387–1398.

Cicirelli, V. G. (1982). Sibling influence throughout the lifespan. In M. E. Lamb & B. Sutton-Smith (Eds.), *Sibling relationships: Their nature and significance across the lifespan* (pp. 267–284). Hillsdale, NJ: Lawrence Erlbaum Associates.

Corter, C., Abramovitch, R., & Pepler, D. J. (1983). The role of the mother in sibling interaction. *Child Development, 54,* 1599–1605.

Dunn, J. (1983). Sibling relationships in early childhood. *Child Development, 54,* 787–811.

Dunphy, D. C. (1963). The social structure of urban adolescent peer groups. *Sociometry, 26,* 230–246.

Ellis, S., Rogoff, B., & Cromer, C. C. (1981). Age segregation in children's social interactions. *Developmental Psychology, 17,* 399–407.

Foa, U., & Foa, E. B. (1975). *Resources theory of social exchange.* Morristown, NJ: General Learning Press.

Freud, A. (1969). Adolescence. In *The writings of Anna Freud: Research at the Hampstead child-therapy clinic and other papers (1956–1965)* (Vol. 5, pp. 136–166). New York: International Universities Press. (Original work published 1936)

Furman, W., & Buhrmester, D. (1983). The contribution of siblings and peers to the parenting process. In M. Kostelnik (Ed.), *Child nurturance: Patterns of supplemental parenting* (pp. 66–69). New York: Plenum.

Furman, W., & Buhrmester, D. (1985a). Children's perceptions of the personal relationships in their social networks. *Developmental Psychology, 21,* 1016–1024.

Furman, W., & Buhrmester, D. (1985b). Children's perceptions of the qualities of sibling relationships. *Child Development, 56,* 448–461.

Furman, W., & Buhrmester, D. (in press). Age differences in perceptions of social networks. *Child Development.*

Furman, W., Jones, L., Buhrmester, D., & Adler, T. (1989). Children's, parents', and observers' perceptions of sibling relationships. In P. G. Zukow (Ed.), *Sibling interaction across culture* (pp. 165–183). New York: Springer-Verlag.

Gavin, L. A., & Furman, W. (1989). Age differences in adolescents' perceptions of their peer groups. *Developmental Psychology, 25,* 827–834.

Grotevant, H., & Cooper, C. (1986). Individuation in family relationships: A perspective on individual differences in the development of identity and role-taking skill in adolescence. *Human Development, 29,* 82–100.

Hartup, W. W. (1983). The peer system. In E. M. Hetherington (Ed.), *Handbook of child psychology: Vol. 4. Socialization, personality, and social development* (pp. 103–196). New York: Wiley.

Hill, J. P., & Holmbeck, G. N. (1986). Attachment and autonomy during adolescence. *Annals of Child Development, 3,* 145–189.

Howes, C. (1987). Peer interaction in young children. *Monographs of the Society for Research in Child Development, 53*(1, Serial No. 217).

Hunter, F. T. (1985). Adolescents' perceptions of discussions with parents and friends. *Developmental Psychology, 21,* 433–440.

Hunter, F. T., & Youniss, J. (1982). Changing functions of three relationships during adolescence. *Developmental Psychology, 18,* 806–811.

Kandel, D., & Lesser, G. (1972). *Youth in two worlds.* San Francisco: Jossey-Bass.

Kelley, H. H. (1979). *Personal relationships: Their structures and processes.* Hillsdale, NJ: Lawrence Erlbaum Associates.

Maccoby, E. E. (1988). Gender as a social category. *Developmental Psychology, 26,* 755–765.

Maccoby, E. E. (1990). Gender and relationships: A developmental account. *American Psychologist, 45,* 513–520.

Maccoby, E. E., & Jacklin, C. N. (1987). Gender segregation in childhood. In H. W. Reese (Ed.), *Advances in child development and behavior* (Vol. 20, pp. 239–288). New York: Academic Press.

Minuchin, S. (1974). *Families and family therapy.* Cambridge, MA: Harvard University Press.

Montemayor, R. (1983). Parents and adolescents in conflict: All families some of the time and some families most of the time. *Journal of Early Adolescence, 3,* 83–103.

Olson, D. H. (1977). Insiders' and outsiders' views of relationships: Research studies. In G. Levinger & H. L. Raush (Eds.), *Close relationships: Perspectives on the meaning of intimacy* (pp. 115–135). Amherst: University of Massachusetts Press.

Parker, J., & Gottman, J. M. (1989). Social and emotional development in relational context: Friendship interaction from early childhood to adolescence. In T. J. Berndt & G. W. Ladd (Eds.), *Peer relationships in child development* (pp. 95–131). New York: Wiley.

Peplau, A. (1979). Power in dating relationships. In J. Freeman (Ed.), *Women: A feminist perspective* (pp. 121–137). Palo Alto, CA: Mayfield.

Piaget, J. (1932). *The moral judgment of the child.* New York: Harcourt.

Raffaelli, M., & Larson, R. W. (1987, April). *Sibling interactions in late childhood and early adolescence.* Paper presented at the biennial meeting of the Society for Research in Child Development, Baltimore, MD.

Reis, H. T. (1986). Gender effects in social participation: Intimacy, loneliness, and the conduct of social interactions. In R. Gilmour & S. Duck (Eds.), *The emerging field of personal relationships* (pp. 91–105). Hillsdale, NJ: Lawrence Erlbaum Associates.

Savin-Williams, R. C. (1980). Dominance hierarchies in groups of middle- to late-adolescent males. *Journal of Youth and Adolescence, 9,* 75–85.

Sharabany, R., Gershoni, R., & Hoffman, J. (1981). Girl-friend, boy-friend: Age and sex differences in intimate friendships. *Development Psychology, 17,* 800–808.

Shaver, P., Furman, W., & Buhrmester, D. (1985). Aspects of a life transition: Network changes, social skills, and loneliness. In S. Duck & D. Perlman (Eds.). *The Sage series in personal relationships* (Vol. 1, pp. 193–217). London: Sage.

Steinberg, L. (1988). Reciprocal relations between parent–child distance and pubertal maturation. *Developmental Psychology, 24,* 122–128.

Stocker, C., Dunn, J., & Plomin, R. (1989). Sibling relationships: Links with child temperament, maternal behavior, and family structure. *Child Development, 60,* 715–727.

Sullivan, H. S. (1953). *The interpersonal theory of psychiatry.* New York: Norton.

Weiss, R. S. (1974). The provisions of social relationships. In Z. Rubin (Ed.), *Doing unto others* (pp. 17–26). Englewood Cliffs, NJ: Prentice-Hall.

Wheeler, L., Reis, H. T., & Nezlek, J. (1983). Loneliness, social interaction, and sex roles. *Journal of Personality and Social Psychology, 45,* 943–953.

Youniss, J., & Smollar, J. (1985). *Adolescent relationships with mothers, fathers, and friends.* Chicago: The University of Chicago Press.

Chapter 3

Siblings and Their Parents

Frits Boer
Arnold W. Goedhart
Philip D. A. Treffers
University of Leiden

Long before the introduction of the systems perspective (Minuchin, 1985) to the study of child development, clinicians reported interactions between the quality of the relationship between siblings and the quality of parental care.

Within this clinical perspective, two notions stand out particularly. First, there has been a common assumption about the effects of parental unavailability that may be called the *compensating siblings hypothesis.* This hypothesis posits that siblings may develop a closer relationship when they experience a relative lack of parental care.

An even more popular assumption is made about the ill effects on the sibling relationship of parental favoritism toward one child. This we call the *favoritism breeds hostility hypothesis.*

The rise of sibling research since the 1980s has not rendered these notions obsolete. On the contrary, they are prominent in contemporary research and theory building, although they appear far more complex than before. In this chapter we review some recent findings and insights that relate to these two notions. Results of two studies relevant to them are then presented, and their implications are discussed.

"COMPENSATING SIBLINGS"

In their classic study of large families Bossard and Boll (1956) wrote:

> [When] the parents are tired and weighed down with cares and responsibilities, they may not have the time, inclination, energy, or affectional resources to satisfy

41

the respective emotional needs of their children. In such cases, it is natural for children to turn to other persons; and often this means other siblings. (p. 156)

Ritvo (cited in Lindon, 1967) pointed out that an older sibling may serve as a substitute for a parent when the actual parents are unable to carry out their nurturing and protective functions, and Bank and Kahn (1982) summed up these and many other observations when they wrote: "A variety of studies conducted over the last 50 years support the notion that parental over-involvement diminishes sibling loyalty while under-involvement can emphasize it" (p. 123). However, they warned against a thoughtless application of this "rule," by reminding us that parental deprivation can also lead to vastly different, unhappy, and conflict-ridden sibling relationships.

These observations were mainly based on clinical impressions and are of a global nature. The findings of empirical research conducted over the last decade are necessarily restricted to the specific aspects under study and usually allow only limited generalization. Nevertheless, with respect to the assumption about compensating siblings, some empirical findings do appear to reflect a compensatory or inverse association between the quality of the parent–child relationship and the quality of the sibling relationship. Other findings, however, point in the direction of a more congruous association between the two, and indicate that a more positive sibling relationship will be found in families with a more positive parent–child relationship. Still other research illustrates the complex character of these associations by showing that the type of association is dependent on other factors.

Bryant and Crockenberg (1980), for example, found that maternal ignoring in a laboratory situation was correlated with an increase in prosocial behavior by the older of two sisters in middle childhood; Dunn and Kendrick (1982) reported, in a longitudinal study, that a tired or depressed state of the mother following the birth of a second child predicted a more positive relationship between the first- and the second-born child 14 months later; and Hetherington (1988) found an enmeshed relationship between sisters growing up in a family without an affectionately involved adult. All these observations, as different as they are, seem to support the notion of an inverse relationship between the quality of parenting and the quality of the sibling relationship.

On the other hand, Bryant and Crockenberg also found a positive correlation between maternal responsiveness and prosocial sibling behavior; Dunn and Kendrick reported a positive correlation between the mother's talking to the older child about the feelings of the sibling with a higher level of friendly behavior between the children 6 months later; and Hetherington found an association between a companionate, caring sibling relationship, and the presence of authoritative, warm, and responsive parents. These observations are derived from the same studies mentioned before, but appear to reflect, instead, a congruous relationship between parenting quality and the sibling relationship quality.

In a review of these and related studies about parenting and the sibling relationship, Dunn (1988) wrote:

> The results suggest that a number of different processes are involved in mediating the influences of one relationship upon another. . . . Individual differences in children and the developmental stage of the child will influence which of these processes is developmentally significant. (p. 178)

"FAVORITISM BREEDS HOSTILITY"

When adults report a negative sibling relationship in childhood, they often attribute this to favoritism of the parents toward one of the children (Ross & Milgram, 1982; Vauhkonen, 1968). Parental favoritism is a well-known phenomenon, engrained in our culture, as the Biblical stories about Jacob and Esau, and Joseph and his brothers, and fairy tales, such as Cinderella, tell us.

Survey studies demonstrate that parents of children in middle childhood show a very low agreement with their children on parental partiality (Boer, van Diest, & Speckens, 1989; Furman, Jones, Buhrmester, & Adler, 1989). Parents differ from their adolescent children as well in their perceptions of how they treat their children: Parents believe they are more impartial than their adolescents do (Daniels, Dunn, Furstenberg, & Plomin, 1985).

The extent of difference in perceived maternal closeness predicts difficulties in emotional adjustment in the child (Daniels et al., 1985). Reported parental favoritism toward a sibling of an adolescent child, correlates with reports of depressed and angry feelings and some identity confusion in adolescents (Harris & Howard, 1984).

Parental favoritism can be conceptualized and assessed in different ways. It can be seen as a perception of the child; it may be seen as a phenomenon of which a parent is aware; or it can be observed by an outsider to the family. Of course, these three forms may overlap completely or partially. A child who complains about the preferential treatment of a sibling may be referring to something the parents are aware of and/or to a phenomenon quite obvious to a good friend of the family, but it is equally plausible that a child may feel favored or not without any obvious foundation in the behavior of the parents.

When parental favoritism is defined as something that outsiders can observe, it is usually referred to as *differential treatment*—a topic that has received considerable research attention. Compared to parental favoritism seen as a perception on the part of the child, differential treatment of children seems to be a more objective phenomenon, and one more easy to describe empirically. However, this phenomenon is not without complexity either, because differences in age, gender, and personality of children make it impossible (and even undesirable) for parents *not* to treat their children differently. These issues come to the fore in the research on the consistency of maternal treatment of different children within the same family at different points in time.

CONSISTENCY OF MATERNAL TREATMENT

In a classic study, Lasko (1954) compared mothers' behavior toward their first and second children when the children were 3, 6, and 9 years old, using the Fels Parent Behavior Rating Scales (Baldwin, Kalhorn, & Breese, 1949). She found that parental behavior toward their first children was on average less warm and more restrictive and coercive than toward their second, and this difference was more evident in the preschool years than later.

Jacobs and Moss (1976), in an observational study of 3-month-old first- and second-born siblings, reached a very different conclusion: "The primary finding of the study was that mothers exhibited less social, affectionate, and caretaking behaviors with their second-born than with their first-born offspring . . . [but] . . . second borns who had the attribute of being male and being a novel gender in the family matrix counteracted the maternal tendency toward diminished interaction with second-born offspring" (p. 319). Dunn, Plomin, and Nettles (1985) pointed out that the data that Jacobs and Moss offer would also allow the conclusion that the mothers were, in fact, quite consistent in their behavior toward their two children. They emphasized the importance of studying the behavior of mothers toward their different children at equivalent age-points and in similar situations because studies of different-aged siblings might assess differential responding of mothers to younger and older children rather than differential responding to the two children per se.

In a series of studies these researchers (Dunn et al., 1985; Dunn & Plomin, 1986; Dunn, Plomin, & Daniels, 1986) indeed found a high consistency in maternal behavior with 12-month-olds on all measures. At 24 months they found similar stability for affection and verbal responsiveness, but a difference in controlling behavior. When comparing the maternal behavior toward the same child at two points in time (24 and 36 months), however, they found little stability. The authors stress that most of the children's time at home is not spent in a mother–child dyad, but in the mother–child–child triad and that the change in behavior toward the oldest child simply means that there is little stability in the triad over time.

In a study of attachment Ward, Vaugh, and Robb (1988) found high stability in the behavior of most mothers toward their children at 12 and 24 months. There was a group of mothers (34.5% of their sample), however, that did not show this similarity in caregiving. Dunn and Plomin (1986) took a closer look at the correlation between maternal characteristics and the relative consistency of their mothering behavior, and found that mothers who were more sociable and extraverted differentiated less between their children than mothers who scored high on emotionality and impulsivity on a temperament survey.

These studies teach us that most, though not all, mothers show consistent behavior toward their children when assessed at the (child's) same chronological age, but that at a particular point in time the respective children may be treated quite differently because they are of different ages. The complexity of the phenomenon of "differential treatment" of children becomes apparent. Indeed, as parents will often tell us, it is impossible to avoid treating children differently. When, for instance, an 8-year-old boy is sent to bed half an hour earlier than his 10-year-old sibling, he may accuse his parents of favoring the 10-year-old, but when they are both sent to bed at the same time, the 10-year-old will find this "unfair," because he was not allowed to stay up so late when he was 8.

It is possible that these mild and common forms of differential treatment, which find a balance over a longer period of time, will have to be distinguished from more extreme and consistently one-side treatment. It may be these latter differences that are usually referred to in studies of differential treatment.

DIFFERENTIAL TREATMENT

In their study of the correlates and dimensions of prosocial behavior between female siblings in middle childhood, Bryant and Crockenberg (1980) noticed an association between the behavior of the child, the way she was treated by her mother, and the way her sister was treated. If there was a discrepancy in treatment, she tended to show more negative behavior toward her sister, even when her own needs were well met.

Brody, Stoneman, and Burke (1987), in a study of home observations of siblings between 4½ and 9 years of age with their mothers, found that both an imbalance of maternal verbalizations and an imbalance of maternal positive behavior toward the younger child were associated with less prosocial behavior between siblings. (However, when mothers directed more management behaviors toward their younger children the younger siblings verbalized less and engaged in less agonistic behavior toward their older siblings.)

The greatest number of significant correlations between dimensions of parental behavior and sibling relationships involving differential treatment were found by Hetherington (1988). If one sibling was treated with less warmth and affection, and more coercion, punitiveness, irritability, and restrictiveness than the other, that sibling was more likely to behave in an aggressive, rivalrous, avoidant, and unaffectionate manner toward his or her sibling. It was the *disparity* in treatment rather than the absolute levels of parental behavior that had the most profound effect. In agreement with Bryant and Crockenberg (1980), Hetherington found that the more advantageously treated sibling also showed more aggressive, avoidant, and unaffectionate behavior. When preferential treatment occurred, rivalry, aggression, and avoidance were more intense when

both parents favored the same child than if the mother and father favored different siblings.

Some of the issues concerning siblings and their parents were addressed in
two studies we conducted. Like most clinicians, we were convinced that *some*
siblings compensate a lack of parental care for each other, and that in *some*
cases perceived favoritism contributes to a negative relationship between siblings. We had no idea, however, how common these phenomena are. We were
particularly interested to know whether, and to what extent, these connections
would be found in a general rather than clinical sample of the population.

We were also curious to know whether such connections would primarily
be due to the child's *perception* of the different family relationships (parental
care, interaction with the sibling), or whether there would also be a more objective, behavioral basis to them.

With these questions in mind, we decided that families with children in middle childhood were particularly suitable for out studies: At this age children
are still very involved in family life, yet are old enough to be able to share
their opinions with an adult.

STUDY 1

All Dutch citizens are registered in their municipality, which makes it possible
to select families on the basis of their composition. For our first study we approached all two-parent families with two children in middle childhood in three
municipalities: Leiden and some sections of The Hague and Voorschoten. One
child had to be about 9 years old (i.e., between 8½ and 9½), and the other
child was not to differ in age by more than 30 months. Thus, the studies included children between 6 and 12 years old.

Two hundred families took part in the first study, which focused on the connections between parental care and the sibling relationship as perceived by the
child. Although more families were invited to take part, 42% of all the families approached by letter did not want to cooperate. We have to keep this in
mind when considering our results. Families from all social strata took part,
but we have to assume that there were differences between those families that
took part and those that refused to. With respect to parental care, it is likely
that there was an overrepresentation of well-organized families providing ade-
quate care in our sample.

In order to investigate the child's perception of the family relationships, we
developed two questionnaires. The first one, the *Leiden Sibling Relationship Questionnaire* (LSRQ) is somewhat similar to the Sibling Relationship Questionnaire
developed by Furman and Buhrmester (1985), but made suitable for the younger children in our study by using statements phrased in terms of concrete be-

havior (see Boer, 1990, for details about the instruments used in our studies). This questionnaire yields measures of *prosocial behavior, quarreling/antagonism, competition, parental partiality toward the child* and *toward the sibling,* as perceived by the child.

The second questionnaire, the *Leiden Parental Care Questionnaire* (LPCQ), is partially based on the Child's Report of Parental Behavior Inventory (CRPBI; Schaefer, 1959), but focuses on those parental behaviors that are indicative of the presence or absence of an unresponsive, indifferent style of parenting. This questionnaire yields measures of perceived *child-centeredness, hostile/detached behavior* and *laissez-faire* approach of the parent.

To be able to engage children as young as 6 in the administration of a questionnaire, it is necessary to use a playful technique. We therefore printed each statement on a card and asked the child to drop each card in one of four miniature mailboxes, carrying the labels *right, somewhat right, somewhat wrong,* and *wrong.* The reactions of the children during the administration and afterwards indicated that in general they enjoyed taking part in the study, especially because we explicitly asked for their opinion.

Results

Prosocial behavior of the sibling (expressed in the statement, "My sibling tells me everything"), quarreling (expressed in "My sibling is often angry with me") and competition (e.g., "My sibling makes a contest out of everything") generally found moderate affirmation by the children. Parental partiality (expressed in a statement such as, "My mother always says I am right and my brother/sister is wrong" or "My mother always says my brother/sister is right and I am wrong"), however, was denied rather strongly by most children, and even more so when this partiality concerned favoring the sibling rather than the child. First-born 9-year-olds showed a stronger denial of parental partiality towards the sibling than second-born 9-year-olds [F (5, 188) = 4.15, $p < .05$].

Another finding was rather unexpected. Of the children who did report parental partiality, there were some that reported parental favoritism toward themselves along with parental favoritism toward the sibling (the correlation between these two scales for 9-year-old children was $r = .39, p < .001$). Apparently, favoritism is not necessarily perceived as a one-sided phenomenon by children.

The perception of parental care, as measured by the LPCQ, reflected that these children, on average, felt treated in a child-centered way (expressed by an item such as: "When I'm frightened my mother always comforts me"), and reported little hostility and detachment from their parents. In general the mothers in our study were described as slightly more child-centered and slightly less hostile or detached than the fathers. However, when negativity on the part of the mother was reported, it was often expressed in terms of active antagonism (expressed in a statement such as "My mother often says other children behave better than I do''), whereas in the case of the father it took the form of indifference (e.g., ''My father often forgets the things he promised me''). This different expression of negativity may be due to the fact that in most families there was much more contact during a day between the children and their mothers than between the children and their fathers.

When we combined the child's perception of parental care with the perception of the sibling relationship, we did find connections between the two. First, we noticed a somewhat unexpected positive correlation between the perception of parental favoritism toward the child him- or herself with perceived hostile/detached behavior of the parent (for 9-year-olds referring to their mothers: $r = .31, p < .001$). This correlation suggests that being favored over the sibling is something children do not necessarily consider a privilege, but something unpleasant.

Second, there was a clear positive association between the negative aspects of the perceived parental care (hostile/detached behavior) and the negative aspects of the sibling relationship (quarreling/antagonism): $r = .43, p < .001$, for 9-year-olds referring to their mothers. A similar positive correlation between the positive aspects of these two relationships (''child-centeredness of parent'' and ''prosocial behavior of sibling'') was only found for the 6- to 8-year-old siblings: $r = .48, p < .001$, with regard to mothers.

In other words, these connections pointed to a congruous relation between parental care and the sibling relationship, rather than the inverse relationship that is assumed in the compensating siblings hypothesis. Of course, all the connections found in this first study were based on self-report by the children.

STUDY 2

In the second study, we added the judgment of outside observers. Fifty families, chosen at random from the original 200, participated. The parents were interviewed extensively about their rearing practices and about their view of the relationship between their children. Within a few weeks after the interview, the children took part in a series of playful tasks designed to elicit different aspects of the quality of the sibling interaction.

Measures of the parenting style and of the sibling relationship were obtained from the audio recordings of the interviews with the parents and the video recordings of the sibling interaction (see Boer, 1990, for details).

Results

A somewhat different course was followed in the analysis of the data from this study. In the first study the sibling relationship was measured by using the judgments of the individual children. In other words, one relationship was described by the two participants, who at times would differ in their appraisal of certain aspects of their mutual relationship. This approach does justice to the unique perception an individual has of his or her relationship with somebody else. However, there is also a dyadic aspect to the relationship, expressed in mutual interactions and emotions. In the second study we attempted to capture this dyadic aspect by creating a combined measure, based on the interview with the parents and the observation of the child. We were only able to do this in a reliable way with respect to the *negative* aspects of the relationship: quarreling, antagonism, and certain forms of competition and dominance.

The parents were judged separately on the different aspects of their parenting behavior, based on the interview. Three different aspects of parenting style could be discerned: *child-centeredness, strictness,* and *control.* Although mothers and fathers certainly differed on these aspects, we found enough similarity between the parents within each family (positive correlations ranging from .40 to .72) to be able to create a combined measure for the child-centeredness and control of the parents.

Notwithstanding the differences in approach, the results found in the second study were quite similar to those of the first. A more negative sibling relationship, now judged in terms of the dyad, proved to be correlated with a lower degree of child-centeredness on the part of the parents, $r = .37$, $p <$ .05, with one reservation: These correlations were only found for the children in the older dyads (in other words, the 9-year-olds with a brother or sister between 10 and 12).

With regard to parental favoritism no significant connections were found with the other measures in the second study. This may have been due to the fact that the recognition or denial of parental favoritism by the parents appeared to be based on very idiosyncratic understandings of this phenomenon. In anticipation of a more systematic analysis of this diversity we describe it here in a somewhat anecdotal way.

When the parents were asked about the possibility that one or both children would feel their sibling was favored by mother and/or father, the answers of the parents could be classified in one or two of the following five categories.

1. Some parents denied the possibility that their children would ever feel this way, in spite of the fact that all through the interview one or both parents indicated that one of their children was more difficult, required firmer handling, and so on.

2. Some parents denied feelings of parental favoritism in their children and added that they made a very conscious effort to prevent the rise of such feelings by treating their two children in a completely equal fashion.

Parents whose responses fell into either of these categories either implicitly or explicitly expressed that they considered parental favoritism a negative phenomenon.

3. Most of these parents recognized their children's feelings of parental favoritism, adding that there was no foundation for such feelings in their handling of the children, but that children will, once in a while, feel that way because they are more aware of instances in which the sibling seems privileged than of the equal number of instances in which the situation is reversed.

Most parents of this group did not consider this a problem. If they did, it was because they felt that one or both children showed an extreme intensity, duration, or frequency of these feelings.

4. Some parents recognized the experience of parental favoritism and said that their children had reason to feel that way. Sometimes this was said in an amused way, sometimes as an accusation of the spouse or as a self-accusation. The phenomenon would often be linked to differences in affinity to the children or to patterns around sharing activities and interests, sometimes linked to gender (mother–daughter vs. father–son).

5. In a few instances parents mentioned deliberate preferential treatment of a child they considered less competent than the other, to prevent or correct a feeling of low self-confidence.

We will have to keep these different forms of perceived parental favoritism in mind as we discuss our findings.

DISCUSSION

Compensating Siblings?

In our studies we did find connections between parental care and the sibling relationship. With the rather global level of our measures, these connections were of a congruous rather than inverse nature.

What is the significance of these findings? In the first place they add to what has been found in other studies on the relation between parenting and the sibling relationship. They suggest that the vicissitudes within one relationship may affect the other, although such studies do not allow us to draw conclusions about causality. At first glance we tend to consider the parenting as the cause and the quality of the sibling relationship as the result, but the direction may very well be reversed. A high frequency of quarreling and antagonism between children can easily cause strains and irritations in parents, which may lead to diminished child-centeredness in their parenting behavior. The findings in some studies (Hinde & Stevenson-Hinde, 1986; Stocker, Dunn, & Plomin, 1989; Stoneman, Brody, & Burke, 1989), pointing to a possible contribution of the temperament of the children to the nature of the sibling relationship, demonstrate the need to be careful in assumptions about causality.

The failure to find an inverse relationship between the quality of parenting and the quality of the sibling relationship could be due to limitations of our method, but also to limitations of our sample. Among the 200 families that took part in our study we found quite a variety in religion, cultural background, and socioeconomic status, but we did not encounter the more extreme forms of parental neglect.

Could it be that an inverse relationship between the quality of parental care and the quality of the sibling relationship is a phenomenon restricted to more extreme groups? With some speculation, it is possible to read the results of Hetherington's (1988) follow-up study this way. In a small percentage of families, the relationship of the (female) siblings she studied showed an enmeshed character. In these families there was no affectionately involved adult available for the children—a clear example of an inverse relation between parenting and the sibling relationship in rather extreme cases. In the other families studied by Hetherington, the relation between the quality of the parenting and the quality of the sibling relationship was clearly more congruous: Companionate, caring sibling relationships were correlated with authoritative parenting, and hostile, alienated sibling relationships were correlated with disengaged and/or authoritarian parenting.

In a somewhat different context Hinde and Stevenson-Hinde (1988) pointed out: "Extreme groups demand study in their own right—usually data from extreme groups can be generalized to more normal families, but different principles may apply in extreme or pathological families from those that apply elsewhere" (p. 370). This may also be true for the compensating siblings phenomenon.

Favoritism Breeds Hostility?

With regard to parental favoritism, in Study 1 there was the somewhat counterintuitive finding of a moderate positive correlation between parental favoritism toward the child and parental favoritism toward the sibling, as perceived by the same child. This finding has not been reported before; this could be due to the format of other questionnaires. Usually perceived parental favoritism is approached as a bipolar phenomenon, with perceived favoritism toward the sibling on one pole, the perception of a balanced treatment of the children at the midpoint, and favoritism toward the child on the other pole. On the LSRQ perceived parental favoritism is represented in a unipolar form. In the light of the current interest in differential treatment by parents (Brody et al., 1987; Hetherington, 1988; Stocker et al., 1989), it is important to realize that the perception of such differential treatment by children may be less one-sided than has been assumed.

When we analyzed the relationship between scores on perceived favoritism, the sibling relationship scales and the parenting behavior scales, positive correlations were found between perceived parental favoritism on the one hand and observed negativity in the sibling relationship on the other hand. There was also a positive correlation between perceived parental favoritism and perceived hostility/detachment on the part of the parent. Interestingly these positive correlations do not just concern perceived favoritism of the sibling, but even perceived favoritism of the child himself.

We hesitate to interpret this correlation, but it forces us to investigate further the different ways in which a child can experience differential treatment. In this (non-clinic) population of children in middle childhood, we have reason to believe that it is the phenomenon of differentiating between children per se, rather than its direction, that is linked to experienced rivalry with the sibling and the perception of a more parent-centered attitude on the part of the favoring parent.

It is tempting to connect this finding with the concept of scapegoating (Tooley, 1975; Vogel & Bell, 1960). This concept supposes a need on the part of some family members (usually the parents) to resolve tensions by choosing another family member (usually one of the children) as a guilt bearer. This concept is a popular one in clinical use, but very likely covers diverse mechanisms. What they have in common, however, is the assumption of the extreme one-sidedness of parents' differential treatment of their children. These findings draw attention to a related but different phenomenon: a susceptibility on the part of some children to differential treatment in general, where triumph about being favored and anger about being subordinated live next to each other in a rivalrous relationship with the sibling.

This susceptibility is related to the perception of having a less responsive parent. We are not able to judge the causal direction of this relation, but hesitate to infer that the parent is always first in creating this situation. It is possible that characteristics of the individual child and of the sibling relationship contribute to this susceptibility, and thereby create a situation that makes it more difficult for the parents to do right in the perception of the child. If we are to gain greater understanding of this clinically important, but complex phenomenon of parental favoritism, this is a possibility that deserves further research consideration.

REFERENCES

Baldwin, A. L., Kalhorn, J., & Breese, F. H. (1949). The appraisal of parent behavior. *Psychological Monographs, 63*(4).

Bank, S., & Kahn, M. D. (1982). *The sibling bond.* New York: Basic.

Boer, F., van Diest, C., & Speckens, A. (1989). "Voortrekken"—een onderzoek naar de beleving van ouderlijke voorkeur ["Favoritism"—a study of the perception of parental preference]. *Kind en Adolescent, 10*, 195–203.

Boer, F. (1990). *Sibling relationships in middle childhood: An empirical study.* Leiden, The Netherlands: DSWO Press, University of Leiden.

Bossard, J. H. S., & Boll, E. S. (1956). *The large family system.* Philadelphia: University of Pennsylvania Press.

Brody, G. H., Stoneman, Z., & Burke, M. (1987). Child temperaments, maternal differential behaviour, and sibling relationships. *Developmental Psychology, 23,* 354–362.

Bryant, B., & Crockenberg, S. (1980). Correlates and dimensions of prosocial behavior. *Child Development, 51,* 529–544.

Daniels, D., Dunn, J., Furstenberg, F., & Plomin, R. (1985). Environmental differences within the family and adjustment differences with pairs of siblings. *Child Development, 56,* 764–774.

Dunn, J. (1988). Connections between relationships: Implications of research on mothers and siblings. In R. A. Hinde & J. Stevenson-Hinde (Eds.). *Relationships within families* (pp. 168–180). Oxford: Oxford University Press.

Dunn, J., & Kendrick, C. (1982). *Siblings: Love, envy, and understanding.* Cambridge, MA: Harvard University Press.

Dunn, J., Plomin, R., & Nettles, M. (1985). Consistency of mothers' behavior toward infant siblings. *Developmental Psychology, 21,* 1188–1195.

Dunn, J., & Plomin, R. (1986). Determinants of maternal behaviour towards 3-year-old siblings. *British Journal of Developmental Psychology, 4,* 127–137.

Dunn, J., Plomin, R., & Daniels, D. (1986). Consistency and change in mothers' behavior toward young siblings. *Child Development, 57,* 348–356.

Furman, W., & Buhrmester, D. (1985). Children's perceptions of the qualities of sibling relationships. *Child Development, 56,* 448–461.

Furman, W., Jones, L., Buhrmester, D., & Adler, T. (1989). Children's, parents', and observers' perspectives on sibling relationships. In P. G. Zukow (Ed.), *Sibling interaction across culture* (pp. 165–183). New York: Springer.

Harris, I. D., & Howard, K. J. (1984). Correlates of perceived parental favoritism. *Journal of Genetic Psychology, 146,* 45–56.

Hetherington, E. M. (1988). Parents, children and siblings: Six years after divorce. In R. A. Hinde & J. Stevenson-Hinde (Eds.), *Relationships within families* (pp. 311–331). Oxford: Oxford University Press.

Hinde, R. A., & Stevenson-Hinde, J. (1986). Relating childhood relationships to individual characteristics. In W. W. Hartup & Z. Rubin (Eds.), *Relationships and development* (pp. 27–50). Hillsdale, NJ: Lawrence Erlbaum Associates.

Hinde, R. A., & Stevenson-Hinde, J. (Eds.). (1988). *Relationships within families.* Oxford: Oxford University Press.

Jacobs, B. S., & Moss, H. A. (1976). Birth order and sex of sibling as determinants of mother-infant interaction. *Child Development, 47,* 315–322.

Lasko, J. K. (1954). Parent behavior toward first and second children. *Genetic Psychology Monographs, 49,* 97–137.

Lindon, J. A. (Ed.). (1967). A psychoanalytic view of the family. *Psychoanalytic Forum, 3,* 13–65.

Minuchin, P. (1985). Families and individual development: Provocations from the field of family therapy. *Child Development, 56,* 289–302.

Ross, H. G., & Milgram, J. I. (1982). Important variables in adult sibling relationships: A qualitative study. In M. E. Lamb & B. Sutton-Smith (Eds.), *Sibling relationships: Their nature and significance across the lifespan* (pp. 225–249). Hillsdale, NJ: Lawrence Erlbaum Associates.

Schaefer, E. S. (1959). A circumplex model for maternal behavior. *Journal of Abnormal and Social Psychology, 59,* 226–235.

Stocker, C., Dunn, J., & Plomin, R. (1989). Sibling relationships: Links with child temperament, maternal behavior, and family structure. *Child Development, 60,* 715–727.

Stoneman, Z., Brody, G. H., & Burke, M. (1989). Sibling temperaments and maternal and paternal perception of marital, family, and personal functioning. *Journal of Marriage and the Family, 51,* 99–113.

Tooley, K. (1975). The choice of a surviving sibling as "scapegoat" in some cases of maternal bereavement. *Journal of Child Psychology and Psychiatry, 16,* 331–339.

Vauhkonen, K. (1968). On the pathogenesis of morbid jealousy. *Acta Psychiatrica Scandinavica, Suppl. No. 202.*

Vogel, E. F., & Bell, N. W. (1960). The emotionally disturbed child as the family scapegoat. In N. W. Bell & E. F. Vogel (Eds.), *A modern introduction to the family* (pp. 382–397). New York: Free Press.

Ward, M. J., Vaugh, B. E., & Robb, M. D. (1988). Social-emotional adaptation and infant-mother interaction in siblings. *Child Development, 59,* 643–651.

Chapter 4

Sibling Caretaking:
Providing Emotional Support
During Middle Childhood

Brenda K. Bryant
University of California, Davis

Families are caretaking, stress-buffering units, and siblings can participate in the caretaking functions of this central social unit (Bryant & DeMorris, in press). Caretaking means addressing the needs of others, and as such, families are stress-buffering units. Well-functioning families mitigate stress of family members in part because they define and address the stressful situations of their individuals as familial concerns rather than as individual concerns (Barbarin, 1983). Families do this because they define themselves as a cooperative unit.

Incidents creating emotional stress within a family unit can be viewed as a critical opportunity for the family to react in a cooperative fashion, and whether or not families "come together" in times of stress has implications for children's functioning. For example, Patterson (1981) found that children who are aggressive with peers were living in families that differed from families without an aggressive child with respect to how crises involving child discipline were handled in a family setting. Fathers who actively entered into disciplining when mothers were being ineffective (i.e., during periods of crises involving child discipline) had children who were unaggressive with peers. Fathers of aggressive children, on the other hand, were likely to remain uninvolved when there was a crisis involving the mother–child dyad. In this instance, when the family fails to function as a cooperative unit (e.g., mother and father united in establishing a consistent limit with the child), the quality of the child's relation with others suffers.

From another perspective, it appears that the extent to which children's stress experiences are aided, children are predisposed to respond prosocially to others.

The evidence for this is correlational in nature and can be illustrated in terms of children's expressions of empathic arousal. I have shown (Bryant, 1987) that it is not general, ongoing parental support but rather mothers' apparent expressive support in situations that are specifically stressful to children that is conducive to the development of empathy. Consistent with these data I also found that children from large families who turned to grandparents, and older children (aged 10 as compared to age 7) who turned to pets for intimate talks in response to stress, reported greater empathy with others. These findings suggest that when parents are relatively less available to children, as is thought to be the case in large as compared to small families, and as children age and are viewed as more capable of being self-sufficient, the availability of extended family members for stress buffering appears to be linked to children's greater sensitivity to the emotional needs of others.

I propose that the impact of a child's experience of parental support and warmth during middle childhood is in part dependent on the child's experience with other significant individuals. When parents are not available to help, or to respond effectively or sensitively to their children (as at times all parents are not), are there others who step in to help, and does the extra help affect both the child's experience of the mother and the skills and predispositions he or she will take to interactions with others? It appears that the answer is "yes," and, when we widen our vision beyond the dyad of parent–child relations, we begin to see how this occurs. I explore here the role of siblings in this regard.

THE SIBLING COMPONENT OF COMPLEX FAMILY FUNCTIONING: THE MYTH OF SIBLING RELATIONSHIPS AS SIMPLY DYADIC

Although many children now live part of their childhood in one-parent homes and an increasing number of children have no siblings, most children in the United States and Western Europe still live with two parents and have at least one sibling (Veenhoven & Verkuyten, 1989). Despite this reality, we have a research literature that, for the most part, operates as though this were not the case. Everyday parent–child interactions are not accurately portrayed when they are presented as pure dyadic interchanges. Virtually all the literature on the influences of parenting are suspect in this regard because there is good reason to believe that dyadic "findings" carry with them the unrevealed phenomena of how parenting behavior directed toward one family member impinges on others who in turn respond toward the child of interest or are "objects" of child observation with concomitant witness/bystander effects. Bryant and Crockenberg (1980), in observing mother–sibling triads, found that the effect of a mother's behavior on her children's social interaction with one another depended in part on how she treated each child relative to the other. Dunn and Munn (1985) also demonstrated that children responded to comments spoken directly to them as well as to those made by one family member to another. Similarly, sibling effects must be considered in relation to parent-child functioning, as the two subsystems are not independent. In other words, dyadic interactions within the family will influence and/or be influenced by whomever else is present.

What appears, then, to be a parental caretaking effect or what appear to be independent sibling caretaking effects may actually reflect a coordinated system of relationships among family members, including parents and siblings. Research designs and analyses have not typically addressed children's social development in this manner, so we have very little empirical evidence of how relationships are coordinated in families to effect certain outcomes. Consider the following example linking children's experiences in the family with their predisposition toward accepting individual differences among peers of the same age: In Bryant (1989), I started with the traditional, direct dyadic parent-child or sibling–child relations vis-à-vis the child's attitudes toward peers, and then followed up with a more complex analysis of indirect effects within the family system, in order to begin to understand the family process by which the apparent direct effects were obtained.

Acceptance of individual differences was defined as allowing close physical proximity to a range of peers, including children known to be relatively negatively evaluated by their peers (Bryant, 1982). Caretaking experiences of the children's mothers, fathers, and siblings were assessed by a modified version of the Cornell Parent Behavior Inventory (Devereux, Bronfenbrenner, & Rodgers, 1969; see Bryant, 1989, for a more complete description).

The simplest indication that parents' and siblings' actions are, in part, interdependent is the direct correlation between sibling and parental caretaking along comparable factors. Punishment was the only factor comparable across all caretakers (mothers, fathers, brothers, and sisters). The extent of punishment children reported their mothers giving them was correlated to that administered by older siblings, $r(166) = .39$, $p < .001$, whereas no significant correlation was found between fathers and older siblings in this regard (Bryant, 1989). Mothers and older siblings shared a concern factor in common, and older sibling demonstrations of concern were also comparably related to mothers' expressions of concern. Sibling relationships, then, are in part moderated by the relationship that children have with their mothers or, conversely, mother–child relationships are in part moderated by the relationships that siblings have. In this sense, family relationships are not accurately described in terms of mere dyadic exchanges.

Siblings' and parents' relationships with children can be similarly moderated by other categories of behavior, not simply the prototype of behavior. To consider these possible moderating effects, I followed up complex, three-way interaction effects pertaining to sibling behavior in predicting children's acceptance of individual differences in peers. Minuchin's (1974) concepts of *enmeshed* and *disengaged* family systems were used to organize an interpretation of these indirect family influences on peer relations. In Minuchin's system, members of "healthy" families know they are connected but have a good sense of separateness as individuals as well, whereas enmeshed families lack well-defined separateness between family members and disengaged families lack a sense of connection between family members. According to this approach, supplementarity of sibling and parental functioning, in which both a parent and a sibling coordinate the giving of support (to enmesh the child), or giving of punishment (to disengage the child), would lead to family enmeshment and family disengagement, respectively. Both enmeshment and disengagement in the family system is considered to impact unfavorably on children's social development.

Table 4.1 presents the three-way interaction effects from Bryant (1989) based on sibling dyadic relationships, and the follow-up analyses on these data consider more complex family functioning. Congruent with an image of enmeshed family functioning, sibling nurturance and supportive challenge, when paired with parental concern or support, was related to children's reduced acceptance of individual differences among peers. Similarly, and congruent with an image of disengaged family functioning, sibling punishment (boundary setting behavior), when paired with paternal punishment (also boundary setting behavior), was related to reduced acceptance of individual differences among peers.

Not only do these follow-up analyses of complex interactions help clarify how context (such as family size) and individual differences (such as age of child) operate in socializing children, they also define conditions under which the family system may be the more revealing unit of analysis. In the last example, neither sibling punishment nor paternal punishment alone was sufficient to "effect" lower acceptance of individual differences among peers. A system of punishment within the family involving both the father and the older sibling was required to impact on children's functioning vis-à-vis acceptance of individual differences among peers. Until we begin to recognize, both in research designs and in analytic strategies, that much of sibling relations and parenting occurs, not in isolation of each other as our research literature predominantly implies, but rather in concert with other family members, we will not understand how dyadic relations (neither parent–child or sibling relations) operate within larger social systems to affect children's social development.

Sibling Caretaking in Dyadic Exchange

Siblings can have even more direct effects on each other in setting and maintaining standards, providing models to emulate and advice to consider, enacting complementary and reciprocal roles in relation to one another through which social skills can be developed and practiced, and, as children get older, serving

TABLE 4.1

Sibling Effects Within the Context of Family Functioning

Sibling Three-Way Interaction #1—Sibling Nurturance × Sex of Child × Family Size

---

Description of interaction: Among females in large families, experiences of older sibling nurturance was associated with lowered acceptance of individual differences of peers.

Family system follow-up analysis: Sibling Nurturance interacted with Maternal Concern, Sex of the Child, and Family Size. The correlation between sibling nurturance and maternal concern was $r(40)$ = .39, $p < .05$, for girls in large families but negligible for girls in small families and for all boys.

Sibling Three-Way Interaction #2—Sibling Supportive Challenge × Family Size × Sex of Older Sibling

---

Description of interaction: For children in large families with older brothers, sibling supportive challenge was associated with lowered acceptance of individual differences of peers.

Family system follow-up analysis: Sibling Challenge tended to interact with both Maternal and Paternal Support in conjunction with Family Size and Sex of Sibling. In each case, the highest obtained correlation between Sibling Challenge and Parental Support (Maternal and Paternal) was found for the group of children in large families with older brothers, $r(40)$ = .61, $p < .001$, and $r(40)$ = .43, $p < .01$, respectively.

Sibling Three-Way Interaction #3—Sibling Punishment × Age × Sex of Sibling effect

---

Description of interaction: Among 10-year-olds with older sisters, sibling punishment was related to lesser acceptance of individual differences.

Family system follow-up analysis: Sibling Punishment tended to interact with both Maternal and Paternal Punishment in conjunction with Age of child and Sex of Child's Older Sibling. Among 10-year-olds with older sisters, the correlation between Sibling and Paternal punishment was $r(46)$ = .55, $p < .001$.

---

as confidants in times of emotional stress (e.g., break-ups with steady dates, menarche, pregnancy scares and so on; Lamb 1982; Mendelson, Aboud, & Lanthier, 1990).

In addition to roles directly learned, siblings frequently introduce aspects of culture outside the family to other siblings within the family. Sometimes siblings import friends, unique language, styles of dress, and games into the family system. They introduce to parents the needs for new rules or adjustments in relation to peers and others outside the family. At other times, children take their siblings to new places. Younger siblings are often able to go out farther in their neighborhoods without being directly supervised by a parent because older siblings (usually sisters) provide supervision (Hart, 1978). Thus, range restrictions imposed on first-borns are generally not imposed on later-borns both because parents think that the older siblings can chaperone the younger ones and because parents gradually change and relax their ideas regarding the need for control (Hart, 1978). Exceptions to this seem to occur for children of single parents and last-born children, over whom parents exert greater control (Holt, 1975). At times then, siblings are companions who directly link one another to larger social worlds.

Clinical Regard for Sibling Relations as Part
of a Family System

Under what circumstances can we best use siblings as therapeutic agents? Although a therapeutic relation may focus on the dyadic interchange between siblings, sibling relations are frequently influenced by the context of a larger group. These influences require consideration.

Consider in particular the family system. Because parent–parent, parent–child, and child–child relationships operate simultaneously within the family, interactions between any two members of the subsystem can be affected by the behavior of other family members (Cicirelli, 1976). In studying sibling relations, then, it is useful to credit the ways in which family members outside the sibling subsystem affect sibling relations in general, and explore the implication of such indirect effects for siblings providing care for siblings. One such indirect effect is now examined.

Impact of Parental Availability/Unavailability on Sibling Relations. Studies covering a wide range of ages suggest that maternal psychological and physical unavailability stimulates interactive, prosocial behavior between siblings by creating the opportunity for an older child to engage more actively in helping a younger child and by encouraging the younger child to use the older sibling as a resource (Bryant & Crockenberg, 1980; Bryant & Litman, 1987; Corter, Abramovitch, & Pepler, 1983; Dunn & Kendrick, 1982; Samuels, 1980; Stewart, 1983). Consider that parental unavailability can take several forms, including (a) physically distant, (b) physically absent, (c) physically and/or mentally ill, and (d) interpersonally conflictual and combative with the child. In research it has been maternal unavailability that has been most closely monitored, and under all these conditions of parental distancing, sibling bonds are generally enhanced (Bryant & Litman, 1987).

The very presence of mothers has been found to reduce sibling interaction, particularly prosocial behavior (Corter et al., 1983). When mothers are absent or physically distant, older siblings appear to comfort their younger counterpart and younger siblings seek out older available siblings. Stewart (1983) studied the responses of preschool children to their younger siblings' distress at being separated from their mothers. More than half of the older siblings in the study responded to the distress of a younger sibling with some form of therapeutic response (i.e., approaching or hugging the infant). Under more stressful conditions, such as the entrance of a strange adult when the mother was still absent, younger siblings approached and sought reassurance from older siblings, whether brothers or sisters. Samuels (1980) found that when mothers were instructed to be physically distant (remain seated at the periphery of an unfamiliar backyard) and to be responsive but refrain from directing the actions of their children, children benefited from having older siblings present. When an older sibling was present, infants left their mothers sooner, inspected features of the environment more, displayed less distress, and were more independent (often following the sibling to some location in the yard and then remaining to explore after the older sibling moved on). In other words, in the absence (absolute or relative) of their mothers, older siblings offered and younger siblings requested and/or accepted a therapeutic alliance. The benefits of this alliance for the younger sibling include less distress and greater orientation toward learning through exploration.

With respect to psychological unavailability, Dunn and Kendrick (1982) found that when mothers were very tired or depressed following the birth of their second-born children, the two siblings had a particularly friendly relationship 14 months later. Results from this study also documented that in families where mothers and older daughters engaged in frequent confrontations at the time of the younger sibling's birth, sibling relations were especially friendly when the younger child was 14 months old. Similarly, Bryant and Crockenberg (1980) found that when mothers frequently ignored requests for help from their school-age daughters, older daughters displayed increased prosocial involvement with their younger sisters. Younger sisters, in turn, were more willing to accept help from older sisters under this condition. These data suggest that siblings may be a particularly valuable resource for those children whose parents (due to either personal or interpersonal problems) are limited in their ability to meet their child's needs. At least, this appears to hold true for younger siblings.

A word of caution is warranted lest these findings be interpreted purely as parental unavailability solely benefiting sibling relations. Sibling abuse is far more common than is typically recognized (Brenner, 1984). Based on statistics of injuries that would warrant a charge of child abuse against a parent, Straus, Gelles, and Steinmetz (1980) found in their nationally representative study of family violence that severe *sibling* abuse occurred in more than half of the families they studied over the course of a year; parental lack of supervision or intervention has been implicated in this phenomenon (Bank & Kahn, 1982; Tooley, 1977). Bryant and Crockenberg (1980) also found that maternal unavailability in response to requests for help was associated with increased conflictual or antisocial interchanges between siblings. Thus, although parental unavailability may promote enhanced sibling bonding, this bonding is not always beneficial and indicates the need for adult watchfulness.

Parental unavailability, then, makes siblings a salient resource with a potential for ameliorating caretaking that may be lacking from the parental constituency of the family. The nature of sibling caretaking when parents are not available is an arena for considering sibling relations in dyadic interchange and as part of a family system.

SIBLING CARETAKING IN FAMILIES WHERE
A CHILD DOES NOT FIND THE PARENT
APPROACHABLE AS A CONFIDANT ABOUT
STRESSFUL LIFE EXPERIENCES:
A PRELIMINARY EMPIRICAL ANALYSIS

In the present study, in which we are just beginning to analyze children's intimate conversations with family members, one kind of caretaking was considered: caregiving focused on discussing events that children have found to be emotionally stressful—situations in which children have been sad, angry, or worried. This focus on discussions per se was a response to what I found to be surprisingly little maternal acknowledgment (much less discussion) of emotional expressions made by 7 and 10- to 11-year-old daughters who were engaged in challenging and at times competitive, conflictual sibling situations (cf. Bryant & Crockenberg, 1980). Puzzled by this paucity of acknowledgment of feeling states of their school-aged children, I began to work from an assumption that mothers (and I assume fathers also) do not typically discuss school-aged children's emotions unless they decide to have a "heart-to-heart" talk with them. So, in developing the protocol for the data I am currently coding, I decided to tell parents (and siblings) directly that I was interested in hearing how they talked to their children (or siblings) about sad, angry, and worried experiences when they decided to do that. This forms the basic data set I began with: a series of private discussions within dyads: the mother–child, father–child, and sibling–sibling dyad for each child. The older person in the dyad, the caregiver, was asked to talk with the younger person in the dyad about experiences in which the younger person had been sad, angry, or worried. Each dyad talked about all three effects and each child participated on three different occasions with one of these caregivers.

To examine sibling caretaking vis-à-vis parental unavailability, I decided to examine families in which the parents were, from the child's perspective, emotionally unavailable or unapproachable, at least in the sense that these children thought they would not seek the parents out for help in any of the three "crises" being examined (crises of sadness, anger, or worry). In particular, I began with those families in which children reported that when they were sad, angry, and worried, they wanted to talk with a sibling and not their mother nor their father.

Three questions are examined:

1. Can we identify reasons that children choose not to seek out either parent and seek out a sibling instead when they are sad, angry, and worried and want to talk to someone about the situation?

2. In what sense can siblings "substitute" for parenting? With respect to providing emotional support, are sibling caretaking and parent caretaking comparable experiences?

3. When children seek out siblings to discuss their stressful experiences, do they present themselves in comparable ways to those used with their parents? What is the differential child input in these dyadic discussions about stress with varying family members?

Subjects

For the present discussion, I selected a subsample of families from a larger sample (described in Bryant, 1985), that varied with respect to the child's perception of their choice of caregiver for discussions of personal distresses. The larger sample included 168 families, 96 with a 10-year-old and 72 with a 7-year-old. Half the families were large (with three or more siblings); half were small (with two siblings). Half the families had a male target child; half had a female target child. Half of the boys had older sisters and half had older brothers; similarly, half of the girls had older sisters and half had older brothers. Family size, sex of target child, and sex of sibling were equally balanced across all of these factors for each age group. All children had a brother or a sister 2 to 3 years their senior. It was these siblings who participated in "stress discussions," as did all of the parents, even if they were not sought out by the children. (Order of caretaker, i.e., discussion partner was balanced over the sample, for mothers, fathers, and siblings.)

The subsample that provided the data for the preliminary analyses that follow includes all children who did not name their mother or father as someone with whom they would want to talk about sad, angry, or worried experiences, but did choose their sibling who was 2 to 3 years older. There were 9 such subjects out of the 168 and I have labeled this group Sib/No Parent. Out of these 9 subjects, 3 were 7-year-olds and 6 were 10-year-olds. Four were boys and 5 were girls. Seven were from large families and 2 were from small families. Four were older sisters and 5 were older brothers. Six were same-sex sibling pairs and 3 were not. Family size, age of child, sex of child, and sex of older sibling did not appear to play decided roles as factors in why children chose to seek them out. It is important to note that brothers were chosen for this caretaker role as well as sisters.

The major comparison group became children who sought out their parents (mothers and fathers combined) for at least five of the six possible emotional situations (i.e., three emotions by two parents) and did not choose their older siblings. This group was labeled Parent/No Sib. There were 8 families that fit this description. Two of the target children were 7-year-olds and 6 were 10-year-olds. Two were girls and 6 were boys. Four were older brothers and 4 were older sisters. Four were from large families and 4 were from small families. Six were same-sex sibling pairs and 2 were not.

For comparisons that involved only sibling dyads, I included a third group:

children who did not seek out a parent or a sibling to discuss any of the three distressful experiences. This group was labeled No Parent/No Sib. There were 5 such children. Three were 7-year-olds and 2 were 10-year-olds. Two were girls and 3 were boys. One was from a small family, and 4 were from large families. Three were same-sex siblings and 2 were not. Three were older brothers and 2 were older sisters.

Procedure

On Day 1, the target child in the family was taken on a "neighborhood walk" to assess personal, home, and neighborhood/community resources, including whom children would turn to in times of stress (i.e., turn to talk to about sad, angry, worried experiences). Following this a battery of social-emotional measures was administered. (See Bryant, 1985, for details.)

On Days 2, 3, and 4, either a mother, father, or older sibling participated with the target child. Included in these sessions was a dialogue within each dyad (child–father, child–mother, and child–older sibling), which was tape-recorded. For the first 5 minutes, the caretaker shared with the target child some important and interesting experience that had occurred in the caretaker's life. Following this, the child was asked to recall and share with the caretaker experiences when he or she was happy, sad, angry, or worried (i.e., stress experiences). The discussions pertaining to sad, angry, and worried provided the data for the analyses that follow.

Coding of Discussions About Stressful Events. In developing a coding scheme for analyzing caretaking in the context just described, I began with Lazarus and Folkman's (1984) dichotomy of palliative versus direct action coping modes. According to these researchers' analysis of adult coping, *direct actions* are designed to alter a problematic relationship in one's social or physical environment, and *palliative modes,* which are intrapsychic in nature, are aimed at relieving the emotional impact of stressful events but do not alter the external environment (i.e., they are only meant to make the person feel better). What follows is a description of eight categories I am using to analyze children's discussions of stressful events with different family members participating in the caretaker role.

Two forms of direct action coping strategies were distinguished: direct action positive and direct action negative. *Direct action positive* was defined as caregiver attempts to instruct the child in how to solve the problem or prevent its recurrence (e.g., "Running away from dogs is the right thing to do.") *Direct action negative* indicates that the caregiver focused on the child's "incorrect" behavior or actions, on what the child didn't do, can't do, or won't do (e.g., "Don't make the dog angry"; "You didn't feed the cat, so we gave her away.").

Two major kinds of palliative responses were distinguished: expressive and cognitive. In addition, palliative responses can make the child feel better or worse, depending on the nature of the palliative responding, so positive and negative, expressive and cognitive responses were distinguished.

Expressive responses indicate that the caregiver focused on the child's feelings (past, present, or future). *Expressive positive responses* focused on the child's feelings by accepting or validating them (e.g., I saw how sad you were). *Expressive negative responses* indicate that the caregiver rejected, questioned, or invalidated the child's feelings (e.g., "Don't feel that way. I don't know what you have to feel angry about—you had a hamster, too").

Cognitive responses indicate that the caregiver attempted to change the child's thinking or re-focus his attention concerning an event so that the child will think of the event in either a more positive or a more negative way than he did originally. *Cognitive positive* scoring indicates that the caregiver focused on a positive interpretation, or attempted to minimize the stress of the emotional experience or event (e.g., "I protected you and took care of you, didn't I?"). *Cognitive negative* scoring indicates that the caregiver focused on a negative interpretation of the event, or provided a rationalization to justify not responding to the child's needs (e.g., "You always think he's crazy").

Two other codes were also used: *Information management* indicates that the caregiver attempted to gather or provide information during the conversation or failed to gather or provide information by ignoring the child or listening inaccurately (e.g., "He said it'll heal by itself"); *digression* indicates that the caregiver engaged in dialogue not relevant to the event or the emotional experience regardless of whether the child accepted the change of topic (e.g., "Tell the woman that we are done").

Finally, although these codes are stated to refer to the caregiver, the same codes were also used to describe the child's behavior in these conversations in order to provide information on the target child's role in these discussions.

Reliability for the coding scheme was calculated on those statements that the coders did not find questionable and was based on percent agreements between two coders reviewing 21 conversations. All questionable statements were coded by two persons to insure comparable treatment throughout the data for ambiguous statements. Direct action positive had 89% agreement, direct action negative had 100% agreement, expressive positive had 94% agreement, expressive negative had 85% agreement, cognitive positive had 94% agreement, cognitive negative had 100% agreement, information management had 97% agreement, and digressions had 100% agreement.

Analysis of Caretaking. Because of the skewed distribution of the data, nonparametric tests were used: Friedman's test was used to compare the three groups (mothers vs. fathers vs. siblings) which were not independent, with Wilcoxon tests used as follow-up for comparisons between two groups. The Kruskal-

Wallis test was used when there were independent comparisons across three groups (e.g., siblings from the three family types), and Mann-Whitney tests were used to compare two independent groups. A criterion of $p < .05$ was established to report significant differences.

Results

I present the data in terms of answers to the original questions I posed.

Question 1: Why do Children Seek Out a Sibling Instead of a Parent to Talk With? First, the behavior of mothers with whom children want to discuss emotionally distressing events was compared to the behavior of those mothers whom children rejected for such discussions. Mothers not chosen showed significantly more expressive negative behavior toward their children during their discussions of children's stressful experiences. (This finding held for percentage of expressive negatives using all coded behavior as the denominator.)

Using a similar analysis, fathers with whom children want to talk when they are distressed used fewer expressive negatives in absolute numbers and in percent of expressive negatives (of all coded behavior) than did fathers who were not sought out by their children.

Mothers and fathers who were chosen, when compared to those not chosen, did not differ in their use of cognitive or direct action strategies (positive and negative) nor did they differ in their use of expressive positives, information management, or digressions. One interpretation of this pattern of results is that children anticipate parents' feedback that their feelings would be unacceptable, and thus avoid creating a situation destined to be fraught with negative feedback about their feelings.

To evaluate whether siblings differ according to whether or not they were chosen to discuss distressing experiences, two groups of siblings not chosen for discussions were considered: those from families in which the target children sought out both parents (the Parents/No sib group) and those for whom parents were not sought out either (No Parents/No sibs group). Siblings who were chosen offered fewer direct action negative comments than siblings in the No parent/No sib group. Non-chosen siblings from the Parent/No sibling group showed more cognitive positive and information management strategies than chosen siblings. Both groups of nonchosen siblings displayed more direct action positive behavior than did chosen siblings.

It appears, then, that children are not capricious in choosing a sibling over either parent to discuss emotionally stressful experiences. Parents who negate or reject their child's feelings, despite a "full" complement of positive cognitive and direct action coping responses are, from the child's perspective, emotionally unavailable. In addition, when parents are unavailable, older siblings who tell their younger siblings that they have "messed up" (i.e., use direct action negatives) are also emotionally unavailable to these younger siblings. Children whose parents negate or reject their feelings and whose siblings tell them they have "messed up," despite receiving other positive and helpful messages, are the children who do not, when given the choice, want to turn to the members of their immediate families for care when they encounter emotionally distressful events and feel the need for emotional care.

Question 2: Can Sibling Caretaking "Substitute" for Parent Caretaking?
First, most children reported going to parents to discuss at least some of these emotionally stressful experiences. Still, although parents are typically wanted for the provision of emotional care, some children prefer receiving emotional care from their siblings. Do child and adult caregivers who are sought out actually provide equivalent responses to children? No. When the behavior of chosen (primary caregiving) mothers and fathers was compared to that of chosen (primary caregiving) siblings, the primary caregiving mothers showed more of every coping strategy except for digressions. Mothers showed more cognitive positive, direct action positive, expressive positive, cognitive negative, direct action negative, expressive negative, and information management. This held for percent cognitive positive, percent direct action positive, percent cognitive negative, and direct action negative, as well. In comparison to primary caregiving siblings, primary caregiving fathers also showed more of every coping strategy except digressions. This also held for percent cognitive positive, percent direct action, percent direct action negative, and percent expressive negative comments.

From these data, sibling caretaking does not appear comparable to adult caretaking. Sibling caretaking lacks the richness and complexity of adult caretaking in terms of the types of coping strategies provided in discussions with children examining experiences the children have found to be emotionally stressful. Thus, these data echo the caution recommended by Boer (1990): to proceed with prudence when we talk about sibling relations as compensating for a parent–child relationship. This is not to say that sibling discussions do not have an influence on a child's development, but rather that sibling caretaking, even when it may be chosen as a substitute for adult caretaking, may not be a comparable experience to that which other children receive when they choose a parent.

Question 3: As Children Seek Out Others to Discuss Their Stressful Experiences, Do They Present Themselves in Similar Ways? Children behaved similarly toward mothers who were chosen and mothers who were not chosen. Likewise, children behaved similarly to fathers they identified as desired for intimate talks and to fathers they did not. This was not the case for siblings. The behavior of children who reported turning to siblings for intimate discussions and not to their parents was compared to that of children who did not want emotional support from siblings. In this comparison, children exhibited fewer direct action positive, fewer direct action negative, and fewer expressive negative comments to the siblings chosen to provide emotional support than to the siblings not chosen. The sibling relationship appears to be more sensitive to factors other than status than the parent–child relationship in this regard. This also means that older siblings have differing challenges in discussing emotionally distressing experiences, depending on the extent to which their younger sibling prefers to talk about an event or not.

Finally, comparing child input to parents with that to siblings, children exhibited more cognitive positive statements to mothers and fathers than they did to siblings, more cognitive negative comments to mothers than to either fathers or siblings, more expressive positive revelations to mothers than to fathers, and more direct action statements to mothers than to siblings. As we consider family processes, further appreciation of the unique challenges a child brings to different family members, even if he or she is engaged in what appears to be the same activity will help define family dynamics. The clinical implication of this is that different family members will need different skills to respond to the ''same'' caretaking task. One family member cannot simply stand in for another family member without changing the caretaking experience, and this is true for both the child and the caregiver. Development will proceed regardless of who does the caretaking. It is our job to first understand what is experienced in sibling as well as in parent–child caretaking and then to proceed in an examination of the pattern of caretaking experiences children have with an array of family members to assess how these experiences relate to children's social-emotional functioning and development. Do children have the same needs in their sibling caretaking experiences if their experiences with parental caregiving differ? Future research is needed to enable us to answer this question.

ACKNOWLEDGMENTS

The funding for the data analyses was provided by the USDA Agriculture Experiment Station Research Program. I wish to thank Curt Acredolo for his timely assistance in data analyses.

REFERENCES

Bank, S., & Kahn, M. D. (1982). Intense sibling loyalties. In M. E. Lamb & B. Sutton-Smith (Eds.), *Sibling relationships: Their nature and significance across the lifespan* (pp. 251–266). Hillsdale, NJ: Lawrence Erlbaum Associates.
Barbarin, O. (1983). Coping with ecological transitions by Black families: A psychosocial model. *Journal of Community Psychology, 11*, 308–311.

Boer, F. (1990). *Sibling relationships in middle childhood: An empirical study.* Leiden, The Netherlands: DSWO Press, University of Leiden.

Brenner, A. (1984). *Helping children cope with stress.* Lexington, MA: D. Heath.

Bryant, B. (1982). An index of empathy for children and adolescents. *Child Development, 53,* 413–425.

Bryant, B. (1985). The neighborhood walk: A study of sources of support in middle childhood from the child's perspective. *Monographs of the Society for Research in Child Development, 50*(3, Serial No. 210).

Bryant, B. (1987). Mental health, temperament, family and friends: Perspectives on children's empathy and social perspective taking. In N. Eisenberg & J. Strayer (Eds.), *Empathy and its development* (pp. 245–270). New York: Cambridge University Press.

Bryant, B. (1989). The child's perspective of sibling caretaking and its relevance to understanding social-emotional functioning and development. In P. Zukow (Ed.), *Sibling interactions across cultures* (pp. 143–164). New York: Springer-Verlag.

Bryant, B., & Crockenberg, S. (1980). Correlates and dimensions of prosocial behavior: A study of female siblings with their mothers. *Child Development, 51,* 529–544.

Bryant, B., & DeMorris, K. (in press). Beyond parent–child relationships: Potential links between family environments and peer relations. In R. Parke & G. Ladd (Eds.), *Family–peer relationships: Modes of linkage.* Hillsdale, NJ: Lawrence Erlbaum Associates.

Bryant, B., & Litman, C. (1987). Siblings as teachers and therapists. *Journal of Children in Contemporary Society, 19,* 185–205.

Cicirelli, V. G. (1976). Mother-child and sibling-sibling interactions on a problem-solving task. *Child Development, 47,* 588–596.

Corter, C., Abramovitch, R., & Pepler, D. J. (1983). The role of the mother in sibling interaction. *Child Development, 54,* 1599–1605.

Devereux, E. C., Bronfenbrenner, U., & Rodgers, R. R. (1969). Child-rearing in England and the United States: A cross-national comparison. *Journal of Marriage and the Family, 31,* 257–270.

Dunn, J., & Kendrick, C. (1982). Siblings and their mothers: Developing relationships within the family. In M. E. Lamb & B. Sutton-Smith (Eds.), *Sibling relationships: Their nature and significance across the lifespan* (pp. 39–60). Hillsdale, NJ: Lawrence Erlbaum Associates.

Dunn, J., & Munn, P. (1985). Becoming a family member: Family conflict and the development of social understanding in the second year. *Child Development, 56,* 480–492.

Hart, R. (1978). *Children's sense of place.* New York: Halstead.

Holt, J. (1975). *Escape from childhood: The needs and rights of children.* Baltimore: Penguin.

Lamb, M. (Ed.). (1982). *Non-traditional families: Parenting and child development.* Hillsdale, NJ: Lawrence Erlbaum Associates.

Lazarus, R., & Folkman, S. (1984). *Stress, appraisal, and coping.* New York: Springer.

Mendelson, M., Aboud, F., & Lanthier, R. (1990, August). *Sibling relationships and popularity in kindergarten.* Poster presented at the annual meeting of the American Psychological Association, Boston, MA.

Minuchin, S. (1974). *Families and family therapy.* Cambridge, MA: Harvard University Press.

Patterson, G. R. (1981). Mothers: The unacknowledged victims. *Monographs of the Society for Research in Child Development, 46* (Whole No. 5).

Samuels, H. R. (1980). The effect of an older sibling on infant locomotor exploration of a new environment. *Child Development, 51,* 607–609.

Stewart, R. B. (1983). Sibling attachment relationships: Child–infant interactions in the strange situation. *Developmental Psychology, 19,* 192–199.

Straus, M. A., Gelles, R. J., & Steinmetz, S. K. (1980). *Behind closed doors: Violence in the American family.* Garden City, NY: Anchor Books.

Tooley, K. M. (1977). The young child as victim of sibling attack. *Social Casework, 58,* 25–28.

Veenhoven, R., & Verkuyten, M. (1989). The well-being of only children. *Adolescence, 24*(3), 155–166.

Chapter 5

Social Norms and the
One-Child Family:
Clinical and Policy Implications

Toni Falbo
University of Texas at Austin

At the beginning of this century, G. Stanley Hall, a founder of modern American psychology, reportedly said that, "Being an only child is a disease in itself" (Fenton, 1928, p. 547). His views were shared by other psychologists of his generation. For example, Frank and Lillian Gilbreth, early industrial psychologists, were efficiency experts who wrote several classics of American industrial management in the early part of this century, including *The Primer of Scientific Management,* in 1912. Two of their 12 children, Frank, Jr. and Ernestine (Carey) wrote the American classics, *Cheaper by the Dozen* (1948) and *Belles on their Toes* (1950), which chronicled the lives of these two psychologists and their children. It seemed to both generations of Gilbreths that the one-child family was inefficient: Why should two adults devote their resources to 1 child when, with the same resources, they could produce 12?

WESTERN LITERATURE

To test this wisdom, several objective studies of birth order and family size were conducted during the 1920s, and the results of these studies generally indicated that only children were either much like others, in terms of their personalities, or a little advantaged, in terms of their intelligence. For example, Fenton (1928) published an article that focused on the personality and social adjustment of a sample of Californians, ranging in age from kindergarten to young adulthood. He found that only children scored very similarly to their peers. Teachers' ratings of schoolchildren on such attributes as self-confidence, aggressiveness, sociability, and emotional stability, indicated little reliable difference between onlies and others. Among college students, the picture was much the same, with onlies showing no proclivity toward neuroticism.

Investigations of the mental health of only children were also ongoing in Europe. In addition to reviewing this early literature, Van Krevelen (1946) studied the records of adult and child patients admitted to major psychiatric clinics in Leiden, The Netherlands, between 1931 and 1941 and found that the prevalence of only children was similar to or lower than their incidence in the general population. Based on a survey he conducted in The Netherlands during 1942–1945, he concluded that only children benefited from attending kindergarten more than others because it gave them the opportunity to learn the lessons from classmates that children with siblings learn at home.

Since then, hundreds of studies have been published in psychological, medical, sociological, and educational journals in Europe and North America, comparing the personality and social outcomes of only children to that of their peers with siblings. The goal of this chapter is to review this Western literature with a special emphasis on understanding the power of social norms in creating and maintaining negative views about only children in North America, Europe, and most recently, China.

Overall, the research studies done in the West have examined a wide range of social and personality attributes and have used an equally wide array of instruments to assess them. With Denise Polit, I have reviewed over 500 of these studies (Polit & Falbo, 1987). We grouped the many personality and social attributes included in these studies into 16 categories, described in Table 5.1. These represent the types of attributes that have been thought to be associated with birth order or family size during the last 60-plus years.

Polit and I conducted several quantitative reviews of this literature in order to examine the extent of the difference between only children and others on these 16 attributes. Using standard meta-analytic techniques, studies were included in these analyses if they provided enough information to produce d, a statistic reflecting the size of the difference between the two groups. Cohen's (1977) d is defined as follows:

$$d = \frac{M_o - M_n}{s}$$

where M_o is the mean for only children, M_n is the mean for the non-only child comparison group, and s is the pooled within-group standard deviation. Thus, the effect size represents the mean difference between groups relative to the within-group variation. In many cases, d could not be computed from the means and standard deviations, because this information was not provided in the study. When either of these statistics was not provided, the effect size was estimated through a variety of alternative techniques (see Glass, McGaw, & Smith, 1981, chap. 5).

TABLE 5.1
Personality and Social Traits Thought to be
Associated with Birth Order and/or Family Size

Trait	Number of Studies Extant	Example
Achievement motivation	30	Helmreich & Spence's work & Family Orientation Scales
Leadership/Dominance	22	Bernreuter Dominance Scale
Citizenship	13	Berkowitz-Daniels Social Responsibility Scale
Maturity	13	Teacher Ratings of Maturity
Generosity/Cooperativeness	13	Altruistic Behavior
Dogmatism	8	Rokeach's Dogmatism Scale
Autonomy	26	Autonomy Scale (EPPS)
Locus of control	6	Rotter's Locus of Control Scale
Self-control	15	Self-Control Scale (CPI)
Self-esteem	22	Rosenberg's Self-Esteem Scale
Anxiety/Neuroticism	32	Q4 (Tension) from High School Personality Questionnaire
Emotional stability	21	Teacher Ratings of Moodiness, Crying
Contentment	12	Cantril Ladder
Extraversion	20	Extraversion Scale (EPI)
Social participation	29	Club Memberships, Dating
Peer popularity	21	Sociometric Choices

Note: For complete references for the specific instruments, please see Polit and Falbo (1987).

Table 5.2 presents the mean sample sizes and ages of the subjects of each group of studies. This table reveals considerable variation in sample sizes and the fact that certain traits, such as emotional stability and generosity, are more likely to be studied among schoolchildren, while others, such as locus of control, are more likely to be studied among adults.

The third column presents our ratings of the average quality of the studies within each category. Studies were assigned 1 point for each of the following: (a) a large sample ($N > 500$), (b) used probability sampling, (c) controlled for extraneous variables, (d) used multivariate methods of analysis, and (e) used an established or reliable measurement instrument, yielding quality ratings ranging from 0 (poor) to 5 (excellent). Quality ratings were independently assigned by Polit and me; the values shown are means of our separate ratings. The five studies deemed by both of us as having 0 quality were omitted from the meta-analysis.

The fourth column in Table 5.2 lists the weighted effect sizes. Given the diverse sample sizes of the studies included in this meta-analysis, we considered it undesirable to use equal weighting for all studies: Obviously, an effect size based on a large sample would be more reliable than one based on a smaller

TABLE 5.2
Description of Samples and Results of Meta-Analyses

Trait	Mean Sample Size	Mean Age of Subjects	Mean Quality Rating	Mean Weighted Effect Size
Achievement motivation	2778.1	16.0	2.3	.17**
Leadership/Dominance	1044.0	17.6	2.3	.04
Citizenship	705.2	21.5	2.3	.05
Maturity	1050.7	13.6	2.2	.01
Generosity/Cooperativeness	1888.0	12.4	1.5	− .04
Dogmatism	494.6	20.3	1.8	− .08
Autonomy	1092.5	16.7	1.5	.04
Locus of control	2065.0	23.8	2.8	.07
Self-control	1177.1	14.7	2.5	.00
Self-esteem	796.2	17.8	2.3	.11*
Anxiety/Neuroticism	785.4	18.7	1.9	.02
Emotional stability	2246.1	11.0	1.8	− .04
Contentment	1883.2	23.5	2.4	− .01
Extraversion	1026.6	18.4	2.3	.06
Social participation	2108.7	17.7	2.3	− .02
Peer popularity	929.5	15.4	2.0	.02

$*p < .05; **p < .001.$

sample. Therefore, all statistical analyses were conducted with weighted data, using the weighting procedure proposed by Rosenthal and Rubin (1982a, 1982b). This procedure essentially weights the effect size by the number of subjects on whom the effect size is based.

Only 2 of the 16 attributes yielded statistically significant results: They were that only children scored higher than others on achievement motivation and on self-esteem. These results are consistent with previous quantitative reviews of only children and achievement (Falbo & Polit, 1986), which have found onlies to achieve more than others and also explains why, at least in the United States, only children have been found to obtain more education than others (Blake, 1989), and at least for men, attain more prestigious occupations (Blake, 1981).

What is more remarkable, however, is the finding that for 14 of these attributes, only children scored similarly to those who have siblings. Despite Hall's early pronouncement about the pathology of only children, they seem to be no different from others on a variety of significant attributes, including their dominance, generosity, autonomy, anxiety, and peer popularity.

Two European scholars, Ernst and Angst (1983), completed a qualitative review of the Western literature published between 1946 and 1980, and reached conclusions similar to ours: that being an only child was not a disadvantage. Since then, other investigators have published their studies of only children and have arrived at the same conclusion. I confine my presentation here to the works of two investigators, one a demographer and the other an epidemiologist.

Judith Blake (1989) examined the relationship between family size and educational attainment in the United States. She based her conclusions on the study of several large surveys of the American population, including one conducted in 1955 and another containing information as recent as 1986. Altogether, the sample was about 150,000. She found that only children were much more likely to come from single-parent homes and to have had major health problems as infants. Statistically controlling for these disadvantages, she found that adult onlies outscored others in intelligence and educational attainment.

Furthermore, Blake's analyses indicated that the home lives of only children were more likely to promote the pursuit of intellectual activities. For example, such children were more likely to have been read to early in life, to have taken music and dance lessons, and to have traveled outside the United States than children from large families. Although only children spent more time playing alone, they were not less popular with their peers.

Deborah Dawson (1991) analyzed data from the 1988 National Health Interview Survey on Child Health, a large, nationally representative sample of 17,110 American children, ranging in age from birth to 17 years. The outcome measures studied included several indicators of physical health, school performance, and emotional well-being.

Dawson also found an association between being an only child and coming from a single-parent home. For example, only children were much more likely than children with siblings to live with a never-married mother.

Included in her statistical models were such variables as age, gender, minority status, SES, and maternal education, as well as whether the child was an only child. Being an only child did not have a significant relationship to the rates of accidental injury or asthma, or to the child's health vulnerability index, but onlies were significantly less likely to have headaches, to stammer, and to wet their beds. In terms of school performance, only children were no more likely to repeat a grade, be expelled or suspended, or be the subject of a special parent–teacher conference. They were, however, significantly less likely to have milder forms of problems, such as antisocial behavior, anxiety or depression, headstrong behavior, hyperactivity, dependency, or withdrawal from peers (see Tables 1 and 2 in her Appendices).

THE PARENT–CHILD RELATIONSHIP

Do these results mean that siblings have no impact on children's development? Of course, siblings have an impact on children's development, but this impact is limited to those children who have siblings. The data described suggest that the absence of siblings can be compensated for by others, particularly their parents, who not only interact more with only children than do parents of multiple children, but also may be more likely to act as brokers in arranging peer interactions for their only children.

There is evidence that only children and their parents have a special relationship. Polit and I were able to find 19 studies that focused on the nature of the parent–child relationship and compared only-borns to others. These studies included teenagers' descriptions of their parents, parents' ratings of their children, and observers' evaluations of the degree of positive contact between parents and children. The results of these studies indicated a small, but statistically significant advantage for only children and their families (Falbo & Polit, 1986). Why would this be so?

When people have one child, they have more opportunity to pay attention to that child and to spend time interacting on a one-on-one basis. The results of several studies in the United States demonstrate that only children receive much more personal attention from their parents than do other children (Falbo & Cooper, 1980). Rather than leading to neurosis in the child, being able to give greater attention allows the parents to adjust their childrearing when their child is not behaving up to their standards, in not achieving in school or in making friends. This self-correcting relationship nurtures the child's sense of self-worth. Furthermore, the relative inexperience of one-child parents leads them to have relatively high standards for their children at relatively early ages. These high expectations probably foster the development of achievement motivation.

THE PERSISTENCE OF BELIEFS

If the differences between only children and others range from nonexistent to mildly advantageous, why do so many of us continue to believe that only children are at a disadvantage? I speculate about the cause of this persistence at least in contemporary North America, and suggest that negative beliefs about only children may have persisted in Europe for similar reasons.

The scenario goes like this. Most adult Americans alive today grew up with siblings (Blake, 1989). This simple fact has many psychological implications. First, it helps to determine what we think of as normal. In general, what we think of as normal is largely determined by what is common. But there is more to it than that. What is normal is also largely determined by traditional views about what is right. The United States, like most industrialized countries, was predominantly rural when G. Stanley Hall made his pronouncements about only children. Most agrarian societies value large families because the more children a farmer has, the more work he can get done in the fields. Yet, despite the Gilbreth family's shining example, few regarded the 12-child family as ideal. Between 1936 and 1961, the 2- to 4-child family was seen as ideal among White

Americans (Blake, 1966), and since 1973 there has been a solid preference among Americans for the 2-child family (U.S. Bureau of the Census, 1974). Having no children or one child has never been regarded as ideal.

A second psychological implication of the fact that most Americans grew up with siblings is that our relationships with our siblings become part of our self-concepts. As Tesser (1980) has theorized, many of our evaluative notions about ourselves are based on our early experiences of comparing ourselves to our siblings. Siblings judge themselves as taller, smarter, clumsier, than their siblings. Given this, how do people without siblings develop evaluative notions about themselves?

Although no systematic study of this process exists, it seems likely that only children acquire evaluative notions from other children, such as cousins, classmates, and neighbors, as well as from their parents and other adult caretakers. Our finding that only children have slightly higher self-esteem than others suggests that the net sum of these evaluative notions about the self are more positive for only children than for non-onlies.

Nonetheless, for some being an only child is associated with loss. As reported by both Blake (1989) and Dawson (1991) American only children are disproportionately likely to grow up in single-parent homes; that is, they are more likely to have divorced parents, to have lost one parent by death, or to have no contact with their fathers. A child from such a background may idealize the two-parent, multiple-child family, particularly if their single parent repeatedly expresses regret about not having more children and a "more normal family life."

Polit (1980) found that children expressed regret about not having more siblings or having too many siblings depending on the mothers' expressed desires. Single or married mothers reported that their only children strongly wanted a brother or sister if the mother had also expressed to the interviewer a strong desire for more children. Conversely, mothers of three children (the largest family size in Polit's sample) would report that their first-born children frequently expressed a desire to have no siblings if the mother had independently expressed her belief that she had had too many children. The apparent correlation between mother's and children's desire for siblings could reflect the mother's projection of her own wishes onto her child. This correlation could also reflect the child's identification with his or her mother and their shared values and feelings.

Thus, it is not surprising that among American only children, there are some who are neutral about being an only child and there are some who are negative about their status. It would be a truly rare only child who has strong, positive feelings about his or her status because it is and continues to be nonnormative. The ones who are negative associate their lack of siblings with their mothers' regrets about not having additional children (perhaps because she divorced the child's father or the father died or the family was extremely poor, etc.). When grown up, such people give normative answers about ideal family sizes, adding that growing up without siblings is a disadvantage. If they seek psychotherapy, they may be likely to tell therapists that their problem lies in the fact that they lack siblings. This naive explanation seems right to them because it is consistent with the cultural wisdom that only children are psychologically defective. It is also a convenient explanation because it absolves them of assuming responsibility for their own problems. These only children can simply avoid assuming the burden of change because it was not their fault that they had no siblings.

Those only children who are neutral about being an only child probably are so because their parents expressed no regret about having just one child. These are probably more likely to be those only children who grow up with both biological parents. If they enter into psychotherapy, they are not likely to see their problems as related to their lack of siblings. As adults, these only children are less likely to say that having one child is ideal because they know that this is not the normative answer. However, since they do not associate their lack of siblings with a loss, they are more likely to respond to questions about being an only child by viewing it as more of an advantage than a disadvantage. This explains why surveys of American adults conducted in 1950 and again in 1972 consistently found that although 78% of White Americans found only children to be disadvantaged, the only children in this group were much more likely to say that only children were advantaged (Blake, 1974).

Thus, although the results of hundreds of studies have indicated that only children are not disadvantaged in terms of their own outcomes, many only children believe that their problems are caused by their lack of siblings. They have these beliefs because social norms and cultural wisdom portray normal development as requiring sibling interaction.

CHINA'S ONE-CHILD POLICY

Perhaps these data on only children could be attributed to something unique to the American context. To test this possibility, I have been conducting surveys of schoolchildren in the People's Republic of China. At present, most of the schoolchildren in urban China have no siblings (Hardee-Cleveland & Banister, 1988), as a result of an intensive, government-sponsored family planning program. This was initiated in early 1979 for the purpose of promoting economic development and averting famine (Croll, Davin, & Kane, 1985). With about 21% of the world's population, but only 7% of its arable land, China believed that it needed to take drastic actions in order to avert disaster. Initially, the policy was rigidly implemented in urban and rural areas alike. After a few years, however, it became clear that the one-child policy was not practical in the rural areas, which account for about 60% of China. Thus, implementation of the policy was relaxed somewhat, so that now most rural families formed after 1979 have two or more children. This is in sharp contrast to the United States, where there is no national family planning policy at all; the varying incidence of only children in the United States has been attributed to fluctuations in the economy, wars, changing women's roles, and the relatively high incidence of divorce (Falbo, 1982).

I found it plausible that the outcomes of only children produced by a relatively coercive family planning policy would be different from those observed in American only children. In urban China, during the last 10 years, newlyweds knew even before their child was conceived that they would have just one child. In the United States, intending to have just one child is extremely rare, ranging between 1% and 7% of ever-married women of childbearing age. Nonetheless, the incidence of ever-married women with just one child has varied this century roughly between 13 and 25% (Falbo, 1982). Thus, because more Americans have only one child than intended to, it is likely that these parents do not realize that they will have just one child until later in their child's life. In contrast, urban Chinese couples who became parents since 1979 knew from the very beginning of their child's life that they would have just one child. Consequently, one might hypothesize that such parents would tend to treat their only child differently than American parents do. Specifically, they might be more likely to overindulge or overprotect their only child than would American parents, suggesting that Hall's pronouncements about only children could be applicable to the current Chinese situation.

In the Chinese press soon after 1979, there were stories about the spoiled only children, called locally "little emperors." Overindulgent parents and grandparents were blamed for ruining the future generation. Given this concern, in 1985 I was asked by UNICEF to work with the Child Development Center of China to address their concerns and to do research on Chinese only children. UNICEF helped me conduct a survey of 800 schoolchildren in the urban part of Beijing Municipality that year. What was interesting about this sample was that the children had been born just before the one-child policy and, therefore, had grown up with one older sibling or with the expectation of being a first-born, not an only child.

The Beijing survey (Falbo et al., 1989) indicated that only children scored better on their school-based achievement tests than their non-only counterparts. Teachers rated the social and personality attributes of their students and evaluated only children no differently than they rated others. These results are surprisingly consistent with those found in the United States. However, Beijing is a very political city with a high concentration of well educated people. These results may not be typical of other places in China.

With the aid of Poston and several Chinese colleagues, I conducted another survey (Poston & Falbo, 1990), using 1,460 first and fifth graders in Jilin Province, which shares a border with North Korea. This sample included both urban and rural children. What we found was that the only-child effect varied depending on whether the only child lived in a rural or urban environment. Urban only children outscored their peers in school-based achievement scores, but there were no significant differences between rural onlies and others. In addition, the personality and social attributes of only children were not seen by their mothers or teachers as significantly different from other children, and this was true in urban as well as rural regions.

In both surveys, however, the samples were determined by convenience, and were not representative of the province. With the substantial help of the National Institutes of Health, Poston and I were able, in 1990, to conduct an additional four surveys, each consisting of 1,000 schoolchildren in each of four provinces: Anhui, Beijing Municipality, Gansu, and Hunan. The sampling method guaranteed that we would have a representative sample of third and sixth graders in each province.

In addition to this sampling improvement, we collected personality and social attributes ratings from the children themselves and from one randomly selected peer. This will provide information about how these children regard themselves and how they are regarded by their peers. We also have ratings, using the same attributes checklist, from the children's teachers and from one parent.

Furthermore, we improved our measurement of scholastic achievement by creating and administering the same mathematics and language tests to all third and sixth graders in the sample. This information will be used to evaluate the scholastic competence of these schoolchildren in addition to their school-based scores. Our new survey even includes precise measurements of height and weight so that we can consider physical development outcomes as well as scholastic and personality outcomes.

Our results (Falbo & Poston, 1991) indicate that significant differences between Chinese only children and first and later born children are not consistently found across the four provinces. In the two provinces where significant achievement differences were found, only children scored higher than others in verbal tests, but lower than others in mathematics tests, the difference being particularly pronounced in the rural parts of Beijing. Although the only child advantage in intelligence has been found to be greatest in verbal forms of intelligence (Polit & Falbo, 1988), the urban/rural difference in the outcomes of only children is unknown in the Western literature largely because one-child families have been extremely rare among rural families in the West and, moreover, no one has attempted to study these regional differences.

Few personality differences were found between only children and others, with teachers in all provinces and parents in three of the provinces consistently rating them similarly to other children. The children's evaluations from classmates were unrelated to being an only child in three of the provinces. In the fourth province, only child boys were given the highest peer ratings. This paucity of significant differences between only children and others in China is not surprising, given that few personality differences have been consistently found between only children and others in the West.

In two provinces, only children were found to be larger than children with siblings. This result suggests that the incentives used to reward parents for having just one child are used to enhance the nutritional value of the food given only children in at least some of the provinces.

Thus, although these results about only children are not identical to the results of Western studies, they suggest that Chinese only children are not at risk of attaining negative outcomes, by Chinese standards. Rather than demonstrating that children without siblings in China have problematic outcomes, the results of the 1990 survey suggest that in China, the differences between only children and others are few in number and small in magnitude.

REFERENCES

Blake, J. (1966). Ideal family size among White Americans: A quarter of a century's evidence. *Demography, 3,* 154–173.

Blake, J. (1974). Can we believe recent data on birth expectations in the United States? *Demography, 11,* 25–44.

Blake, J. (1981). The only child in America: Prejudice versus performance. *Population and Development Review, 7,* 43–54.

Blake, J. (1989). *Family size and achievement.* Berkeley: University of California Press.

Cohen, J. (1977). *Statistical power analyses for the behavioral sciences.* New York: Academic.

Croll, E., Davin, D., & Kane, P. (1985). *China's one-child policy.* New York: St. Martin's Press.

Dawson, D. A. (1991). Family structure and children's mental health and well-being. *Journal of Marriage and the Family, 53,* 573–584.

Ernst, C., & Angst, J. (1983). *Birth order: Its influence on personality.* Berlin: Springer-Verlag.

Falbo, T. (1982). Only children in America. In M. Lamb & B. Sutton-Smith (Eds.) *Sibling relationships* (pp. 285–304). Hillsdale, NJ: Lawrence Erlbaum Associates.

Falbo, T., & Cooper, C. R. (1980). Young children's time and intellectual ability. *Journal of Genetic Psychology, 137,* 299–300.

Falbo, T., & Polit, D. (1986). A quantitative review of the only-child literature: Research evidence and theory development. *Psychological Bulletin, 100,* 176–189.

Falbo, T., & Poston, D. L. (1991). *The academic personality and physical outcomes of only children in China.* University of Texas Population Research Center Papers, No. 12.12.

Falbo, T., Poston, D., Ji, G., Jiao, S., Jing, Q., Wang, S., Gu, Q., Yin, H., & Liu, Y. (1989). Physical, achievement, and personality characteristics of Chinese children. *Journal of Biosocial Science, 21,* 483–495.

Fenton, N. (1928). The only child. *Journal of Genetic Psychology, 35,* 546–556.

Gilbreth, F. B., & Gilbreth, L. M. (1912). *The primer of scientific management.* New York: Van Nostrand.

Gilbreth, F. B., Jr., & Carey, E. G. (1948). *Cheaper by the dozen.* New York: Crowell.

Gilbreth, F. B., Jr., & Carey, E. G. (1950). *Belles on their toes.* New York: Crowell.

Glass, G. V., McGaw, B., & Smith, M. L. (1981). *Meta-analysis in social research.* Beverly Hills, CA: Sage.

Hardee-Cleaveland, K., & Banister, J. (1988). Fertility policy and implementation in China. *Population and Development Review, 14,* 245–286.

Polit, D. F. (1980). *The one-parent/one-child family: Social and psychological consequences.* Cambridge, MA: American Institutes for Research.

Polit, D. F., & Falbo, T. (1987). Only children and personality development: A quantitative review. *Journal of Marriage and the Family, 49,* 309–325.

Polit, D. F., & Falbo, T. (1988). The intellectual outcomes of only children. *Journal of Biosocial Science, 20,* 275–285.

Poston, D. L., & Falbo, T. (1990). Academic performance and personality traits of Chinese children: "Onlies" versus others. *American Journal of Sociology, 96,* 433–451.

Rosenthal, R., & Rubin, D. B. (1982a). Comparing effect sizes of independent studies. *Psychological Bulletin, 89,* 500–503.

Rosenthal, R., & Rubin, D. B. (1982b). Further meta-analytic procedures for assessing cognitive gender differences. *Journal of Educational Psychology, 74,* 708–712.

Tesser, A. (1980). Self-esteem maintenance in family dynamics. *Journal of Personality and Social Psychology, 39,* 77–91.

U.S. Bureau of the Census. (1974). *Fertility expectation of American women: Current Population Reports, June 1973* (Series P-20, No. 265). Washington, DC: U.S. Government Printing Office.

Van Krevelen, D. A. (1946). *Het eenige Kind* [The only child]. Utrecht, The Netherlands: Erven J. Bijleveld.

Part II

Clinical Issues

Children's Experiences With Disabled and Nondisabled Siblings: Links With Personal Adjustment and Relationship Evaluations

Susan M. McHale
Vicki S. Harris
The Pennsylvania State University

Sibling relationship experiences may be altered in significant ways when children grow up with a disabled sister or brother. These experiences may have important implications for children's well-being and development. Indeed, much of the literature on children with disabled siblings centers around the concern that their family experiences may be harmful to their social and emotional adjustment (e.g., Breslau, Weitzman, & Messenger, 1981; Dyson, 1989; Gath, 1972; Lobato, Barbour, Hall, & Miller, 1989).

In addition to its practical significance, research on sibling relationships in families with disabled children also may provide important insights about "normal" sibling relationship processes. This is based on the assumption that experiences common to most sibling relationships may be particularly salient in families with disabled children. For example, some writers (e.g., Crocker, 1981; Powell & Ogle, 1985) have suggested that the special needs of a disabled child mean that sisters and brothers in these families are more frequently involved in sibling caregiving activities and/or are expected to spend more time supervising and entertaining their disabled siblings. The affective tone of sibling interactions also may be affected by a child's disabling condition. Limitations in a child's communication skills, self-control, or social understanding, stemming from cognitive or physical disabilities, may set the stage for more frequent sibling conflict. Alternatively, in some sibling dyads, a child's disabling condition may elicit more need and opportunity for prosocial and altruistic behavior on the part of a nondisabled sister or brother. Finally, the special care disabled children often require means that many parents must devote extra time, attention, and family resources to these youngsters, possibly at the expense of the interests of other nondisabled siblings in the family. In turn, such differential treatment may lead to feelings of rivalry, jealousy, or hostility by nondisabled brothers and sisters. By studying families in which sibling activity patterns, sibling interaction styles, parents' differential treatment, or other sibling relationship processes are altered in important ways, we may highlight the central dimensions of children's sibling relationship experiences.

Although many writers have speculated about the special challenges children face when growing up with a disabled sibling, there is a paucity of hard evidence regarding sibling relationship processes in families with disabled children. Following the lead of early research on sibling relationships, most investigations of children with disabled siblings have examined what Bronfenbrenner and Crouter (1983) term *social address* variables. In this tradition, differences in children's adjustment or sibling relationship evaluations are linked to family size and socioeconomic status (SES), children's birth order, gender, and age, and the severity and nature of a child's handicapping condition (see Lobato, 1983; McHale, Simeonsson, & Sloan, 1984; Powell & Ogle, 1985; Simeonsson & McHale, 1981, for reviews). Such analyses provide clues about *which* children may be at risk for adjustment or relationship problems, but tell us very little about the relationship *processes* that are responsible for the effects that have been observed.

This gap in the literature provided the impetus for our work on the sibling relationship experience of children with younger mentally retarded siblings. In this chapter, we provide an overview of our research, paying special attention to the links between children's sibling relationship experiences and both their subjective evaluations of the relationship and their personal adjustment.

In our work, we began by documenting whether differences between children with and without disabled siblings occur in experiences surrounding their sisters and brothers. In turn, we examined the connections between children's sibling experiences and the measures of their socioemotional adjustment and their sibling relationship evaluations. In assessing sibling relationship processes, we focused on three issues emphasized in the literature on the potential adjustment problems of children with disabled siblings, as well as in the general literature on children's sibling relationships: (a) children's involvement in daily activities with their siblings, including sibling caregiving; (b) conflict and negativity between siblings and children's strategies for coping with such relationship problems; and (c) parents' differential treatment of children and their siblings. Before discussing our findings regarding these relationship processes, we first provide a brief overview of our research methodology. Further details about this research including the sample and measures can be found in Gamble and McHale (1989), Harris and McHale (1989), McHale and Gamble (1989), and McHale and Pawletko (in press).

STUDY

Subjects

We interviewed 62 youngsters (target children) between 8 and 14 years of age and their mothers. The youngsters all had at least one younger brother or sister. In half of these families the younger siblings were mentally retarded, and in the other half the younger sibling had no identified disability. These younger children (target siblings) ranged from 3 to 11 years of age. Both groups consisted of 7 pairs of sisters, 12 pairs of brothers, 7 girls with younger brothers, and 5 boys with younger sisters. The average family size (including parents) was between five and six, with a range from four to eight. All but two families had two parents living in the home and most families were from lower middle-class backgrounds, as judged by the parents' incomes and occupations.

Methods

We used two different means of data collection: (a) during home interviews, we obtained mothers' and children's ratings of the target children's psychological well-being and the sibling relationship; (b) during telephone interviews, we asked target children and their mothers to recall specific events of the day using a cued-recall procedure.

Home Interviews. Mothers and older siblings were interviewed in separate rooms by different interviewers about the sibling relationship and about the personal well-being of family members. Analyses of group (i.e., disabled vs. nondisabled siblings) and gender differences on measures of adjustment—the Childhood Depression Inventory (Kovacs, 1981), the Revised Children's Manifest Anxiety Scale (Reynolds & Richmond, 1979), the Perceived Competence Scale (Harter, 1982), and the Conners' Parent Rating Scale (Goyette, Conners, & Ulrich, 1978)—revealed that children with disabled siblings scored more poorly on all measures of adjustment except perceived cognitive competence and mothers' reports of conduct. On the measure of general self-worth, girls with disabled siblings reported lower scores than any other group of children (see McHale & Gamble, 1989). In contrast, when sibling relationship evaluations were the dependent measures, children with nondisabled siblings scored more poorly on both mother and child ratings on the Sibling Inventory of Behavior (Schaefer & Edgerton, 1981), as well as on the Relationship Satisfaction Questionnaire (McHale & Gamble, 1989). (The data on relationship evaluations are described more fully further on.)

Phone Interviews. At the end of the home interviews, seven telephone interviews were scheduled for the subsequent 1- to 3-week period. The phone interviews were conducted within about 30 minutes of the children's bedtimes, so that the children could report on all of their activities with their siblings for the day, and took place on four weekdays and three weekend days.

To collect the data on children's daily activities, a list of 22 activities (e.g., babysitting, watching TV, playing ball, going on an outing) was read to the children, and they were asked to recall how many times, if at all, they had engaged in each activity with their sibling that day. For each activity, they also were asked to recall how long the activity lasted, who initiated the activity, and who else (if anyone) was present during the activity. Mothers were questioned about the activities of the older and younger siblings at separate points in the telephone interview, and the order of reporting was counterbalanced across calls. In reporting on each sibling, mothers first recalled the frequency and duration of each of 28 activities they themselves had undertaken with the child that day (i.e., helping with homework, helping with dressing, eating, bathing, reading books, visiting). Mothers then reported on the frequency and duration of 18 household chores (e.g., making his or her bed, cleaning the bathroom, taking out the garbage) the child had performed during the day of the call.

Mothers and children were asked about specific activities that had occurred during the past 12- to 15-hour period in an effort to facilitate the accuracy of their recall. The data were summed across the seven days of calls and aggregated to construct the measures of interest for the analyses. Assessments of the reliability of these data have been reported elsewhere (McHale & Gamble, 1989).

SIBLING RELATIONSHIP EXPERIENCES
IN FAMILIES WITH DISABLED
AND NONDISABLED CHILDREN

In the following pages we address the three issues identified earlier in this chapter:

1. children's involvement in daily activities with their siblings,
2. conflict and negativity in the relationship and children's strategies for coping with such experiences, and
3. parents' differential treatment of siblings.

Although we consider previous work regarding this issue, our discussion focuses on results of our research described earlier.

Children's Daily Activities With Siblings

Although empirical research tends to focus on the affective quality of sibling interactions, we believe that the extent and nature of sibling activities represent important dimensions of children's sibling relationship experiences as well. Assessing not only how well siblings get along when they spend time in joint activities but how much time siblings actually spend in joint activities may be essential for understanding individual differences in some sibling relationships. When a sibling is handicapped by severe mental and/or physical disabilities, brothers and sisters may react by avoiding contact with that child. In these families, the sibling interactions observers witness may be nonconflictual or even mildly positive, despite the fact that, in their daily lives, social contact between the siblings may occur very rarely. This concern was one basis for our focus on siblings' daily activities.

A further goal was to provide empirical data to test several assertions that are prominent in the literature on the psychological adjustment of children with disabled siblings. The finding that older sisters of disabled children are most vulnerable to mental health problems has led some writers to speculate that many children are "burdened" by heavy sibling caregiving responsibilities (Cleveland & Miller, 1977; Farber, 1959; Gath, 1972; Grossman, 1972). Their responsibilities may lead to feelings of resentment and, in turn, to guilt about their reactions. The likely consequence, it has been thought, is adjustment problems and sibling relationship difficulties. Another way in which the needs of disabled siblings may put children at risk is by limiting the amount of time they have to spend on other activities they might enjoy (e.g., peer or extracurricular activities). That is, the time children spend supervising or caring for their disabled siblings may constrain their opportunities for activities outside the home.

Findings from some previous research have suggested that children with disabled versus nondisabled siblings do, indeed, differ in the kinds of activities they undertake together. For example, based on observations of siblings interacting together, some investigators (e.g., Stoneman & Brody, 1984) have argued that the activities of children with disabled siblings tend to be more *instrumental* or task-oriented (helping, teaching, caregiving) in contrast to those of nondisabled siblings, which are more often *expressive* in nature, as in play. Although observational strategies may be the method of choice when the focus is on the affective tone of sibling interactions, the constraints of observational data collection strategies (which usually involve an hour or two of data collection in the home on one or two occasions with an observer present) mean that such measures may provide an inaccurate portrayal of the kinds of sibling activities children engage in in their everyday lives. Furthermore, prior to conducting our study, we could find no empirical work linking children's *temporal involvement* in instrumental versus expressive activities with their siblings to indices of children's adjustment.

In examining children's sibling activities and their correlates, we used data from our telephone interviews. We first assessed differences between children with disabled versus nondisabled siblings in their daily activities and then examined the links between children's sibling activities and indices of both children's personal adjustment and their evaluations of the sibling relationship (see McHale & Gamble, 1989). Analyses of children's daily activities with siblings revealed that children (particularly girls) spent more time in *caregiving* activities with disabled than with nondisabled siblings (see Table 6.1). In contrast, children with nondisabled siblings spent more time performing chores with their sisters and brothers. We found no group differences, however, in siblings' joint leisure or recreational activities, nor did we find evidence that the daily activities of children with disabled siblings were unduly constrained. There were no differences in the total amount of time children spent with disabled versus nondisabled sisters and brothers. As we have noted elsewhere (McHale & Gamble, 1989), the gender differences indicating that girls perform more caregiving, whereas boys are more frequently engaged in play, parallel the gender differences between mothers' and fathers' parenting activities that several investigators have noted (e.g., McHale & Huston, 1984), and suggest that there may be continuities between children's roles with younger siblings and the activities associated with their parental roles.

Our findings on group differences in the nature of sibling activities imply that children with disabled and nondisabled siblings are not differentially involved in work or "instrumental" versus play or "expressive" activities with their sisters and brothers. To the extent that instrumental activities, such as caregiving or chores, are inherently less enjoyable than expressive ones, at the most general level, we have no reason to expect that the affect attached to the nature of the activities children perform with their siblings should lead to differences in children's evaluations of their relationships. Although caregiving and

TABLE 6.1
Duration (in Minutes Per Day) of Children's Activities
with Disabled Versus Nondisabled Siblings

| | Disabled Siblings | | Nondisabled Siblings | | |
	Boys (n = 17)	Girls (n = 14)	Boys (n = 17)	Girls (n = 14)	F
Caregiving	17.9	25.3	8.5	16.1	5.20* (G) 3.30*** (S)
Chores	2.5	3.1	7.8	17.4	7.44** (G)
Meals	35.5	37.4	35.1	31.0	
Television	43.3	25.7	40.3	35.7	
Outings	38.0	60.6	43.8	47.6	
Play	21.8	15.9	24.1	12.8	3.69* (S)
Total Involvement	159.0	167.9	160.0	157.6	

*$p < .05$; **$p < .01$; ***$p < .10$.
(G) = Group
(S) = Sex

chores may both be classified as instrumental, these categories of activities may differ along a second dimension, that is, their degree of egalitarianism: Two siblings can play equal roles in performing household tasks such as washing dishes or cleaning their room, whereas caregiving, teaching, or helping are activities that presuppose unequal status of the two members of the sibling dyad. Indeed, we suspect the degree of egalitarianism in sibling experiences to be the source of differential evaluations of the sibling relationship across these two family contexts, an issue we consider more fully shortly. First, however, we review our findings on the correlates of children's sibling activities.

Our analyses revealed slight support for the idea that high levels of involvement, particularly in sibling caregiving, may be problematic for some children's adjustment (McHale & Gamble, 1989). Specifically, we found that time spent in caregiving was significantly related to children's reports of anxiety symptoms, $r = .25$, $p < .05$, but we detected no significant associations with other kinds of activities or between sibling activities and children's evaluations of their sibling relationships (i.e., satisfaction, warmth, hostility). More importantly, separate analyses conducted by child gender and group also provided some evidence that the implications of sibling caregiving may differ for girls with disabled versus nondisabled siblings: For example, the correlation between sibling caregiving and depression for girls with disabled siblings was $r = .53$, $p < .01$, whereas that for girls with nondisabled siblings was $r = -.43$, $p < .01$ (Mutcher, 1987). Given the small sample size of these groups ($ns = 14$), however, such findings require replication.

In future research it also will be important to collect information on children's feelings and attitudes toward sibling activities, such as caregiving. As we and others have noted, the meanings children attribute to their family responsibilities may mediate the connection between task performance and children's well-being and development (Elder, 1974; McHale, Bartko, Crouter, & Perry-Jenkins, 1990).

Finally, it is important to expand our conceptualization of the potential implications of children's responsibilities for their siblings. As a first step, in this study we examined "adjustment" measures, including self-esteem, depression, and anxiety, and conduct problems. Other research has shown that some individuals with disabled siblings are more empathic and altruistic, more idealistic, more tolerant toward others, and more oriented to humanistic and social welfare concerns (Caldwell & Guze, 1960; Farber & Jenne, 1963; Grossman, 1972): As adults, eldest sisters are most likely to pursue the helping professions in choosing their careers (Cleveland & Miller, 1977). Future investigators may wish to include measures of social-emotional maturity or social understanding in assessing the effects of children's daily activities with, and responsibilities for, their siblings as "consequences" of these kinds of sibling experiences. A focus on the potential growth-enhancing implications of children's experiences with a disabled sibling, however, will require longitudinal designs, given that these implications may not become apparent until late adolescence or adulthood. As we have argued elsewhere (McHale & Gamble, 1989), the slightly higher levels of anxiety and lower self-esteem exhibited by children with disabled siblings in our study may be the price of a more mature outlook on oneself and one's world. The youngsters in our research were on the brink of adolescence, a time of introspection, self-awareness, increased self-criticism, and growing awareness of the needs and concerns of others (Elkind, 1967), all of which may be (mistakenly) characterized as "internalizing symptoms." We would expect to find quite different implications for children whose internalizing "symptoms" have different developmental underpinnings. Longitudinal designs are essential if we are to determine whether any short-term costs that we observe for children will pay dividends in terms of self and interpersonal understanding later in life.

Coping With Conflict and Negativity in the Sibling Relationship

Another process through which sibling experiences may affect children's well-being or their feelings about the sibling relationship pertains to the affective tone of siblings' interactions during their activities together. As we have suggested, some writers have speculated that interactions with disabled siblings may be more negative (due, for example, to delays in these siblings' social development, to their communication difficulties, or to associated behavior problems). Thus far, however, the empirical evidence does not provide clear support for this proposition.

For example, two studies of children's behavior toward their siblings that used Schaefer and Edgerton's (1981) Sibling Inventory of Behavior (SIB) revealed that when group differences occurred, it was the behavior of children with disabled siblings that was rated more positively by mothers (McHale, Sloan, & Simeonsson, 1986; Ogle, 1982). In a recent study, Begun (1989) examined the sibling relationship evaluations of females aged 12 to 69 years, comparing the same individual's evaluations of her relationships with a disabled versus a nondisabled sibling. Experiences with disabled siblings, evaluated using Furman and Buhrmester's (1985) Sibling Relationship Questionnaire, were described as involving less intimacy, similarity, admiration, and competition, as well as more dominance by the (nondisabled) sister. Further, these sisters reported that they exhibited more nurturance toward their disabled sibling but received less in return relative to their experiences with their nondisabled sisters and brothers. These findings may reflect the fact that relationships with disabled siblings involve less reciprocity and more complementarity than those with nondisabled sisters and brothers (see Dunn, 1983).

Further evidence that relationships with disabled siblings may differ along this dimension comes from our analyses of mothers' and children's reports of children's versus siblings' behavior in the sibling relationship. Using the SIB, we compared mothers' and children's independent reports of each sibling's behavior (collected on separate occasions) using a 2 (Rater: mother vs. child) × 2 (Sibling: older vs. younger) × 2 (Group) design with repeated measures on the Rater and Sibling factors. The results, shown in Table 6.2, revealed a significant Rater × Sibling × Group overall effect, $F(4,55) = 3.44$, $p <$ .01, and significant univariate effects for the three measures of hostility (e.g., "tease or bother sibling"), acceptance (e.g., "complain about trouble sibling makes"), and initiation of contact (e.g., "makes plans that include sibling"). Follow-up tests revealed that although the behaviors of siblings were *not* rated differently by either mothers or children in the comparison group, mothers of disabled children evaluated their two children's behavior very differently. They reported less hostility toward the sibling and more contact initiated toward the sibling but less acceptance of the sibling by the nondisabled than by the disabled child. Differences were also apparent in children's evaluations of their own versus their disabled siblings' initiation of contact. These mean level differences were found in the face of generally significant correlations between both mothers' and children's ratings of the older versus younger siblings' behaviors conducted separately by group (*r*s range from .25 to .66 and .27 to .79 for ratings involving children with disabled and nondisabled siblings, respectively). Though the latter correlational results reveal one kind of reciprocity in

TABLE 6.2
Children's and Mothers' Ratings of Child and Sibling
Behavior in the Sibling Relationship

Behavior toward sibling	Disabled Sibs (n = 31)		Nondisabled Sibs (n = 31)		Rater × Sibling × Group Interaction
	Mother Report	Child Report	Mother Report	Child Report	F
Hostility					
Child	27.1	25.6	23.3	22.9	7.18**
Maternal	21.9	21.4	23.2	20.5	
Acceptance					
Child	24.9	23.3	22.3	21.3	4.01*
Maternal	26.5	23.6	22.9	22.7	
Contact					
Child	25.3	24.8	23.6	23.8	5.19*
Maternal	16.4	17.5	21.8	20.9	

Note: High scores represent more frequent positive and less frequent negative behavior toward the sibling.
**p < .01; *p < .05.

the behaviors of children and their disabled siblings (i.e., both have similar standing relative to the larger groups of which they are a part), the results of the repeated measures analyses suggest that children with disabled siblings may often give more than they receive in their sibling relationships. Further, these differences in what siblings contribute to their interactions may constitute experiences that set the stage for the ratings of lower levels of intimacy and competition in relationships with disabled siblings that Begun (1989) reported. Do these group differences in sibling interaction experiences have implications for children's adjustment or relationship satisfaction? Correlational analyses revealed that only children's reports of their own behavior were linked to the adjustment indices; neither maternal reports of either child's behavior nor children's reports of their siblings' behavior were related to children's adjustment (for simplicity's sake, in these analyses we created a total score on the SIB, summing across the three subscales). Further, correlations were stronger and more consistent in the case of children with disabled siblings (rs of $-.60$; $p < .01$; $-.35$, $p < .01$; and $-.52$, $p < .01$, for correlations between relationship ratings and depression, anxiety, and self-worth, respectively) as compared to those involving children with nondisabled siblings (rs of $-.24$, ns; $-.31$, ns; and $-.02$, ns, for correlations between relationship ratings and depression, anxiety, and self-worth, respectively). One possible basis of these different patterns is the greater variability in both relationship ratings and adjustment found in children with disabled siblings.

We were surprised by this pattern of results because we had anticipated that the younger siblings' aversive behavior (particularly that of disabled siblings) would constitute a source of stress for children, stress that would be the most proximal correlate of children's adjustment problems or relationship satisfaction. Research on children's experiences of stressful events, however, has given rise to a growing conviction that children's efforts to avoid, eliminate, or reduce stress (i.e., their coping strategies) can buffer, to a significant degree, the negative impact stressors may have on physical, psychological, and social well-being (e.g., Garmezy & Rutter, 1983). For this reason, we investigated children's strategies for coping with sibling negativity as a potential mediator linking aversive sibling behavior and children's adjustment (see Gamble, 1985; Gamble & McHale, 1989).

In this component of our study, we initially generated a list of troublesome events involving siblings by asking children in nightly phone calls to describe at least two different times during the day of the call when something happened with their sibling that "bothered them, made them worried or mad, or caused a problem for them." In all, children reported 195 such "stressors," which were then collapsed into seven categories of events (see Gamble, 1985). During the home interviews previously described, children rated the frequency of each of these events and also evaluated their affective response to each event (i.e., *not at all mad* to *very mad*). Finally, children reported on the strategies they used to cope with such problematic sibling experiences.

Correlational analyses revealed that children's affective reactions to sibling stressors were related more systematically to children's well-being and sibling relationship ratings than was the actual frequency of sibling stressors, and these findings were consistent both for children with disabled and for those with non-disabled siblings (Gamble & McHale, 1989). Further, for both groups, two categories of coping responses were linked to children's adjustment and relationship ratings. Specifically, "self-directed cognitions" (e.g., "try to calm down"; "think about ways to solve the problem") were positively related, and "other-directed cognitions" (e.g., "I think that my sibling is a creep"; "I wonder why my parents don't do something" to control the sibling) were negatively related to adjustment and relationship reports.

Following the reasoning of theorists such as Seligman (1975), we have argued that self-directed cognitions (the use of which is positively related to adjustment and sibling relationship indices), may represent children's active efforts to control their reactions to troublesome sibling experiences or to resolve negative emotions (Gamble & McHale, 1989). In contrast, other-directed cognitions (the use of which is negatively related to well-being and relationship measures) seem to involve children's ineffectual "fuming" at others (i.e., the sibling, parents) who are seen as being in control of, or culpable for these problem situations. Note that neither of these cognitive strategies reflects children's attempts to actively change the stressful situation itself. Although these cognitive strategies were linked to the "outcome" measures of interest, the use of overt coping strategies (i.e., self- or other-directed behaviors) was related to neither the adjustment nor the relationship measures. It may be that at this age there is little children can do to control sibling relationship experiences effectively. Another possibility is that controlling one's affective reactions is actually more important for children's psychological adjustment and relationship evaluations than are more objective situational factors. If these findings are replicated, they will have important implications for intervention strategies directed at children with disabled siblings, given the tendency for these children to use less effective coping styles. This work also may be important for research on children's stress and coping, which thus far has provided limited information on coping in the context of children's social relationship experiences.

Differential Treatment of Siblings by Parents With Disabled and Nondisabled Children

A third component of our research focused on the differential treatment children experience at the hands of their parents and its potential implications for children's adjustment and sibling relationships. A number of researchers have speculated that the special demands involved in caring for a disabled child may lead parents to devote a large portion of their time and attention to that child, leaving less for other children in the family (e.g., Crocker, 1981; Farber, 1959). In addition, the physical, cognitive, and social limitations of disabled children mean that these children may not be held to the same standards of behavior as nondisabled siblings in the family (Crocker, 1981). In short, there has been a clear expectation in the literature that differential treatment by parents may occur in a more extreme form in these families than in others, and give rise to feelings of jealousy and rivalry in nondisabled children. Children's reactions to differential treatment, in turn, were expected to have negative implications for their adjustment. Our review of the literature, however, yielded no previous empirical data bearing on the questions of: (a) whether siblings are actually treated more differently when one has a handicapping condition; or (b) whether greater levels of differential treatment are linked to adjustment and relationship difficulties in these youngsters.

To address these issues, we examined four dimensions of differential treatment of older and younger siblings:

1. Maternal involvement in activities with the older versus the younger sibling.
2. Household responsibilities assigned to the older versus the younger child.
3. Disciplinary responses employed by mothers toward the older versus the younger child in response to sibling conflict.
4. The older child's satisfaction with parents' differential treatment.

Consistent with speculations in the literature, our findings revealed greater levels of differential treatment in families with a disabled child than in those without (see McHale & Pawletko, in press). Mothers spent relatively more time involved in activities with younger than with older siblings, and this difference was greater in the case of families with disabled siblings. It is important to note, however, that relative to other older siblings, children with disabled siblings actually spent *more* time with their mothers. Turning to children's chores, we found that older children in both groups were relatively more involved in household tasks than were their younger siblings; again, however, the difference in task performance was greater when the younger sibling had a handicapping condition. Finally, in terms of discipline strategies, we found no differences in mothers' use of what Steinmetz (1979) referred to as "positive love" (e.g., reasoning, compromise), "negative love" (e.g., ignoring, criticizing) or "power assertive" discipline (e.g., physical punishment, tangible reinforcement) strategies in families without disabled siblings (see Steinmetz, 1979, for a complete description of these strategies). However, mothers used more positive love strategies with older siblings and more power assertive strategies with younger siblings in families with disabled children.

Taken together, these findings present a more complex picture of group differences in differential treatment than had previously been supposed. Although we may initially conclude that younger disabled siblings receive "preferential" treatment in terms of the time they spend with their mothers and the few household responsibilities they are assigned, when it comes to disciplinary strategies, the older siblings are the recipients of preferential treatment (more positive love, less power assertive discipline). Neither can we ignore the results of comparisons of older siblings with and without disabled brothers and sisters. These analyses indicated that children with disabled siblings were not "neglected" by their mothers relative to other children their age; nor did they experience a different form of discipline. The only dimension along which these children differed from both their disabled siblings and nondisabled agemates was in their higher level of household tasks.

Analyses of the connections between differential treatment and children's satisfaction with differential treatment, as well as their evaluations of their personal well-being and sibling relationships illuminate the importance of understanding the meanings children attribute to different forms of differential treatment. First, despite the greater levels of differential treatment in families with disabled children, we detected no group differences in children's satisfaction with differential treatment (McHale & Gamble, 1989). Further, our analyses revealed that satisfaction with differential treatment was correlated only with differential maternal involvement: The more satisfied children were, the less time they spent (relative to their younger siblings) with their mothers, $r = .40$, $p < .01$ (see Pawletko, 1988). Finally, we found evidence that children's satisfaction with differential treatment was systematically related both to measures of children's well-being and to their sibling relationship evaluations (rs range from $-.41$, $p < .01$, for the correlation between satisfaction and depression to $.52$, $p < .01$, for the correlation between satisfaction and relationship ratings). The pattern of associations between the dimensions of differential treatment and children's well-being and sibling relationship evaluations, however, was more complicated (McHale & Pawletko, in press). In general, the correlates of differential treatment differed depending upon: (a) the domain of differential treatment under consideration (i.e., maternal involvement, chores, or discipline); (b) the particular outcomes of interest (well-being vs. sibling relationship evaluations); and (c) whether or not the child had a disabled sibling.

More negative "outcomes" to children were evident when they experienced relatively more time with their mothers than did their siblings, when they undertook relatively more chores, and when they experienced relatively more power assertive discipline. Whereas children with disabled siblings expressed their "vulnerability" in lower ratings of personal well-being, children with nondisabled siblings who received less preferential treatment evaluated their sibling relationships more negatively. In some cases, we found that children who reported the most positive sibling relationships (e.g., those with disabled siblings who received relatively more positive love) also reported the poorest adjustment.

We also found different links between differential treatment and well-being for children with disabled versus nondisabled siblings (e.g., relatively greater levels of positive love were linked to more negative well-being in the former group but more positive well-being in the latter).

Again, these findings underscore the importance of collecting information about the *meanings* children attribute to family experiences, such as differential treatment. Not only might differential treatment be perceived differently by different children, but the same children might experience a host of contradictory emotional reactions when they perceive preferential treatment exhibited to themselves or their siblings. For example, preferential treatment may raise a child's self-esteem, but, to the extent to which such treatment implies a parent's more negative evaluation of a sibling, the child may also develop a negative attitude toward the brother or sister. A child with a disabled sibling, while finding some pleasure in preferential treatment, may at the same time feel guilty that the sibling's special needs are being neglected.

Future research on differential treatment in families with disabled versus nondisabled children may reveal that children perceive differential treatment to be more legitimate when their siblings are disabled, and further, we may discover that children find preferential treatment more tolerable when its reasons are clear (McHale & Pawletko, in press).

> The legitimacy of differential treatment may be a salient factor only to children who have the cognitive capabilities or moral reasoning skills to appreciate that fairness does not always mean being treated the same. . . . [Further,] the perceived legitimacy of differential treatment may be orthogonal to children's affective reactions to such experiences: Children may harbor feelings of jealousy despite recognizing that differential treatment is ''fair.''

At a more general level, these patterns of findings illustrate the utility of including special populations of children or children from different family contexts in research on sibling relationships. In addition to its practical importance for families who face special challenges, studying differences in the implications of objectively similar relationship experiences may illuminate elements of sibling relationship processes that otherwise would be ignored.

SUMMARY AND CONCLUSIONS

In this chapter, we have highlighted the results of our research comparing the sibling relationship experiences of children with and without disabled siblings. Moving away from an examination of the ''effects'' of status variables, we focused on three sibling relationships processes: children's daily activities with siblings, sibling conflict and negativity, and parents' (mostly mothers') differential treatment. Our research goals were to provide empirical evidence pertaining to speculations in the literature on children with disabled siblings: (a) that these children's sibling experiences are more demanding and/or more aversive than are those of children with nondisabled siblings; and (b) that experiences with disabled siblings lead to both negative attitudes about the sibling relationship and problems in children's personal adjustment. In the process of studying the experiences of children who face special challenges in negotiating their sibling relationships, we also hoped to illuminate dimensions of sibling experiences that might be missed in studies of more homogeneous samples of children.

Our findings portray a picture of children with disabled siblings that is more complicated than previous literature suggests. We found both differences and similarities in the two groups' sibling experiences, as well as a great deal of within-group variability, particularly in the relationship experiences of children with disabled siblings. Although we uncovered links between children's sibling experiences and indices of children's adjustment and relationship satisfaction, our findings did not lead us to conclude that any one set of experiences will necessarily put children with disabled siblings at risk for adjustment or relationship problems.

The results, however, did highlight an important direction for future research. In addition to measuring the more objective, potentially observable differences that are evident both between and within groups of siblings (such as activity patterns or differential treatment by parents), it will be important to learn more about children's subjective evaluations of their experiences and the meanings they attribute to relationship events. We expect that the larger context in which particular sibling experiences occur may imbue objectively similar experiences with very different meanings. For example, having one's room ransacked or one's property wrecked by an 8-year-old brother whose motives are seen as hostile will probably receive a very different (possibly less complicated) reaction than will the same events precipitated by an 8-year-old mentally disabled brother who is temporarily out of control. We expect that analyses of the combination of the objective properties of sibling experiences and children's personal "definition of the situation" (Lewin, 1946) will better illuminate the links between sibling relationships and their consequences for children.

In understanding the meanings children attribute to their social exchanges with siblings, it will be particularly important to place these events within the larger context of their sibling relationship experiences. In the present study we examined the correlates of three dimensions of sibling experiences—sibling activities, sibling negativity, and differential treatment—independently. It is clear, however, that these dimensions of the sibling relationship are intertwined in children's everyday lives. For example, the implications of the sibling relationship for children who spend a great deal of time with their siblings and who report largely negative interaction experiences may be quite different than those for children who spend similar amounts of time with their siblings but whose interaction experiences are more positive. Considering yet a third dimension of sibling relationship experiences, parents' differential treatment, adds to the complexity of such integrative analyses. Unfortunately the sample size of our study precluded such a "multivariate" description of children's relationships. We expect, however, that it will be necessary to place specific relationship processes within the larger context of other relationship experiences if we are to understand individual differences in children's sibling relationships and their implications for children's development and well-being.

ACKNOWLEDGMENTS

We thank Wendy Gamble and Terese Pawletko for their help in conducting this research, and Linda Roth for her assistance in preparing the manuscript. We are also very grateful to the families who participated in the study. Funding was provided by the March of Dimes Foundation.

REFERENCES

Begun, A. (1989). Sibling relationships involving disabled people. *American Journal on Mental Deficiency, 93,* 566–574.

Breslau, N., Weitzman, M., & Messenger, K. (1981). Psychological functioning of siblings of disabled children. *Pediatrics, 67,* 344–353.

Bronfenbrenner, U., & Crouter, A. (1983). The evolution of environmental models in developmental research. In W. Kessen (Ed.), *The handbook of child psychology: Vol. 1. History, theory, and methods* (pp. 358–414). New York: Wiley.

Caldwell, B., & Guze, S. (1960). A study of the adjustment of parents and siblings of institutionalized and non-institutionalized retarded children. *American Journal of Mental Deficiency, 64,* 845–855.

Cleveland, D., & Miller, N. (1977). Attitudes and life commitment of older siblings of mentally retarded adults: An exploratory study. *Mental Retardation, 3,* 38–41.

Crocker, A. (1981). The involvement of siblings of children with handicaps. In A. Milunsky (Ed.), *Coping with crisis and handicap* (pp. 219–223). New York: Plenum.

Dunn, J. (1983). Sibling relationships in early childhood. *Child Development, 54,* 787–811.

Dyson, L. (1989). Adjustment of siblings of handicapped children: A comparison. *Journal of Pediatric Psychology, 14,* 215–229.

Elder, G. (1974). *Children of the Great Depression.* Chicago: University of Chicago Press.

Elkind, D. (1967). Egocentrism in adolescence. *Child Development, 38,* 1025–1034.

Farber, B. (1959). Effects of a severely mentally retarded child on family integration. *Monographs of the Society for Research in Child Development, 21*(2, Serial No. 75).

Farber, B., & Jenne, W. (1963). Family organization and parent–child communication: Parents and siblings of a retarded child. *Monographs of the Society for Research in Child Development, 28*(7, Serial No. 91).

Furman, W., & Buhrmester, D. (1985). Children's perceptions of the qualities of sibling relationships. *Child Development, 56,* 448–461.

Gamble, W. (1985). *The experiences and coping strategies of children with handicapped and nonhandicapped siblings.* Unpublished doctoral dissertation, The Pennsylvania State University, University Park.

Gamble, W., & McHale, S. M. (1989). Coping with stress in sibling relationships: A comparison of children with disabled and nondisabled siblings. *Journal of Applied Developmental Psychology, 10,* 353–373.

Garmezy, N., & Rutter, M. (Eds.). (1983). *Stress, coping and development in children.* New York: McGraw-Hill.

Gath, A. (1972). The mental health of siblings of cognitively abnormal children. *Journal of Child Psychology and Psychiatry, 13,* 211–218.

Goyette, C., Conners, C., & Ulrich, R. (1978). Normative data on revised Conners' Parent and Teacher Ratings Scales. *Journal of Child Psychology and Psychiatry, 13,* 211–218.

Grossman, F. (1972). *Brothers and sisters of retarded children.* Syracuse, NY: Syracuse University Press.

Harris, V., & McHale, S. (1989). Family life problems, daily caregiving activities, and the psychological well-being of mothers of mentally retarded children. *American Journal on Mental Retardation, 94,* 231–239.

Harter, S. (1982). The Perceived Competence Scale for Children. *Child Development, 53,* 87–97.

Kovacs, M. (1981). Rating scales to assess depression in school-aged children. *Acta Pacdopsychiatrica, 46,* 305–315.

Lewin, K. (1946). Behavior and development as a function of the total situation. In L. Carmichael (Ed.), *Manual of child psychology* (pp. 918–970). New York: Wiley.

Lobato, D. (1983). Siblings of handicapped children: A review. *Journal of Autism and Developmental Disorders, 13,* 347–364.

Lobato, D., Barbour, L., Hall, L., & Miller, C. (1987). Psychosocial characteristics of preschool siblings of handicapped and nonhandicapped children. *Journal of Abnormal Child Psychology, 15,* 329–338.

McHale, S., & Gamble, W. (1989). Sibling relationships of children with disabled and nondisabled brothers and sisters. *Developmental Psychology, 10,* 353–373.

McHale, S., Bartko, W., Crouter, A., & Perry-Jenkins, M. (1990). Children's housework and psychosocial functioning: The mediating effects of parents' sex-role behaviors and attitudes. *Child Development, 61,* 1413–1426.

McHale, S., & Huston, T. (1984). Men and women as parents: Sex role orientations, employment and parental roles with infants. *Child Development, 55,* 1349–1361.

McHale, S., & Pawletko, T. (in press). Differential treatment of siblings in two family contexts: Implications for children's adjustment and relationship evaluations. *Child Development.*

McHale, S., Simeonsson, R., & Sloan, J. (1984). Children with handicapped brothers and sisters. In E. Schopler & G. Mesibov (Eds.), *Issues in autism: Vol. 2. The effects of autism on the family* (pp. 327–342). New York: Plenum.

McHale, S., Sloan, J., & Simeonsson, R. (1986). Sibling relationships with autistic, mentally retarded, and nonhandicapped brothers and sisters: A comparative study. *Journal of Autism and Developmental Disorders, 16,* 399–414.

Mutcher, D. (1987). *Sibling caregiving and the well-being of girls with disabled sisters and brothers.* Unpublished master's thesis, The Pennsylvania State University, University Park.

Ogle, P. (1982). *The sibling relationship: Maternal perceptions of nonhandicapped and handicapped/nonhandicapped dyads.* Unpublished doctoral dissertation, University of North Carolina at Chapel Hill.

Pawletko, T. (1988). *Correlates of maternal differential treatment of disabled and nondisabled siblings.* Unpublished doctoral dissertation, The Pennsylvania State University, University Park.

Powell, T., & Ogle, P. (1985). *Brothers and sisters: A special part of exceptional families.* Baltimore: Paul H. Brookes.

Reynolds, C., & Richmond, B. (1979). Factor structure and construct validity of "What I think and feel": The Revised Children's Manifest Anxiety Scale. *Journal of Personality Assessment, 43,* 281–283.

Schaefer, E., & Edgerton, M. (1981). *The Sibling Inventory of Behavior.* Unpublished manuscript, University of North Carolina, Chapel Hill, NC.

Seligman, M. (1975). *Helplessness: On depression, development, and death.* San Francisco: Freeman.

Simeonsson, R., & McHale, S. (1981). Research on handicapped children: Sibling relationships. *Child: Care Health and Development, 7,* 153–171.

Steinmetz, S. (1979). Disciplinary techniques and their relationship to aggressiveness, dependency, and conscience. In W. Burr, R. Hill, F. Ney, & I. Reiss (Eds.), *Contemporary theories about the family* (Vol. 1, pp. 405–438). New York: Free Press.

Stoneman, Z., & Brody, G. H. (1984). Research with families of severely handicapped children: Theoretical and methodological considerations. In J. Blacher (Ed.), *Severely handicapped young children and their families: Research in review* (pp. 179–214). New York: Academic Press.

Chapter 7

The Brothers and Sisters
of Mentally Retarded Children

Ann Gath
The Maudsley & Bethlem Royal Hospitals, London

THE INITIAL REACTION

How the other members of the family will react to the presence of a mentally retarded child depends, in part, on the timing of the realization that a child has a severe degree of mental retardation. In some conditions, notably Down Syndrome, the facial stigmata and other physical anomalies alert the parents to the probability of a life-long handicap shortly after the child is born. Some of the older children in the family will see for themselves that the child has a distinct appearance. To quote one 16-year-old girl, whose mother had just had a baby by a second marriage, "It's all gone wrong. Mummy has just had one of those mongols." Some siblings, unable to appreciate that the newborn baby does look different from others, are still able to appreciate that all is not well and that their parents are distressed rather than expressing the long antic-ipated joy at the birth. Children who were very young themselves at this criti-cal time or who were born subsequently may only gradually come to appreci-ate the difference between their own growing up process and the slow progress of the retarded sibling. By the time the extent of the handicap is appreciated, the relationship between the children has been established without the influence of damaging and often inaccurate prejudice.

The findings discussed here are based on a group of longitudinal studies that followed each other so that the successive cohorts were about 5 years apart. The researchers learned from the earlier studies and methodology improved. The results, however, are consistent across the cohorts even though services were improved and parents were better informed in the later studies.

The chance to form affectionate bonds unsullied by preconceptions concerning mental retardation are experienced by the parents and all the siblings of children whose disability only becomes evident during the first few years of life. In most cases, the recognition of the limitations of the child's developmental progress is very gradual, but there are a few conditions, of which Rett Syndrome is a good example, where the child develops in an apparently normal way, but then progress stops, followed by an acutely distressing phase with loss of skills and severe emotional instability, and apparent fear of, or even hostility toward, family members. Such a catastrophe produces intense shock and grief in the parents and extends to the other children, who are terrified by this course of events. Clinical anecdotes lead to the suspicion that there is a greater likelihood of parents of a Rett syndrome child being unable to cope and having to request permanent placement of the child away from home than parents of other retarded children.

THE DISTRESS AND DISAPPOINTMENT OF PARENTS

Most, if not all, parents are very distressed when told of their child's handicap. Even if they are unable to understand the feelings of their parents, other children in the family commonly share the grief and are affected by it, though not invariably adversely. The pain at the time is great, of course, but many families feel themselves drawing closer together and so it is only a few vulnerable families that are disrupted or even permanently broken up by this crisis in their lives. The presence of other normal children in the family is a great comfort to the majority of parents, but conversely, the arrival of a second handicapped child in the same family increases the grief many times over and the presence of two children with mental retardation or other long standing disability in one family adds up to very much more than twice the burden of one.

Unresolved grief persists for years, as I observed in a long-term study of children with Down syndrome when parents, 14 years after the event, still recalled the impact of the news of the disorder with tears (Gath, 1990). Such grief did not interfere with parenting, but when it continues as a chronic depression, it does cause severe limitation of the ability to cope. In such a case, there is loss of some of the skill required in parenting the normal child as well as the handicapped one.

THE PREOCCUPATION OF PARENTS
WITH A VERY DEPENDENT CHILD

The possibility of neglecting their other children is an additional worry to parents whose new baby has to be cared for in a special care nursery (Gath, 1978). Most understandably, such parents feel torn between their acute concern for the new member of the family and their desire to be with and continue caring for the older children. Clearly, the families most affected by this dilemma will be those parents who are for some reason isolated and who cannot rely on the support of their own parents and close relatives.

Later on in infancy, there may be other periods, such as when a multi-handicapped child is very difficult and slow to feed, that the parents may again feel unhappy about how little time or energy is left over for the others. However, over the course of childhood, actual neglect of the apparently normal children in favor of a handicapped child is very unusual. No evidence was found in any of the studies of mentally retarded children living at home (Buckley & Sacks, 1987; Byrne, Cunningham, & Sloper, 1988; Shepperdson, 1988), and it is a rare occurrence to find it even in a specialized unit where very difficult children and disturbed families are treated.

SHARING THE LOAD

It is clear that bringing up a mentally retarded child is very hard work, taking up many hours a day, and that most of this extra burden is carried by the mother (Dupont, 1986). In earlier studies, it was concluded that some of this burden was taken up by the sisters, particularly the older ones in large families (Gath, 1974). Acting out as a response to increased domestic responsibility was suggested as the explanation for the high rate of behavioral deviance in this group of children. However, subsequent studies (Gath & Gumley, 1987) found no evidence that the sisters were asked to do more chores or to take more responsibility than what was expected for other girls of the same age. This change is attributed to improved services, particularly educational, since that early survey was carried out.

Studies of the families of children who are retarded show that disturbed behavior in the brothers and sisters of mentally retarded children is more common in families with only two children, indicating that life may be easier for a brother or sister when there is another normal child in the family (Gath & Gumley, 1987). This fits with other clinical findings concerning how children cope in other types of family crises, such as admission to the hospital, bereavement, or divorce.

SIBLING RIVALRY

Competition between a normal sibling and the retarded child can occur in certain circumstances. It is more common when there are only two children in the family. Ambivalent attitudes by the parents toward the affected child have been seen to be more likely to induce hostility from the normal sibling.

On the other hand, the child with the disability may be threatened by, or hostile to, a younger sibling who catches up and then surpasses him or her in particular skills. Under these circumstances, the reaction is usually temporary: When the normal sibling becomes much more competent than the disabled one, the older/younger relationship is effectively reversed from that which existed in early childhood.

Sadly, family problems that were not anticipated early on can emerge when the normal brothers and sisters leave to set up their own homes. Older parents whose youngest child had Down Syndrome sometimes report that although he was adored by his older siblings and was loved by them in return, he became very hostile toward his nephews or nieces, deeply resenting the attention paid by his siblings to their own children and his parents toward their grandchildren.

FAIRNESS

All parents have problems in sharing their time and attention, as well as presents and treats, equally among their children. They all try to avoid the accusation of "It's not fair." To provide equal shares of all sorts of goodies would be unjust to some child in all families where there are children of different ages, interests, and needs, but when the children also have a wide range of ability, understanding, and opportunity, fairness becomes impossible. Attempts to make compensation for the handicap suffered by the retarded child or for the deprivations endured by a normal sibling usually compound the problem. For example, overindulgence of either child in any form merely increases the rivalry, thus adding to the difficulties already present. In a study of children with Down Syndrome and the brothers or sisters closest in age (Gath & Gumley, 1987), I found that parents went to considerable lengths to be consistent within the family about rules of acceptable behavior, such as not allowing jumping on the furniture or staying at the table until the meal was finished, but they did make allowances for the relative abilities and for age when determining responsibilities and privileges, such as traveling unaccompanied by public transport, staying in the house alone, or cooking unsupervised.

A common, but usually short-lived problem in ordinary families concerns interference by a younger member of the family with the belongings, or worse, the homework, of an older brother or sister. In our studies of families with a Down Syndrome child, the affected toddlers were less likely to offend in this way than were the normal children of the same age. However, when a child remains at the developmental level of a 2-year-old, destructiveness can be a troublesome and persistent feature, making life a misery for a brother or sister, especially in a crowded home where no one has much privacy.

BULLYING AND STIGMA

People who are in any way different have always been called uncomplimentary names and subjected to bullying. Over the past years, the terms applied to those who suffer from mental retardation have been changed repeatedly in the forlorn hope that the stigma attached to each term will be lost when the new, presumably unprejudiced term is used. It is frequently the normal brother or sister who is taunted by the bullies about having a "daft sister" or a "cretin for a brother." Children who have been given an explanation well tailored to suit their level of understanding are much better equipped to deal with such persecution than are those left to puzzle out by themselves why the child in their family is different.

PROBLEMS AFFECTING BROTHERS AND SISTERS

Brothers and sisters of children with mild mental retardation for which there is no medical explanation are more likely to have educational problems of their own than are the children in the family of a child with a clear cut chromosomal disorder, such as Down Syndrome, or the siblings of a child with traumatic brain damage (Broman, Nichols, Shaughnessy, & Kennedy, 1987; Gath & Gumley, 1987). There are interesting exceptions, as in the case of Fragile X, the second most common cause of mental retardation, which occurs from sex-linked inheritance. Carrier sisters have been described as having some learning difficulties and greater problems than expected in coping with stress.

Emotional and conduct problems in the potentially normal children are associated with behavior problems in the retarded child and with other sources of family discord, such as marital disharmony between the parents. Treatment of such problems can well be handled on a family therapy basis, but that is unlikely to be effective if the therapist is not well informed about the nature and implications of the handicaps of the affected child.

PLACEMENT AWAY FROM HOME

The interests of the other children in the family are often given as a reason for parents' considering boarding school or seeking other placement away from home. Severe, intractable behavior disorders in the retarded children, and very distressed and exhausted parents, are regarded by many as strong indications for such intervention. Brothers and sisters, however, may not benefit as much as was hoped. In most boarding schools, the holidays are much the same as in other schools, so that the child with the behavior problems will tend to be at home just when there is the least available help, such as in the summer or at Christmas. In addition, many schools (in England) now board weekly only, so the brothers and sisters cannot expect a relaxed and refreshing weekend after their busy week at school. More serious is the problem of generalizing to the home the improvement in behavior noted at school, where there is a high staff ratio and plenty of space out of earshot of neighbors. This improvement often does not carry over, not because the parents do not try to put all of the suggestions into practice, but because conditions are very different, and usually much less easy, at home. The siblings of children who appear to have been sent away to school not infrequently feel insecure and worried that they, too, will be sent away if they fail to live up to expectations.

Respite or link families are less threatening to all concerned, but they are likely to be able to help the children with the most difficult behaviors and can only offer short periods of respite. Furthermore, this sort of help is extremely difficult, if not impossible, to set up in a deprived inner-city area. Should residential placement, either at school or in a hostel become necessary, then contact must be maintained with the family so that brothers and sisters, as well as parents, can continue to see the child as part of the family but in need of special care to help with his or her particular problems.

CONCERNS FOR THE FUTURE

Eventually, the paths of the siblings will diverge still further as the unaffected brothers and sisters make friends outside the family and take part in activities out of the home, before they start to work and then move away permanently. At this point, helping the retarded adolescent or young adult also leave the family nest and achieve some modest level of independence is a positive experience for all members of the family, including the brothers and sisters, relieving them of painful decisions at times of crisis, such as when the parents die or become too frail to continue caring for the one permanently dependent child. The opportunity for the retarded young adult to choose to leave home for him or herself is very limited indeed, but parents need to have the option to ease a handicapped child safely away from the home so they do not have the worry of leaving the responsibility to a sibling.

GENETIC COUNSELING

An understandable worry of the brothers and sisters of any sort of disabled child is whether the same thing will happen again when they have children in the future. This particular worry may not be shared with the parents because the normal siblings often realize the issue is a sensitive one and are very anxious not to cause any more upset. The chance of a recurrence of a specific disorder varies greatly. All brothers and sisters should have the right to discuss this possibility with a well-informed person in private, and that may well mean without the parents being present. However, the timing of such a discussion is important. If it is done too early, the child may be acutely embarrassed or perhaps totally miss the point of what is being said (Berry, 1990). If it is done too late, then a promising relationship may be broken up through fear or ignorance, or if it occurs later still, a recurrence of the disorder may bring even greater grief and resentment. Skilled genetic counseling should be offered to the other children in the family at about the time they are able to assume adult responsibilities.

CONCLUSIONS

There is little evidence to support the idea that families who have a handicapped child are of necessity handicapped in some way themselves. In the research published, there have been many examples found of life being lived fully by the brothers and sisters of a child with mental retardation. The families that do require special help are those who have many other disadvantages, particularly poverty, deprivation, social isolation, and chronic problems of family relationships.

The burden of the double handicap of mental retardation and a serious behavior disorder takes a heavy toll from the most stable and resourceful of parents. Although some such disorders are related to family dysfunction and may be reflected in increased disorder in the siblings, other very disruptive and distressing behavior is independent of such factors and may be more directly attributable to the underlying brain disorder of the child concerned. It is this group that is only just beginning to get attention. The limitations of "community care" for those with this dual diagnosis result in an almost intolerable burden for parents and, inevitably, the brothers and sisters.

REFERENCES

Berry, C. (1990, October). *Genetic counselling.* Paper presented at the meeting of the Association for Child Psychology and Psychiatry, London.

Broman, S., Nichols, P. L., Shaughnessy, P., & Kennedy, W. (1987). *Retardation in young children: A developmental study of cognitive deficit.* Hillsdale, NJ: Lawrence Erlbaum Associates.

Buckley, S., & Sacks, B. (1987). *The adolescent with Down's Syndrome.* Portsmouth, MA: Portsmouth Down Syndrome Trust.

Byrne, E. A., Cunningham, C. C., & Sloper, P. (1988). *Families and their children with Down's Syndrome: One feature in common.* London: Routledge.

Dupont, A. (1986). Sociopsychiatric aspects of the young severely mentally retarded and the family. *British Journal of Psychiatry, 148,* 227–234.

Gath, A. (1974). Sibling reactions to handicap: A comparison of the brothers and sisters of mongol children. *Journal of Child Psychology and Psychiatry, 15,* 187–198.

Gath, A. (1978). *Down's Syndrome and the family: The early years.* London: Academic Press.

Gath, A. (1990). Down Syndrome children and their families. *American Journal of Medical Genetics.* Supplement 7, Trisomy 21 (Down Syndrome).

Gath, A., & Gumley, D. (1987). Retarded children and their siblings. *Journal of Child Psychology and Psychiatry, 28,* 715–730.

Shepperdson, B. (1988). *Growing up with Down's Syndrome.* London: Cassell.

Chapter 8

Siblings as Co-Patients and Co-Therapists in the Treatment of Eating Disorders

Walter Vandereycken
University of Leuven, Leuven, Belgium

Ellie Van Vreckem
Kortenberg, Belgium

Although a voluminous literature exists on the families of eating disorder patients, it chiefly concerns the parents and their relationship with the patient (see Vandereycken, Kog, & Vanderlinden, 1989). For too long a time, both researchers and therapists have overlooked the fact that siblings may be involved in the development of anorexia/bulimia nervosa in their sister.[1] They, too, might suffer from this situation and show signs of psychosocial dysfunctioning (being *co-patients*), but equally neglected is the fact that the so-called "well" siblings may play a constructive role in the treatment of their anorexic or bulimic sister (and play the role of *co-therapist*). In the first part of this chapter we summarize the current knowledge about these siblings from a research perspective. Then we discuss what therapeutic role they may play, according to our own clinical experience.

RESEARCH ON SIBLINGS

Except for twins, siblings are in general a neglected group in research on eating disorders. The findings on this group are scattered in the vast literature on anorexia nervosa and bulimia. We summarize here the major features that

---

[1]Although eating disorders also occur in males, more than 95% of our patients are young women (the majority between 15 and 30 years of age). Hence, unless otherwise indicated, we discuss only female patients.

have been studied in large patient samples and in a systematic way.

Family Size

With regard to family size divergent opinions may be found in the older literature, and recent studies show similarly contrasting findings: Herzog (1982)
reported a greater number of only children among normal-weight bulimic girls
than among anorexics, whereas Bonenberger and Klosinski (1988) found that
12.6% of their anorexic sample were only children compared to 47.3% in the
general population (of the Federal Republic of Germany). Many other comparative studies, however, did not reveal any significant difference in family
size: Dolan, Evans, and Lacey (1989), who compared bulimics with non-eating-
disordered women; A. Hall (1978), who compared anorexics with data from
the general population (in New Zealand); Igoin-Apfelbaum (1985), who compared bulimic with overweight but non-bulimic girls; Johnson, C. Lewis, Love,
L. Lewis, and Stuckey (1984), who investigated bulimic and non-bulimic girls
in a large high school population; and Weiss and Ebert (1983), who studied
normal-weight bulimics and matched normal females.

Birth Order

In the descriptive literature, no consistent pattern can be found with relation
to the patient's birth order. In the older literature it was suggested that anorexic
patients are often first-born children or the second child, usually after an elder
sister. Some reports on large samples mention that first-borns, as well as last-
borns, are found to be anorexic more frequently than children occupying a
middle position (e.g., Bonenberger & Klosinski, 1988; Bruch, 1973; Crisp,
Hsu, Harding, & Hartshorn, 1980; Hall, 1978; Halmi, 1974), whereas no systematic birth order differences were found in other studies (e.g., Garfinkel &
Garner, 1982; Gowers, Kadambari, & Crisp, 1985; Mester, 1981; Theander,
1970). A preponderance of female siblings in families of anorexia nervosa patients has been mentioned by several clinicians (e.g., Bonenberger & Klosinski, 1988; Bruch, 1973; A. Hall, 1978; Mester, 1981; Stierlin & Weber, 1987;
Theander, 1970), but not found by others (Gowers et al., 1985; Gowers & Crisp,
1988). In their sample of 300 anorexia nervosa patients, Gowers and Crisp
(1988) analyzed the sibship structure of 98 cases in which the female patient
came from a family containing one other sibling, and found a trend toward
a relationship between the bulimic subtype of anorexia nervosa and the presence
of a male sibling (this trend disappeared or became inconsistent when a third
sibling was present).

The problem with these findings is that it is difficult to interpret them without
comparison with either a control group or normative data on the general popu-

lation. In the few comparative studies that have been conducted, no significant difference in birth order was observed between bulimics and normal controls (Dolan et al., 1989; Weiss & Ebert, 1983), between bulimic and restricting anorexics (Garfinkel, Moldofsky, & Garner, 1980; Vandereycken & Pierloot, 1983), or between normal-weight bulimics and anorexics (Herzog, 1982). Becker (1980) reported that in his group of anorexia nervosa patients, the number of female siblings was significantly higher than in the general population. Comparing bulimic women with non-eating-disordered women, Dolan et al. (1989) found no difference in sibling sex ratio. In some cases the anorexic patient may have occupied a "special" position because of a previous stillbirth, as A. Hall (1978) observed. Finally, some follow-up studies in anorexics have shown that neither sibship position (A. Hall, Slim, Hawker, & Salmond, 1984) nor the presence or absence of sisters (Casper, 1990) to have prognostic significance.

Eating Disorders in Siblings

One way to explore the possible genetic influences on eating disorders is to document the presence of anorexia nervosa and bulimia in more than one member of the same family, particularly in twins. Several case reports on this issue have appeared in the literature, but these idiographic studies usually suffer from methodological problems and biases (Treasure & Holland, 1990; Vandereycken & Pierloot, 1981). The best information has come from two British twin studies. In the first (Crisp, A. Hall, & Holland, 1985; Holland, A. Hall, Murray, Russell, & Crisp, 1984), 34 pairs of twins and 1 set of triplets were described: of the 30 female twin pairs, 9 out of 16 monozygotic pairs (55%) were concordant for anorexia nervosa, whereas only 1 out of 14 dizygotic pairs (7%) was concordant. In a second more elaborate study, 59 female twins were carefully investigated by Holland, Sicotte, and Treasure (1988): A concordance for anorexia nervosa was found in 68% of the monozygotic twins (8% in the dyzygotics), whereas zygosity made no difference in the concordance for bulimia nervosa (35% and 29%, respectively). The authors conclude that inherited factors account for about three quarters of the liability to develop anorexia nervosa, whereas the familial aggregation of bulimia nervosa probably results from environmental transmission. This conclusion, however, is contradicted by more recent reports: Waters, Beumont, Touyz, and Kennedy (1990) identified 11 anorexia nervosa patients who were members of a same-sex twin pair and found no evidence that the co-twin was concordant for the eating disorder; and Hsu, Chesler, and Santhouse (1990), as well as Fichter and Noegel (1990), reported a marked difference in concordance rates for bulimia nervosa between monozygotic and dizygotic twins. Evidence from (separated) adoptive twins would be especially helpful in teasing apart the contribution of the family environment to these differences.

In contrast to the many twin studies, little has been written on the occurrence of an eating disorder in other siblings of anorexic or bulimic patients. Systematic studies on this issue are scarce. In his extensive study of 94 female anorexic patients, Theander (1970) reported that 6.6% of the siblings had the disorder. Strober, Morrell, Burroughs, Salkin, and Jacobs (1985) studied the lifetime prevalence of eating disorders in the families of 60 anorexic patients and 95 psychiatrically ill control probands. No eating disorders were present in the brothers, but for the sisters, the data for the anorexia (70 sisters) and the control groups (113 sisters), respectively, were: full-blown anorexia nervosa: 2.9% versus 0.9%; subclinical anorexia nervosa: 6.7% versus 0%; bulimia nervosa: 2.9% versus 0.9%. Pooling all diagnoses, significantly more of the anorexics' sisters showed some eating disorder (11.4%) when compared to the control group (1.8%). Later these authors extended their study of the lifetime prevalence of eating disorders in the families of 97 of the anorexia nervosa patients, whom they compared to 66 probands with primary affective disorder and 117 probands with various nonaffective conditions (Strober, Lampert, Morrell, Burroughs, & Jacobs, 1990). Female first-degree relatives of the anorexics had a significantly higher risk of eating disorder than the other groups. None of the brothers (n = 95) developed an eating disorder, whereas 6.1% of the sisters (n = 92) did: 2.0% anorexia nervosa and 4.1% bulimia nervosa. All in all the number of affected siblings was quite low.

In the literature we found only two studies in which a systematic comparison was made between the behavioral characteristics of patients and their sisters. Maloney and Shepard-Spiro (1983) investigated 21 sister pairs (anorexia nervosa patients and their normal sisters) and compared the eating attitudes and behaviors of the closest-in-age sister with those of the anorexic patient. The scores on the Eating Attitudes Test for the sisters differed significantly from the patients and, with the exception of two sisters, fell within the normal range. Casper (1990), in a long-term follow-up study, looked at the closest-in-age sisters of anorexia nervosa patients as a control group. In a group of 15 patient–sister pairs, recovered anorexics did not differ from their sisters in body weight or Eating Attitudes Test scores, and on only two subscales of the Eating Disorder Inventory (ineffectiveness, interpersonal distrust) did they rate slightly higher than their sisters. Compared to normal controls, the sisters scored higher on the same subscales and showed a tendency to admit somewhat more body dissatisfaction and drive for thinness.

Behavioral and Mental Disorders

The incidence of overt sibling disturbance in anorexia nervosa families, according to A. Hall (1978), is low: Of the 110 siblings she studied, there was 1 grossly psychopathic brother, 1 brother with episodes of hysterical amnesia, 2 mentally defective children and a few mildly disturbed children. In the families of 43 bulimic anorexics studied by Collins, Kotz, Janesz, and Ferguson (1985), alcoholism was diagnosed in 3 brothers and 1 sister. These investigations of family psychiatric morbidity, however, were not carried out in a systematic way, unlike the many studies reported more recently. Indeed, the assumption that an association might exist between eating disorders and other mental disorders induced several family history studies. These focused especially on mood disorders, but also on substance abuse and personality disorders. In most of these investigations the findings concerning psychiatric morbidity in first-degree (and second-degree) relatives were pooled, so that no results are specified for siblings.

An analysis of family history information from 40 anorexia nervosa patients and 23 normal control subjects by Rivinus et al. (1984) revealed a tendency toward more depression and substance abuse in the anorexics' siblings, but the comparison with the control group did not reach statistical significance. In 42 siblings of 75 anorexia nervosa patients, Strober, Salkin, Burroughs, and Morrell (1982) found no case of affective disorder, 2 cases of alcoholism and 5 of drug use disorder. A controlled family study by Strober et al., (1990), which was mentioned earlier, found that the lifetime rates of affective disorder in siblings is much higher in the siblings of depressed anorexics compared to the siblings of nondepressed anorexia nervosa patients: 7.1% versus 2.9% for the sisters and 3.7% versus 1.5% for the brothers.

Personality

In Casper's (1990) study, the hypothesis that the sisters' personality would be categorically different from those of former anorexic patients was only partly supported. On most measures of the Multidimensional Personality Questionnaire (MPQ), and the California Psychological Inventory (CPI), sisters scored intermediately between patients and normal controls. Patients tended to be more emotionally and cognitively controlled (exhibiting lower impulsivity on the MPQ) and were less spontaneous than their sisters. Compared to normal controls, sisters reported greater stress reaction (MPQ) and scored lower in all areas testing interpersonal adequacy (CPI): dominance, capacity for status, sociability, social presence, self-acceptance, tolerance, and achievement via independence. Casper concluded:

> Sisters shared the patients' strong endorsement of conventional standards, but these qualities seemed counterbalanced in the sisters by more vigor and a more enterprising nature. . . . A great degree of restraint and control also distinguished recovered women from their sisters. Although sisters were equally authority-bound, this trait was counterbalanced by greater spontaneity and a greater ability toward effective social engagement. (pp. 167–168)

The behavioral and personality characteristics of anorexia nervosa daughters were also compared to the patients' sisters (11 twins and 11 non-twin pairs) in a study by Waters et al. (1990), in which maternal ratings were employed. Pre-anorexic personality scores did not differ between sibling pairs and did not change significantly after the development of anorexia nervosa (even though the patients themselves changed dramatically in a more obsessive-compulsive sense). In comparison with the non-twin normals, twin sisters who were well tended to use logic over sentiment and showed less irritability.

Sibling Rivalry

Both overt or more hidden sibling rivalry, particularly between sisters, has been noticed in the families of both anorexics (e.g., Stierlin & Weber, 1987) and bulimics (e.g., Sights & Richards, 1984). Dally (1977) mentioned "sibling jealousy" as one of the factors possibly causing or perpetuating anorexia nervosa (and if present, possibly related to a less favorable outcome), but all of these findings are just clinical impressions based upon selected cases: Systematic studies are almost non-existent. Even A. Hall (1978), in her description of family relationships in 50 male anorexics, came to a rather general conclusion without exact data on frequency:

> Relationships with individual siblings are a major stress factor in some patients. Two common findings are (i) an intense, ambivalent, rivalrous relationship with the nearest in age sibling whether older or younger, whether brother or sister and (ii) an expectation that the patient would relate well with a close in age sister who was of incompatible personality. (p. 266)

Engel and Höhne (1989) conducted a standardized interview in 33 severely ill anorexia nervosa patients and 111 normal female controls, including an evaluation of their intrafamilial relations. The two items in the interview that concerned sibling rivalry and sibling relationship were rated rather positively and showed no difference between groups.

Comparing anorexics and their sisters (twin and non-twin pairs), Waters et al. (1990) found that, according to the girls' mothers, the patients related significantly less well to their sisters than vice versa; twin sisters who were well tended to be less antagonistic in their relationships toward their anorexic sisters and they were more friendly, loyal, and supportive than were the non-twin well sisters. Finally, some long-term follow-up studies have looked at sibling rivalry as a possible prognostic factor: Without giving details on how they assessed this variable nor how often they observed it in anorexic patients, neither Morgan, Purgold, and Welbourne (1983) nor A. Hall et al. (1984) did find sibling rivalry to be related to outcome.

Sibling Incest

In recent years the "discovery" of incest as an important factor in several forms of psychopathology has drawn attention to the possible association between the development of an eating disorder (particularly bulimia) and sexual abuse during childhood and adolescence. Beckman and Burns (1990) studied this issue in college women and reported no difference between bulimic and nonbulimic women with respect to intrafamilial sexual abuse, but they did not specify the relationship between the woman and the abuser (i.e., whether fathers or brothers were involved). The same lack of specific data applies to other recent studies (e.g., Smolak, Levine, & Sullins, 1990), many of which concern only sexual abuse by adults (e.g., Palmer, Oppenheimer, Dignon, Chaloner, & Howells, 1990). The latter group of researchers, however, had reported earlier (Oppenheimer, Howells, Palmer, & Chaloner, 1985) on coercive incestuous relationships between eating disorder patients and siblings (i.e., five cases of abuse by older brothers). R. C. W. Hall, Tice, Beresford, Wooley, and A. K. Hall (1989) found that 60 of 158 patients with an eating disorder gave a history of sexual abuse; in 10 cases a brother was involved and in 1 case a sister. Now that health care professionals are more aware of this problem (see, e.g., Ascherman & Safier, 1990), we can expect to see more attention to the importance of this issue in both research and treatment of eating disorder patients.

Summary

In the bulk of the literature on families of eating disorder patients (see Vandereycken et al., 1989), siblings occupy a rather marginal position. Moreover, clinicians and researchers are interested primarily in problematic aspects of the sibship and overlook the positive role brothers and sisters can play in either the protection or the recovery from an eating disorder. Some family therapists, working both in anorexia nervosa (Minuchin, Rosman, & Baker, 1978; Stierlin & Weber, 1987) and bulimia (Schwartz, Barrett, & Saba, 1985) have commented on this neglect, but with a few exceptions (e.g., Roberto, 1988), siblings may still be considered an often forgotten group. We, too, only recently realized their important therapeutic potential, which we describe in the next section.

SIBLINGS AND THEIR THERAPEUTIC SIGNIFICANCE

For more than 20 years the University Psychiatric Center in Kortenberg, Belgium, has developed a special interest in the study and treatment of eating disorder patients. The Eating Disorders Unit offers highly structured group treatment for anorexia and bulimia nervosa patients who need inpatient care. The multidimensional approach includes a behavioral program for restoration of weight and eating habits, intensive group psychotherapy, art therapy, and specific body-oriented therapy. In addition to these major therapeutic elements (described in Vandereycken, 1985, 1988), the active participation of the patient's family is considered to be an essential part of the program. It is achieved mainly through parent counseling groups and family and/or marital therapy (see Vandereycken et al., 1989). In recent years we have paid systematic and explicit attention to the patients' siblings and have tried, when possible, to involve them in our therapeutic approach.

It was, in fact, the recurring separation–individuation problems in families of eating disorder patients that directed our attention to the dynamics of the sibling system and the relationships between siblings and parents. Siblings can help us understand and clarify the past and present family interactions. With their often surprising and refreshing conceptions about family functioning they can act as "consultants" to the therapists in the therapeutic process, especially when issues between family members remain unresolved. Finally, they may act as nurturers, using each other for mutual support, for example, in families without good parenting (Lewis, 1990).

Siblings most often react very positively when we invite them to participate in therapy. All of the siblings are invited, especially those who are initially described as "certainly not coming" or "not important." We try to understand each sibling's position within the family and ask for everyone's opinions. We have found that real and genuine help is often provided by those siblings from whom one would expect the least help, for example, "silent" siblings who are having problems themselves. In separate sibling sessions, our treatment principles and goals are explained. Usually they understand the interactional meanings of the eating disorder very well. By understanding what is going on in the treatment, siblings can function as our co-therapists at home, provoking discussions about new topics or expressing more freely their opinions about daily life. We can often use the siblings' perceptions of the family interactions to re-label both the eating disorder and the family problems in constructive terms.

A crucial issue in this is the creation of clear boundaries between siblings and parents, which thereby strengthen both subsystems. Our aim is to restore the executive power of the parents in the eating disordered families: We reinforce their parental role, letting the children function as children. For this reason we organize separate sessions for both subsystems. Whereas the sessions with the parents focus on the separation process, the individuation process is stressed in the sibling subgroup. As to intrafamilial boundaries, working with large families appears to be a confusing and demanding job. In large families (with five or more children) creating clear boundaries as well as defining separate subsystems is very difficult. In general, older brothers and sisters can have a valuable protective role, but they can also reinforce boundary-confusion (e.g., by facilitating sexual abuse) or overprotection and over-involvement.

In the following paragraphs we examine some specific therapeutic issues and strategies, illustrated by case examples.

The "Parentified" Sibling

The *parentified* sibling is often a social worker, nurse, doctor, or somebody with high social status. He or she is the one who brought the patient or the family into treatment. This sibling has a strong position within the family and often seems to be the ideal co-therapist. However, these siblings tend to avoid "hot" topics such as rivalry and vulnerability, keeping some family secrets while revealing others. Bank and Kahn (1982) discouraged these siblings' involvement in the treatment, even in sibling therapy, and dismissed them in order to precipitate a therapeutic crisis within the family. Selvini Palazzoli (1985) went even further: Her treatment staff refused to start family therapy, and made the astonishing claim that the parentified sibling cannot stand any change in the family functioning without becoming ill him or herself.

Our treatment strategy is to stress again and again the importance of clear boundaries between the parental and the sibling subsystems, while dealing with the parentified sibling in separate individual sessions. We consider it important that parentified siblings have confidence in the treatment and in the therapists. We try to get these siblings in touch with their own ambivalence about individuation, and urge them to recognize the burden of their lonely task and position, despite the apparent gratitude of everyone. By anticipating and preparing them for the inevitable crises during treatment, we prevent them from intervening at stress moments, and help them to leave the real responsibilities to the hospitalized sibling.

Sibling Rivalry

In the sessions with the parents, we re-label the eating problems as a sign of ambivalence, as the child's attempt to separate from, as well as to remain dependent on, the parents. In the sibling group, we re-label the eating disorder as a search for identification and individuation. Patterns of identification going from *twinning*—siblings feel as if they are identical—to *de-identification*—siblings feel totally different from their sibling—are described (Bank & Kahn, 1982). Studies suggest that both can be considered as patterns for resolving underlying sibling rivalry. Schachter, Shore, Feldman-Rotman, Marquis, and Campbell (1976) have paid specific attention to de-identification, and found that this striving for special marks of distinction occurs mostly in closely spaced sibling pairs of the same sex. This process of continuous social comparison is very characteristic of eating disorder patients and is frequently noticed in the histories of our patients. Indeed, eating problems could be considered a form of de-identification. What we often encounter, however, is a total negation of the underlying feelings of rivalry and jealousy, and we are often faced with the opposite attitude: Anorexics are especially well known for being very kind and helpful (a sort of twinning attitude). Sometimes only the concerned sibling is able to feel the underlying rivalry, a rivalry often not recognized by the parents.

As far as twinning or de-identification, we try to define the emotional distance between the siblings and work on either their differences or their common experiences (Bank & Kahn, 1982). In fact we are doing exactly the same with the relationships between patients in our group psychotherapy sessions. In a positive and accepting (group) atmosphere, we point out feelings of rivalry and defense mechanisms whenever they appear. We always pinpoint each personal view or interpretation and each way of dealing with conflictual feelings. In order to prevent a dichotomy between good and bad, strong and weak, beautiful and ugly, or to prevent perfectionism and rigidity, we re-label conflicts and oppositions as complementary and enriching differences. Dealing with the issue of rivalry, for example, we deliberately design in our inpatient groups a somewhat hierarchical structure. Group members evolve through three consecutive phases, each with growing responsibilities and rights. Every three weeks, a ''group leader'' is selected from among the members who are in the final treatment phase. This situation elicits feelings of competition, but also helps to channel these feelings into explicit stages of responsibility and experience.

In psychotherapy groups as well as in families, peers or siblings can become engaged in an escalating symmetrical battle. Here, the prescription of an alternative role-script (changing the roles of both parties) serves as an introduction to complementarity. This can act as a refreshing antidote to the escalating symmetry (Wagner, Hunter, & Boeller, 1988).

Family 1.   In a family with five siblings, we noticed a strong rivalry between the first pair of closely spaced girls. The eldest was considered intelligent and independent, living on her own far away from home. The second, an anorexic patient, was viewed as childish, demanding, and controlling the whole family. In the sibling sessions, we explained and discussed extensively the importance of separation from the parents, while noticing the little steps toward assertion and recovery of the anorexic patient. During treatment one sister left home to live on her own and a married brother stopped having a daily meal with his parents. All of a sudden we were confronted with a terrible crisis within the family concerning a seemingly trivial issue: the acquisition by our patient of a washing machine. The parents experienced this as a rejection and the mother, suffering from diabetes, went into a life-threatening coma.

In the sibling therapy with the first sibling pair, we proposed to reverse roles: the eldest, independent sibling should ask her mother to wash temporarily for her again and should come home more frequently while the patient should continue her efforts to separate. This looks like a simple solution, but we had to work intensively with the two sisters because of their intense feelings of rivalry: "Who will now be the best daughter in the eyes of the parents?" "Was separation always the best option in life?" In the sessions with the parents we explained that separation doesn't mean rejection. We convinced the parents to go on vacation for the first time in years, and afterwards they told us they had even made some new friends.

Family 2. This example emphasizes how siblings can become mutual nurturers. An anorexic patient, the youngest of seven children, was a very reticent and suspicious 22-year-old woman. At the age of 12 she began self-mutilating during the period her father was dying of leukemia. All the attention and care of the family was focused on the father's illness and afterward on the siblings' successive marriages. Hence, during her youth the patient was confronted with repeated loss. At age 14 the anorexia nervosa was diagnosed, but the self-mutilation remained secret. In the sibling sessions with a seemingly "not important" older sister, described as having a lot of problems herself, some of our patient's secret memories and impressions were confirmed by her sister. We found out that the mother, known as a very respectable and religious woman, had beaten her children regularly and unreasonably for minor faults or assertions. Talking for the first time in their lives about these events—feeling mutual recognition, warmth, sorrow, and pain—the sisters were able to free themselves from some traumas. From that day on our patient stopped self-mutilation. Similar patterns of change have occurred since in three different sibling therapies.

Obtaining a balanced image of the parents, with both positive and negative elements, being able both to criticize and to like them, is our therapeutic tool for achieving separation and individuation for the children. For this purpose siblings appear to be very helpful.

Triangular Dynamics

A general rule in our approach is that direct therapeutic confrontations between the patient and the conflict-ridden parent should be approached with care. Before engaging in such confrontation (as in cases of incest), one should first build up psychological strength in the vulnerable family member and ensure a strong and positive alliance between the therapist and all family members involved. We carefully prepare balanced confrontations between parents and siblings.

In eating disordered families one conflictual relationship is usually presented more or less openly. Most often it concerns the interaction between the

patient and her mother. However, focusing solely on this dyadic conflict—
frequently crystallized in a battle around food—could be misleading and even
anti-therapeutic if one neglects the total family context in which this conflict
occurs. Many family therapists tend to work on the triangular interactions between parents and patient. It could be more fruitful, however, to look first for
possible triangular conflicts between the patient, the parents, and one or more
siblings. We illustrate this with the following example.

Family 3.   A girl (18 years old) with anorexia nervosa was described by
her parents as the opposite of her brother who was 1 year older. He was depicted
as not very intelligent and strong (even physically), but more flexible and social. The parents tried to stimulate the siblings' feelings of "solidarity" by in-
sisting, for instance, that their daughter help her brother with his lessons. As
long as they were children, the anorexic girl was her father's favorite: She was
"the best" both at school and in sports. The father appeared to compensate
for his own professional disappointments with an overinvolvement as a coach
in the sports competitions of his children. His son played soccer and his daughter
was an excellent swimmer, but she had to stop competitive sport after the discovery of growth retardation. Other events hurt her vulnerable self-esteem very
badly: the neglect by her trainer, in contrast to the admiration of her parents
and brother, and being abandoned by her first boyfriend. In the relationship
between the mother and the daughter, we discovered intense feelings of rivalry concerning clothes, weight, and attention from the father. Our patient men-
struated at the age of 12, but because sexuality was taboo in the family, she
thought she had diarrhea. Confronted with boys and sexuality she felt dirty
and disgusted, so she behaved like a boy and imitated her brother and his
friends. At the age of 16, she had a mysterious close friendship with another
anorexic girl. Her parents reacted with anger and her brother with jealousy.
This "special" friendship was probably a search for differentiation and separation from her family. When this girlfriend left for 1 year, our patient fell
in love with a boy, "who would never fit in with my family." She menstruat-
ed again from that time.

   During her inpatient treatment we also worked intensively with the sibling
relationship. We focused on both siblings' extreme loyalty to each other, their
mutual dependence, their lack of differentiation, and finally, on their underlying rivalry. Both admitted they had selected each other's friends and never
had lovers because of mutual criticism. A few weeks after our patient had decided to choose her own weekend activities and select her own friends, her brother
started a relationship with a girl. In the following sibling sessions, he told his
sister that only the separation through her hospitalization had allowed him to
do so. They quarreled much more than before, but they understood each other
at a deeper level, no longer striving for priority or dominance. The sister
then detached herself from the family myth concerning sports and successful

competition: She could appreciate her brother's efforts in soccer, but no longer wanted to please her father by being "the best" in competition. Finally, against strong opposition from her mother, she decided to go to a university where she could live in a student home. Soon after leaving home she started a relationship with a boy.

CONCLUSION

For many years we had been convinced of the importance of the family context in treating patients with eating disorders, but we only recently became aware of the significance of sibling relationships. It is time to take into consideration the full richness and intensity, however conflictual or ambivalent, of sibling interaction. In this chapter we have touched on only a few aspects of this issue, but we hope the message is clear: We have learned much from siblings. They have deepened our understanding of eating disorders and enlarged the scope and potential of our treatment.

REFERENCES

Ascherman, L. I., & Safier, E. J. (1990). Sibling incest: A consequence of individual and family dysfunction. *Bulletin of the Menninger Clinic, 54*, 311–322.

Bank, S., & Kahn, M. (1982). *The sibling bond.* New York: Basic.

Becker, H. (1980). Die Vater–Tochter-Beziehung in der Familiendynamik bei Anorexia-nervosa-Patientinnen [The father–daughter relationship in the family dynamics of anorexia nervosa patients]. *Nervenarzt, 51*, 568–572.

Beckman, K. A., & Burns, G. L. (1990). Relation of sexual abuse and bulimia in college women. *International Journal of Eating Disorders, 9*, 487–492.

Bonenberger, R., & Klosinski, G. (1988). Zur Elternpersönlichkeit, Familiensituation und Familiendynamik bei Anorexia-nervosa-Patientinnen unter besonderer Berücksichtigung der Vater–Tochter-Beziehung (eine Retrospektivstudie) [The personalities of the parents, the family situation and the family dynamics of anorexia nervosa patients, particularly in terms of the father–daughter relationship: A retrospective study]. *Zeitschrift für Kinder- und Jugendpsychiatrie, 16*, 186–195.

Bruch, H. (1973). *Eating disorders: Obesity, anorexia nervosa, and the person within.* New York: Basic.

Casper, R. (1990). Personality features of women with good outcome from restricting anorexia nervosa. *Psychosomatic Medicine, 52*, 156–170.

Collins, G. B., Kotz, M., Janesz, J. W., & Ferguson, T. (1985). Alcoholism in the families of bulimic anorexics. *Cleveland Clinic Quarterly, 52*, 65–67.

Crisp, A. H., Hall, A., & Holland, A. J. (1985). Nature and nurture in anorexia nervosa: A study of 34 pairs of twins, one pair of triplets, and an adoptive family. *International Journal of Eating Disorders, 4*, 5–27.

Crisp, A. H., Hsu, L., Harding, B., & Hartshorn, J. (1980). Clinical features of anorexia nervosa: A study of a consecutive series of 102 female patients. *Journal of Psychosomatic Research, 24*, 179–191.

Dally, P. (1977). Anorexia nervosa: Do we need a scapegoat? *Proceedings of the Royal Society of Medicine, 70*, 470–474.

Dolan, B. M., Evans, C., & Lacey, J. H. (1989). Family composition and social class in bulimia: A catchment area study of a clinical and a comparison group. *Journal of Nervous and Mental Disease, 177,* 267–272.

Engel, K., & Höhne, D. (1989). An interaction model of anorexia nervosa. *Psychotherapy and Psychosomatics, 51,* 57–61.

Fichter, M. M., & Noegel, R. (1990). Concordance for bulimia nervosa in twins. *International Journal of Eating Disorders, 9,* 255–263.

Garfinkel, P., Moldofsky, H., & Garner, D. (1980). The heterogeneity of anorexia nervosa: Bulimia as a distinct subgroup. *Archives of General Psychiatry, 37,* 1036–1040.

Garfinkel, P. E., & Garner, D. M. (1982). *Anorexia nervosa: A multidimensional perspective.* New York: Brunner/Mazel.

Gowers, S., & Crisp, A. H. (1988). Anorexia nervosa and the structure of the sibship. In D. Hardoff & E. Chigier (Eds.), *Eating disorders in adolescents and young adults* (pp. 117–124). London: Freund.

Gowers, S., Kadambari, S. R., & Crisp, A. H. (1985). Family structure and birth order of patients with anorexia nervosa. *Journal of Psychiatric Research, 19,* 247–251.

Hall, A. (1978). Family structure and relationships of 50 female anorexia nervosa patients. *Australian and New Zealand Journal of Psychiatry, 12,* 263–268.

Hall, A., Slim, E., Hawker, F., & Salmond, C. (1984). Anorexia nervosa: Long-term outcome in 50 female patients. *British Journal of Psychiatry, 145,* 407–413.

Hall, R. C. W., Tice, L., Beresford, T. P., Wooley, B., & Hall, A. K. (1989). Sexual abuse in patients with anorexia nervosa and bulimia. *Psychosomatics, 30,* 73–79.

Halmi, K. (1974). Anorexia nervosa: Demographic and clinical features in 94 cases. *Psychosomatic Medicine, 36,* 18–26.

Herzog, D. (1982). Bulimia: The secretive syndrome. *Psychosomatics, 23,* 481–487.

Holland, A. J., Hall, A., Murray, R., Russell, G. F. M., & Crisp, A. H. (1984). Anorexia nervosa: A study of 34 pairs of twins and one set of triplets. *British Journal of Psychiatry, 145,* 414–419.

Holland, A. J., Sicotte, N., & Treasure, J. (1988). Anorexia nervosa: Evidence for a genetic basis. *Journal of Psychosomatic Research, 32,* 561–571.

Hsu, L. K. G., Chesler, B. E., & Santhouse, R. (1990). Bulimia nervosa in eleven sets of twins: A clinical report. *International Journal of Eating Disorders, 9,* 275–282.

Igoin-Apfelbaum, L. (1985). Characteristics of family background in bulimia. *Psychotherapy and Psychosomatics, 43,* 161–167.

Johnson, C., Lewis, C., Love, S., Lewis, L., & Stuckey, M. (1984). Incidence and correlates of bulimic behavior in a female high-school population. *Journal of Youth and Adolescence, 13,* 15–26.

Lewis, K. G. (1990). Siblings: A hidden resource in therapy. *Journal of Strategic and Systemic Therapies, 9,* 39–49.

Maloney, M. J., & Shepard-Spiro, P. (1983). Eating attitudes and behaviors of anorexia nervosa patients and their sisters. *General Hospital Psychiatry, 5,* 285–288.

Mester, H. (1981). *Die Anorexia nervosa* [Anorexia nervosa]. Berlin-Heidelberg: Springer–Verlag.

Minuchin, S., Rosman, B. L., & Baker, L. (1978). *Psychosomatic families: Anorexia nervosa in context.* Cambridge, MA: Harvard University Press.

Morgan, H. G., Purgold, J., & Welbourne, J. (1983). Management and outcome in anorexia nervosa: A standardized prognostic study. *British Journal of Psychiatry, 143,* 282–287.

Oppenheimer, R., Howells, K., Palmer, R. L., & Chaloner, D. A. (1985). Adverse sexual experience in childhood and clinical eating disorders: A preliminary description. *Journal of Psychiatric Research, 19,* 357–361.

Palmer, R. L., Oppenheimer, R., Dignon, A., Chaloner, D. A., & Howells, K. (1990). Childhood sexual experiences with adults reported by women with eating disorders: An extended series. *British Journal of Psychiatry, 156,* 699–703.

Rivinus, T. M., Biederman, J., Herzog, D. B., Kemper, K., Harper, G. P., Harmatz, J. S., & Houseworth, S. (1984). Anorexia nervosa and affective disorders: A controlled family history study. *American Journal of Psychiatry, 141,* 1414–1418.

Roberto, L. G. (1988). The vortex: Siblings in the eating disordered family. In M. D. Kahn & K. G. Lewis (Eds.), *Siblings in therapy* (pp. 297-313). New York: W. W. Norton.

Schachter, F., Shore, E., Feldman-Rotman, S., Marquis, R., & Campbell, S. (1976). Sibling deidentification. *Developmental Psychology, 12,* 418-429.

Schwartz, R. C., Barrett, M. J., & Saba, G. (1985). Family therapy for bulimia. In D. M. Garner & P. E. Garfinkel (Eds.), *Handbook of psychotherapy for anorexia nervosa and bulimia* (pp. 280-307). New York: Guilford.

Selvini Palazzoli, M. (1985). The problem of the sibling as the referring person. *Journal of Marital and Family Therapy, 11,* 21-34.

Sights, J. R., & Richards, H. C. (1984). Parents of bulimic women. *International Journal of Eating Disorders, 3*(4), 3-13.

Smolak, L., Levine, M. P., & Sullins, E. (1990). Are child sexual experiences related to eating-disordered attitudes and behaviors in a college sample? *International Journal of Eating Disorders, 9,* 167-178.

Stierlin, H., & Weber, G. (1987). Anorexia nervosa: Family dynamics and family therapy. In P. J. V. Beumont, G. D. Burrows, & R. C. Casper (Eds.), *Handbook of eating disorders: Part 1. Anorexia and bulimia nervosa* (pp. 319-347). Amsterdam: Elsevier.

Strober, M., Salkin, B., Burroughs, J., & Morrell, W. (1982). Validity of the bulimia-restricter distinction in anorexia nervosa: Parental personality characteristics and family psychiatric morbidity. *Journal of Nervous and Mental Disease, 170,* 345-351.

Strober, M., Morrell, W., Burroughs, J., Salkin, B., & Jacobs, C. (1985). A controlled family study of anorexia nervosa. *Journal of Psychiatric Research, 19,* 239-246.

Strober, M., Lampert, C., Morrell, W., Burroughs, J., & Jacobs, C. (1990). A controlled family study of anorexia nervosa: Evidence of familial aggregation and lack of shared transmission with affective disorders. *International Journal of Eating Disorders, 9,* 239-253.

Theander, S. (1970). Anorexia nervosa: A psychiatric investigation of 94 female cases. *Acta Psychiatrica Scandinavica,* Suppl. 214.

Treasure, J., & Holland, A. (1990). Genetic vulnerability to eating disorders: Evidence from twin and family studies. In H. Remschmidt & M. H. Schmidt (Eds.), *Anorexia nervosa* (pp. 59-68). Toronto: Hogrefe & Huber.

Vandereycken, W. (1985). Inpatient treatment of anorexia nervosa: Some research-guided changes. *Journal of Psychiatric Research, 19,* 413-422.

Vandereycken, W. (1988). Organization and evaluation of an inpatient treatment program for eating disorders. *Behavioral Residential Treatment, 3,* 153-165.

Vandereycken, W., Kog, E., & Vanderlinden, J. (Eds.). (1989). *The family approach to eating disorders. Assessment and treatment of anorexia nervosa and bulimia.* New York/Costa Mesa (CA): PMA Publications.

Vandereycken, W., & Pierloot, R. (1981). Anorexia nervosa in twins. *Psychotherapy and Psychosomatics, 35,* 55-63.

Vandereycken, W., & Pierloot, R. (1983). The significance of subclassification in anorexia nervosa: A comparative study of clinical features in 141 patients. *Psychological Medicine, 13,* 543-549.

Wagner, V. S., Hunter, R., & Boeller, D. (1988). Sibling rivalry and the systemic perspective: Implications for treatment. *Journal of Strategic and Systemic Therapies, 7,* 67-71.

Waters, B. G. H., Beumont, P. J. V., Touyz, S., & Kennedy, M. (1990). Behavioural differences between twin and non-twin sibling pairs discordant for anorexia nervosa. *International Journal of Eating Disorders, 9,* 265-273.

Weiss, S., & Ebert, M. (1983). Psychological and behavioral characteristics of normal-weight bulimics and normal-weight controls. *Psychosomatic Medicine, 45,* 293-303.

Chapter 9

Sibling Relationships in Disharmonious Homes: Potential Difficulties and Protective Effects

Jennifer Jenkins
Institute of Child Study, University of Toronto

The main focus of developmental psychopathology research has been on identifying factors that increase children's risk of psychological difficulties. In more recent years attention has also been given to factors that might ameliorate or lessen the impact of negative experiences on children. In adults who are under stress, social support has been found to reduce the risk of developing psychopathology (Cohen & Wills, 1985). There has been little work, however, on identifying the factors that protect children who are living in stressful circumstances from developing psychopathology. One could hypothesize that social support might also be protective to children, and might come from parents, siblings, relatives outside the nuclear family, peers, and teachers.

Bank and Kahn (1982) have written about the close and protective sibling relationships that can develop when children are in adverse family circumstances. On the basis of interviews and observations carried out on people in psychotherapy they found that siblings can form an intense relationship with one another to compensate for deficiencies in other aspects of family interaction. For instance, if a mother is very depressed or distances herself from her first-born child when she has another baby, the first child may turn to the second child for love and intimacy. The researchers further suggest that these relationships between siblings, although positively compensatory in some ways, may be too symbiotic to allow for ultimately healthy individuation. These observations have been made on the basis of uncontrolled studies on clinical samples and could valuably be examined with suitable control groups and in a nonclinic population.

There are two important questions to consider in relation to sibling relationships in stressful circumstances. The first relates to whether there is any
difference in the frequency of positive relationships between children in stressful family circumstances and those in non-stressful family circumstances. In
other words, do stressful family relationships allow children the opportunity
to develop more intense sibling relationships than they would in less stressful
family circumstances? The second issue relates to the potential benefit of sibling relationships for children under stress. If these relationships are protective to children, one would expect to find an association between the quality
or presence of a particular kind of sibling relationship and lower levels of emotional and behavioral problems in childhood.

In relation to the first question, Hetherington (1988) compared the quality
of sibling relationships in homes in which the children had experienced a divorce
between the parents with children who were in stepfamilies and children who
were living in intact homes. She found that children in stepfamilies had more
problematic and hostile relationships with siblings than children in intact homes.
Boys in divorced homes were found to be more coercive and aggressive toward
siblings than children in intact homes or in stepfamilies. In this research there
was little evidence that when children were exposed to the adverse circumstance
of their parents' divorce, they used their siblings as sources of support and
built up particularly close relationships with them. MacKinnon (1989) also investigated the quality of sibling interactions in divorced and non-divorced homes
and she, too, found that boys in divorced families had more problematic sibling relationships than boys in intact families, particularly when the boys had
younger sisters. Again, there was no indication that particularly positive relationships developed between children in divorced homes.

In relation to the second question, about the potentially protective influence
of siblings, Sandler (1980) found that the presence of an older sibling was
protective to children under stress. In a group of children from economically
deprived backgrounds, who had experienced a high level of negative life events,
he found that having an older sibling at home was associated with a lower
level of emotional and behavioral problems. Among children who had not
experienced a high level of negative life events, no association was found between the presence of a sibling and the level of emotional and behavioral
problems.

The study by Sandler is the only one I know of to investigate the positive
impact of sibling relationships on children under stress. If, however, we con-
ceptualize sibling relationships as one kind of social support available to children, there is strong evidence from several studies that children with high levels of social support have fewer problems than those with low levels of social
support. Stiffman, Jung, and Feldman (1986) found that relationships with
grandparents were associated with lower levels of emotional and behavioral
problems for children living with a mentally ill parent. Werner and R. S. Smith

(1982) and Rutter (1971) have both found that good parent–child relationships were associated with fewer emotional and behavioral problems for children in adverse circumstances.

In order to examine whether close sibling relationships act to protect children in stressful circumstances, a research design with a high and low stress group, and a statistical analysis allowing one to test for the interaction between the stress and the protective factor is needed. These design features allow one to distinguish between different kinds of factors. Some putative protective factors combine with the independent variable (or stress measure) additively so that each has an independent effect on the outcome variable, and the combined effect is simply the sum of the two individual effects. This type of factor is associated with the outcome variable irrespective of the level of stress that people are experiencing. Factors that, in combination with the stress, show independent effects have sometimes been called protective factors. More accurately these kinds of factors denote an absence of risk.

Some putative protective factors and stress factors combine interactively with one factor acting to multiply or divide the impact of the other. Such factors can be said to *potentiate* one another (when they increase the risk of disturbance) or for one factor to *buffer* the effects of the other (when the factor acts to decrease the risk of disturbance). When a putative protective factor is operating to buffer the effects of stress, the absence of the factor is associated with high levels of disturbance in the high stress group but has no association with the outcome variable in the low stress group. This kind of pattern is tested for by looking for a statistical interaction between the stress and the protective factor. One of the aims of the research described further on was to distinguish among these different kinds of factors.

Marital disharmony was chosen as a stress in this study because of the considerable amount of evidence suggesting a strong relationship between marital disharmony and children's disturbance. Children who live in homes in which the parental marriage is disharmonious are between two and five times more likely to develop significant emotional and behavioral problems than children living in harmonious homes (Quinton, Rutter, & Rowlands, 1976; Richman, Stevenson, & Graham, 1982). It is also a very common stress. M. A. Smith, in a sample from the London area (personal communication, 1983), found that approximately 18% of 7-year-old children were living in disharmonious homes.

My aim in this chapter is to present data pertaining to whether children are protected by close sibling relationships, to distinguish between factors that are protective and those that increase children's risk, and to compare the frequency of negative and positive sibling relationships in disharmonious and harmonious homes. Other aspects of the study, including more detailed accounts of measures, are described elsewhere (Jenkins & M. A. Smith, 1990; Jenkins, M. A. Smith, & Graham, 1989; Smith & Jenkins, in press.)

METHODS

The sample for this study was drawn from a previous general population study examining the effects of lead on children's health and behavior (M. A. Smith, Delves, Lansdown, Clayton, & Graham, 1983). In this study, 452 families from three boroughs in London, England, with a target child between 6 and 7 years old, representative of the population in the boroughs on gender, family size, birth order, and socioeconomic status (SES), were interviewed between 1979 and 1982. A rating of the quality of the parents' marital relationship was made as a control procedure.

For the present study, carried out between 1984 and 1986, families who had been rated in the first study as having a disharmonious marriage were matched on a best-fit basis for gender of child, family size, geographical area, and social grouping with families who were rated as being harmonious (see further on for a description of the rating).

There were 178 families eligible for the present study. These included 83 families in which the marriage had been rated as disharmonious in the initial study and 83 families in which the marriage had been rated as harmonious. There were 12 replacements who were included when original families either refused participation or moved out of the London area. Replacements were made from families with marriages initially rated as harmonious, as all of the families with marriages rated as disharmonious were already included in the sample. The same child in the family was the target for both studies. All children were between 9 and 12 years old at the time of follow-up.

Of eligible families, 22% did not take part. These included 7% (n = 13) who moved out of the London area or whom we were unable to trace, and 15% (n = 26) who refused to participate. These families were compared on a number of variables (using information collected previously) with the families who did take part. They did not differ on any of the variables examined, which were quality of marriage, gender of child, SES, birth order of the index child, family size, maternal IQ, and maternal educational attainments. One hundred thirty-nine families took part in the study. This included 139 primary caretakers (this was the mother in all but 3 families; this dataset will be referred to as the mothers' data), 102 fathers, and 136 children. The 139 families included 16 families in which the parents had separated or divorced since the initial interview and 4 families in which one of the spouses had died. Only those families that remained intact (n = 119) between the first and second interview were included in the following analyses. Twelve families had one child, 78 had two children, 27 had three children and 2 had four or more children living at home. Information collected from mothers was more comprehensive than that collected from either fathers or children. (Unless otherwise specified, the mothers' data are reported.)

Parents were interviewed in their homes simultaneously but separately using a semi-structured interview. The children were interviewed approximately 1 week later. All interviewers were blind to any previous knowledge of the family and the children's interviewer was blind to all details of the present family circumstances. Interrater reliability was assessed by two interviewers rating the same interview and was carried out on 15 mothers and 10 children. Cronbach's alpha (Cronbach, Gleser, Nanda, & Rajaratnam, 1972) was used to calculate reliability and was between a = .73 and a = 1.0 for the measures described here. Test–retest reliability trials were not carried out on the mothers' or fathers' interviews because most of the measures were taken from interviews with previously well established reliability and validity (Brown & Rutter, 1966; Quinton et al., 1976; Richman et al., 1982; Rutter & Brown, 1966; Rutter, Tizard, & Whitmore, 1970).

Parental Marital Relationship

An interview assessment of the marital relationship was used in the initial study and in the present study (Quinton et al., 1976). This measure has been demonstrated to be a reliable rating of the quality of the marital relationship with good predictive validity over a five-year period. Both parents are interviewed on the following measures: help from spouse on care of the children and household tasks, satisfaction with help received, satisfaction with confiding, irritability and quarrels, separations, perceived problems with the marriage, mutual activities, and satisfaction with outings. Global ratings are made on warmth, hostility, and criticism based on content and voice tone. An overall rating from 1 to 6 is made by the interviewer with 1 representing a better than average marriage characterized by mutual warmth and concern and 6 representing a marriage characterized by constant antagonism, hostility, and quarrels or by a complete lack of affection, mutual concern, and cooperation. After each interviewer had made a separate rating for the mother's and father's account of the marriage, the two raters arrived at a joint rating, taking into account all the information collected by the separate interviewers. Marriages rated as 1, 2, or 3 on this rating constituted the harmonious marriage group. Marriages rated as 4, 5, or 6 constituted the disharmonious group.

Children's Emotional and Behavioral Problems

Mothers were questioned in detail about their children's emotional state and behavior with items taken from the interview developed by Graham & Rutter (1968; Rutter & Graham, 1968) and supplemented with items from the *Diagnostic and Statistical Manual of Mental Disorders,* 3rd ed. (DSM-III; American Psychiatric Association, 1980). Thirty-one aspects of children's behavior were asked about and rated in terms of their frequency and severity. Scores from individual items were summed to yield a total symptom score with a higher score indicating many minor problems, a smaller number of serious problems, or both. Children were also interviewed about their own emotional state and behavior on an instrument covering similar items.

Sibling and Mother–Child Relationships

Mothers were interviewed about the quality of the target child's relationships with her and with his or her siblings. Because we were looking to see if sibling relationships could be protective, we looked for the presence of a particularly close and supportive relationship. The presence of a particularly close sibling relationship was rated if the target child chose to spend a lot of time with one sibling, and there was evidence that they comforted one another or supported one another during times of upset in the family. We were also interested in the presence of particularly hostile or antagonistic relationships between the target children and their siblings. A poor relationship was rated if the children showed high levels of hostility toward any of their siblings that was not mitigated by any signs of warmth or closeness between them. Children could not be rated as having both a close relationship and a poor relationship with the same sibling. Children with more than one sibling, however, could be rated as having a close relationship with one sibling and a poor relationship with another.

Mother–child relationships were rated *poor, moderate,* and *good,* based on reported and global ratings of positive and negative elements of the relationship. For further details of all measures see Jenkins and M. A. Smith (1990).

RESULTS

Before turning to the question of the potentially protective effect of close sibling relationships, it is important to establish that marital disharmony is associated with increased emotional and behavioral disturbance in children. Marital disharmony was found to be strongly associated with children's problems using the mothers' report of children's symptoms and the children's report of their own symptoms. This remained the case after controlling for potentially confounding factors such as parental psychiatric health (including depressive symptoms, alcohol abuse, and anxiety symptoms) and SES. (See M. A. Smith & Jenkins, in press, for details on these analyses.)

Potential Protective Effects

The quality of the sibling relationship was found to be significantly associated with the level of the children's symptoms, $F(2,100) = 7.2, p < .001$. The interaction between the parental marriage and sibling relationships was also found

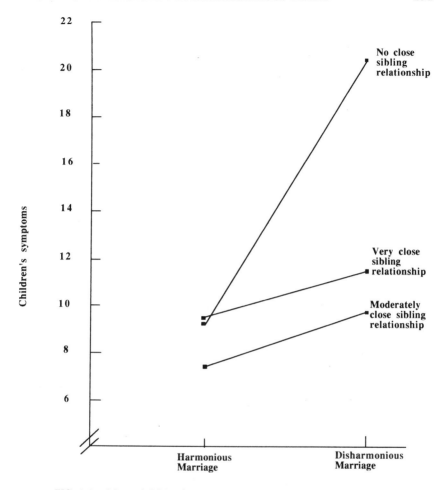

FIG. 9.1.   Mean of children's symptoms (as reported by mothers) as a function of the presence of close sibling relationships (as reported by mothers) in harmonious and disharmonious marriages.

to be significant, $F(1,100)$ = 4.1, p < .02. As Fig. 9.1 shows, children with close sibling relationships in disharmonious homes exhibit a level of disturbance similar to children who live in harmonious homes, whereas children who have no close sibling relationship exhibit a very high level of symptoms. In harmonious homes there is no relationship between the quality of the sibling relationship and children's emotional and behavioral problems.

The summation measure of children's emotional and behavioral problems had included an item on how aggressive the target child was to his or her siblings. The analysis was then redone with this variable excluded from the total symptom score to ensure that the results were not based on any potential confounding. Very similar results were obtained with this variable excluded. The quality of the sibling relationship was significantly associated with the children's symptoms, $F(2,100) = 6.0$, $p < .003$, and the interaction between the parental marriage and the sibling relationship was also significant, $F(1,100) = 3.2$, $p < .05$.

Thus, the results suggest that having a very close sibling relationship does act protectively for children who are experiencing the stress of parental disharmony, whereas the quality of the sibling relationship has little effect on children who are living in harmonious homes. Another kind of social support that we were interested in was the parent–child relationship. The mother–child

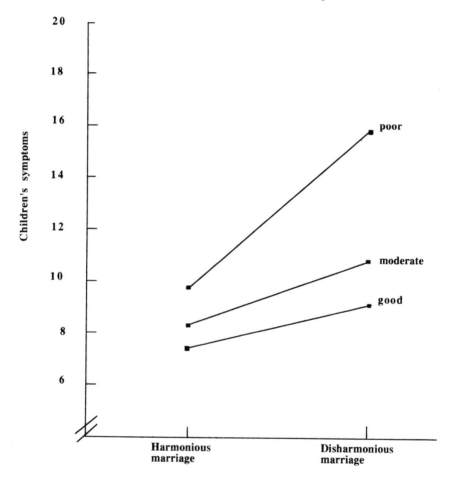

FIG. 9.2.   Mean of children's symptoms (as reported by mothers) as a function of the mother–child relationship (as reported by mothers) in harmonious and disharmonious parental marriages.

relationship was found to have a significant effect on children's symptoms, $F(2,106) = 5.2, p < .007$. The interaction between the quality of the parents' marriage and the mother–child relationship was not significant, $F(2,106) = 1.2$, *ns*. Looking at Fig. 9.2, it can be seen that children with poor mother–child relationships showed a higher level of symptoms than children with good mother–child relationships, irrespective of whether the home was harmonious or disharmonious. The same pattern was seen for the father–child relationship. We therefore found evidence for two different kinds of factors. Parent–child relationships were important for the quality of children's adjustment irrespective of whether they were in a harmonious or disharmonious home, whereas sibling relationships acted in a compensatory way only when the children were in a disharmonious home.

These analyses were based on the mothers' reports, but it was important to confirm the importance of the sibling relationship when using the children's report of their relationships, in order to exclude the possibility that results were due to mothers' reporting on both the children's symptoms and their sibling relationship. A similar pattern was seen in the children's data. The sibling relationship as reported by the children was not significantly associated with children's symptoms, $F(2,105) = 1.5$, *ns,* but the interaction between parental marriage and children's symptoms approached significance, $F(2,105) = 2.3$, $p < .09$. This pattern can be seen in Fig. 9.3.

Further details of other factors found to act protectively to children in disharmonious homes can be found in Jenkins and M. A. Smith (1990).

Using Siblings to Cope With Parental Quarreling

In order to understand more about the process of how children cope with parental quarreling, we asked very detailed questions about children's responses to parental quarrels and whether they turned to their siblings at this time.

Children do use their siblings as a source of comfort during quarrels. Fifty-nine percent who had experienced a parental quarrel in the previous year reported actively seeking contact with their sibling when such a quarrel started at home, and 40% of these children reported discussing something about the quarrel with their sibling. These were very rarely prolonged discussions, but just brief comments made from one child to the other such as "They're at it again," and "Better stay out of their way." These behaviors with siblings during quarrels did not themselves have any association with children's adjustment. Children who sought contact with their siblings or who talked with them about the quarreling did not show lower levels of disturbance than children who did not do these things (Jenkins et al., 1989). It would seem that it is more the global aspect of the sibling relationship that is associated with children's well-being rather than specific ways that children do or do not use their siblings during episodes of parental quarreling.

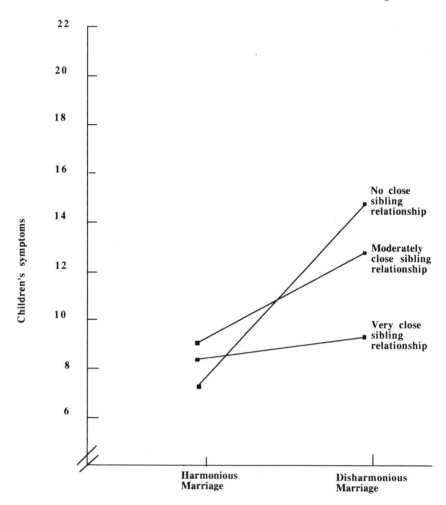

FIG. 9.3. Mean of children's symptoms (as reported by mothers) as a function of the presence of close sibling relationships (as reported by children) in harmonious and disharmonious marriages.

Comparison of the Quality of Sibling Relationships in Harmonious and Disharmonious Homes

One issue of interest, given the previous work on siblings in troubled homes, was to establish whether the frequency of close and poor sibling relationships was different in harmonious and disharmonious homes. Considering positive relationships first, children in disharmonious homes were no more likely to have a close relationship with one of their siblings than children in harmonious homes, $\chi^2 (2, N = 106) = .04$, ns. Thus, experiencing the stress of disharmony did not draw children toward one another and make it more likely that they would develop a strong bond. In considering poor relationships, however, a different picture emerges. In disharmonious homes children were significantly more likely to have a poor relationship with one of their siblings than in harmonious homes, χ^2 (1, N = 106) = 15.8, p < .0001. Marital disharmony increased children's risk of having a poor sibling relationship by a factor of 8, as can be seen in Table 9.1.

As children in disharmonious homes are more likely to have hostile sibling relationships, it is important to consider whether these children have an inability to make relationships or whether they simply have difficulty in specific relationships. If all children who had been rated as having one poor sibling relationship also had *no* positive sibling relationship, the children's inability to make relationships with their siblings might be just another aspect of their disturbance. The direction of effect, in relation to close sibling relationships being protective, would need to be questioned. In fact, 63% of children who had a very hostile relationship with one sibling had a moderately close or very close relationship with other siblings. This suggests that these children are not pervasively poor at making relationships, but that they have poor relationships with certain people.

DISCUSSION

There are two issues of developmental significance in the data that have been presented here. Children who live in disharmonious homes are more likely to develop hostile and aggressive relationships with their siblings than children living in harmonious homes. It is also clear, however, that if children do develop a close and supportive relationship with their sibling, this can offer some protection against the development of psychological disturbance when they are under stress. I consider each of these issues in turn.

There was no evidence from this general population sample that children in disharmonious homes formed closer relationships with siblings than chil-

TABLE 9.1

Number of children who have a hostile relationship with one sibling in the family, as a function of parental disharmony (Row percentages are given in brackets)

	Sibling Relationship	
Parental Relationship	No hostile sibling relationship	Hostile sibling relationship
Harmonious	51	2
	(96)	(4)
Disharmonious	35	18
	(66)	(34)

dren in harmonious homes. Indeed, children in disharmonious homes were found to be much more likely to have overtly hostile relationships with one of their siblings than children in harmonious homes. Hetherington (1988) found that children who had experienced divorce were more likely than children who had not experienced divorce to have hostile relationships with siblings. The question, then, is what is it about marital disharmony (assuming that marital disharmony in an intact family is similar to marital disharmony that results in divorce) that increases the likelihood of children having hostile relationships with siblings? Cummings, Ianotti, and Zahn-Waxler (1985) and Cummings (1987) found that children who watch two adults who are not their parents in a simulated argument demonstrate increased aggression with peers directly after it. In relation to disharmonious homes, it may be that hostility is modeled in the relationship between the parents and that children learn that hostility is an appropriate response to conflict or to certain kinds of negative expressed emotion. The children who have a hostile relationship with a sibling are not incapable of forming close relationships with other siblings, and it would therefore seem that there are specific elements within relationships that elicit or trigger more hostile responses from children. Such an element might, for instance, be parental preference, which has been documented in other studies to affect sibling relationships.

It was also the case, however, that children in disharmonious homes who did manage to have a moderately close or very close relationship with a sibling had a much lower level of emotional and behavioral problems than children who did not have such a relationship. The association between a low level of emotional and behavioral problems and the presence of a close sibling relationship was only evident in the children from disharmonious homes, and no association was present for the children in harmonious homes. Such a pattern was not seen with respect to the mother–child relationship. Mother–child relationships were found to be associated with children's disturbance irrespective of the quality of the parental marital relationship. Thus, if children were in a harmonious home but had a poor relationship with their mother, they were at risk of showing a higher level of emotional and behavioral problems.

One way of conceptualizing the difference between mother–child relationships and sibling relationships in the way that they interact with marital disharmony, is in terms of how central or significant the mother–child or sibling relationship is to a child's development. Perhaps it is the case that the mother–child relationship is more central to the child's well-being than having a good sibling relationship and it is important to the child's adjustment irrespective of other factors in the child's life.

The cross-sectional nature of these data mean that conclusions about the direction of effects between parental marriage, children's disturbance, and putative protective factors must remain tentative. Several interpretations of the data are possible. One is that children living in a disharmonious home lack something in their lives when compared to children in harmonious homes. They may not receive the same care and attention from parents, or they may not have a good internalized image of themselves, as they see themselves to be the product of two unhappy parents. A close relationship with a sibling may compensate for this deficiency by giving the child an experience of caring and love and an opportunity to feel competent by providing comfort to others. This kind of explanation gives some understanding of the interaction between parental marriage and close sibling relationships. According to such an account, it is only the children in disharmonious homes who need to find compensation and close sibling relationships provide it; as a result children's disturbance is reduced to the level that it would be at if they were not experiencing the stress of living in a disharmonious home.

An alternative explanation of the association between the absence of a close sibling relationship and children's emotional and behavioral problems, is that children with emotional and behavioral problems cannot reach out and make close relationships with their siblings because of their disturbance. One would then expect that children with higher levels of disturbance would not have close sibling relationships, and that this pattern should be seen in harmonious as well as disharmonious homes. In the harmonious homes there was no association between the absence of a close sibling relationship and increased disturbance. This makes the second explanation less likely. However, the correlational nature of these data should caution against drawing conclusions about the direction of effects. An intervention study designed to improve the relationship between disturbed children and their siblings in disharmonious homes would provide valuable information on the direction of the effects in the relationship between these factors.

There are several therapeutic implications arising from this work. Clinicians working with disharmonious couples need to be aware that the children in these families are at risk of having hostile relationships with one another. Therapists may want to plan preventive measures that take this risk into account. Second, when children present at clinics for the treatment of emotional and behavioral problems, therapists could assess the possibilities for change in the family system: If a child's disturbance is related to pathology within the marriage, therapists can try to achieve change in the marital relationship. If change does not seem likely or easy in the marriage, this study suggests that an improvement in the child's mental health might be achieved by working for the development of improved relationships between siblings.

ACKNOWLEDGMENT

This work was carried out at the Institute of Child Health, University of London, London, England with Marjorie A. Smith. Parts of this chapter were reprinted with permission from *Journal of Child Psychology and Psychiatry* (Jenkins & Smith, 1991) and *Journal of the American Academy of Child and Adolescent Psychiatry* (1990).

REFERENCES

American Psychiatric Association. (1980). *Diagnostic and statistical manual of mental disorders* (3rd ed.). Washington DC: Author.

Bank, S., & Kahn, M. (1982). *The sibling bond.* New York: Basic.

Brown, G. W., & Rutter, M. (1966). The measurement of family activities and relationships: A methodological study. *Human Relations, 19,* 241–263.

Cohen, S., & Wills, T. A. (1985). Stress, social support and the buffering hypothesis. *Psychological Bulletin, 98,* 310–357.

Cronbach, L. J., Gleser, G. C., Nanda, H., & Rajaratnam, N. (1972). *The dependability of behavioral measurements: Theory of generalizability for scores and profiles.* New York: Wiley.

Cummings, E. M. (1987). Coping with background anger in early childhood. *Child Development, 58,* 976–984.

Cummings, E. M., Ianotti, R. J., & Zahn-Waxler, C. (1985). The influence of conflict between adults on the emotions and aggression of young children. *Developmental Psychology, 21,* 495–507.

Graham, P. J., & Rutter, M. (1968). The reliability and validity of the psychiatric interview with the child. *British Journal of Psychiatry, 114,* 581–592.

Hetherington, E. M. (1988). Parents, children and siblings: Six years after divorce. In R. A. Hinde & J. Stevenson-Hinde (Eds.), *Relationships within families* (pp. 311–331). Oxford: Clarendon.

Jenkins, J. M., & Smith, M. A. (1990). Factors protecting children in disharmonious homes. *Journal of the American Academy of Child and Adolescent Psychiatry, 29,* 60–69.

Jenkins, J. M., & Smith, M. A. (1991). Marital disharmony and children's behaviour problems. *Journal of Child Psychology and Psychiatry, 32.*

Jenkins, J. M., Smith, M. A., & Graham, P. J. (1989). Coping with parental quarrels. *Journal of the American Academy of Child and Adolescent Psychiatry, 28,* 182–189.

MacKinnon, C. (1989). An observational investigation of sibling interaction in married and divorced families. *Developmental Psychology, 25,* 36–44.

Quinton, D., Rutter, M., & Rowlands, O. (1976). An evaluation of an interview assessment of marriage. *Psychological Medicine, 6,* 577–586.

Richman, N., Stevenson, J., & Graham, P. J. (1982). *Pre-school to school: A behavioural study.* London: Academic.

Rutter, M. (1971). Parent–child separation. *Journal of Child Psychology and Psychiatry, 12,* 233–260.

Rutter, M., & Brown, G. (1966). The reliability of family life and relationships in families containing a psychiatric patient. *Social Psychiatry, 1,* 38–53.

Rutter, M., & Graham, P. J. (1968). The reliability and validity of the psychiatric interview with the child. *British Journal of Psychiatry, 114,* 563–579.

Rutter, M., Tizard, J., & Whitmore, K. (1970). *Education, health and behaviour.* London: Longman.

Sandler, I. (1980). Social support resources, stress and maladjustment of poor children. *American Journal of Community Psychology, 8,* 41–52.

Smith, M. A., & Jenkins, J. M. (in press). The effects of marital disharmony on pre-pubertal children. *Journal of Abnormal Child Psychology.*

Smith, M. A., Delves, T., Lansdown, R., Clayton, B., & Graham, P. (1983). The effects of lead exposure on urban children: The Institute of Child Health/Southampton Study. *Developmental Medicine and Child Neurology, 47* (Suppl. 47).

Stiffman, A. R., Jung, K. G., & Feldman, R. A. (1986). A multivariate risk model for childhood behavior problems. *American Journal of Orthopsychiatry, 56,* 204–211.

Werner, E. E., & Smith, R. S. (1982). *Vulnerable but invincible: A longitudinal study of resilient children and youth.* New York: McGraw-Hill.

Chapter 10

Remembering and Reinterpreting Sibling Bonds

Stephen Bank
Wesleyan University
Bank and Hiebel Family & Child Associates
Middletown, Connecticut

And even if you were in some prison the walls of which let none of the sounds of the world come to your senses—would you not then still have your childhood, that precious, kingly possession, that treasure house of memories? Turn your attention there. Try to raise the submerged sensations of that ample past; your personality will grow more firm.
—Rainer Maria Rilke (1962, p. 20)

This chapter invites the reader to enter the world of a clinician who works in a private outpatient clinic where people voluntarily seek psychotherapy. There, seeing families and individuals of all ages and of diverse social backgrounds for the last 20 years, I have made observations of what people who seek psychotherapy have to say about their siblings, how they feel about them, how the connections between sisters and brothers have formed, and how they remember the injuries, the moments of solace, the disappointments, and the terrors of their growing up. I have known many of these people for upward of 10 years, and have followed their family relationships over time; others have been seen only briefly, under crisis conditions. Practicing in the same office in the same New England town for 20 years, I have now begun seeing the offspring of the first children who were patients with *their* parents when I began practicing in 1970. In some families, I have heard the stories and struggles of siblings from members of three generations. Many of these people, who helped me develop my conceptualization of sibling relationships, grew up in desperate family circumstances. Others grew up under more benign conditions, with peaceful periods of developmental time being interspersed with periodic hardships and losses.

I invite you to think about the sibling connection, and about how its powerful

139

effects can be listened to actively in psychotherapy. I make some suggestions about the attitude of the therapist and about the actions that the therapist and the patient can take to bring about understanding, relief, and a new sense of vitality in the sibling relationship. This chapter builds on and extends previous work reported in *The Sibling Bond* (Bank & Kahn, 1982b) and in *Siblings in Therapy* (Kahn & Lewis, 1988).

TRAUMATIC SIBLING MEMORIES: TWO ILLUSTRATIONS

The power of the sibling connection and the way in which sibling memory can saturate one's adult family life unhappily has preoccupied my clinical attention for many years, and I am constantly looking for evidence of these phenomena, even when I am not functioning in my role as a psychotherapist. In 1982, shortly after publication of the *The Sibling Bond,* Michael Kahn and I were invited to appear on TV "talk shows" across the United States. This had not been our original intention, because we had written for a clinical and academic audience. However, the American public hungers to look inside relationships, and it is almost impossible to do sibling research without someone from the media asking for information.

I had many intriguing experiences, and a few that were banal, as I flew around the country discussing siblings, but one encounter touched me deeply because it was so emotionally authentic and because it gave one more bit of evidence for a theory of how siblings attach under conditions of extreme trauma, a theory which Michael Kahn and I have been working on for 15 years (Bank, 1987, 1989; Bank & Kahn, 1975, 1980–1981, 1982a, 1982b; Kahn & Bank, 1981; Kahn & Lewis, 1988).

> One talented producer carefully developed a program on sibling rivalry of unusually high quality, and we were asked to help with the research. I was to interview a young couple about their children's relationship. The network sent a camera crew who virtually lived with this family, day and night, for several weeks, gathering footage of a boisterous 5-year-old boy and his energetic, adorable 3-year-old sister as they played, bathed, quarrelled, ate, got ready for bed, and did things with their parents. The parents came to the television station to meet with me to discuss their emotional reactions to the films of their children.
>
> The films suggested that the children's interactions were normal and what one would expect for preschoolers. The parents wisely stayed out of the children's minor squabbles. When they did intervene, they were gentle and firm, and provided explanations about feelings. Despite the busy pace of their living, this was an affectionate, thoughtful family. If grades were awarded for parental effectiveness, these parents would have gotten an *A*.
>
> A quirk in the interview, however, led to an unexpected emotional episode.

The mother kept pressing me about her son's hostility to his sister, his screaming at her when she would knock over his block tower, his difficulty sharing his toys. My reassurances, I realized, were not sinking in. So I said, "I'm not sure this advice is very satisfying to you. . . . Is there anything else that might be bothering you, inside yourself, as you look at these films?" She replied, "I just wonder if he could leave emotional scars on her, and I worry that he'll really hurt her when they get older. I always wonder if I'm handling them the right way."

I then asked, "Is any part of your concern about the children in any way connected to your own childhood, or to things that might have happened when you were young?" Open-ended questions about siblings can sometimes allow people to gain entrance to a private world of memory and feeling about their brothers and sisters. Freed to generate their own images in their own terms, emotional memories can be retrieved (and eventually reinterpreted).

Suddenly she couldn't speak, her face became serious and pained, and she began to cry. This surprised me at the time because everything had seemed so calm, and now, suddenly, she was remembering something that took her voice away. After what seemed like a very long interval, she told me about her older brother, a boy who had terrified and injured her. "He hit me very often, probably every day," she said. "I had black and blue marks. I was always scared of him. My mother and father were both working, and they never knew." "Why didn't you tell them?", I asked. "Because I don't think they'd have done anything about it," she replied. One day, when she was 17, she hit her brother square in the face. Although that ended his abuse, it did not end the terror she felt in later years. As she remembered her rage and fear, her right hand clenched into a fist in her lap. When he came to a family gathering several years before this interview, she reported, she had developed a stomachache and gone home. Being alone with him in the same room made her anxious.

This was a familiar scenario for me, because I had seen the same kinds of emotional floods unleashed by apparently innocent questions while doing psychotherapy with adult siblings over the previous 20 years. The scenario goes like this: There are two children, cloistered in the private and cut-off world of a household in which emotions cannot be acknowledged. The parents are emotionally unavailable. In this vacuum of parental guidance and disturbed nurturance, the children come to need one another for contact. This contact can become sexual, physically abusive, verbally or emotionally humiliating, or primitively comforting to the point of providing both solace and enmeshing dependency. Furthermore, because the relationship is established before language is fully developed, before cognition and emotional maturity have been acquired, the children develop intense, ambivalent emotions that later form vivid images. The concept of unconscious memory has been the topic of considerable experimental and clinical research in recent years (Kihlstrom, 1987; Neisser, 1982): Unconscious memories evoked by certain current situations that remind us of the emotional situation we found ourselves in as children, can provoke powerful irrational actions and reactions.

Because parents cannot always be available, and do not help the children to limit or understand their relationship, these images are never verbalized and therefore remain out of immediate and conscious awareness. Even in adulthood, these secret inscriptions can affect our reactions to our own children, to our spouse, and of course, to our adult siblings. Esther Salaman (1982) invoked the image of "the submerged ship of childhood." I say more about excavating these secret inscriptions and submerged ships of the sibling connection further on, because such archaeological work can have a crucial place in bringing about therapeutic changes.

The power of unconscious memory of siblings is suggested in a second family, involving a 40-year-old woman undergoing psychotherapy.

> Shortly after her second marriage, Deborah came to see me because she continually overreacted to small signs of what felt like abandonment—by her genuinely attentive husband, by her children, and by her adult siblings. Just prior to Christmas she fell into an angry and anxious mood when her older brother refused to attend a celebration that she had orchestrated as a "real old-fashioned Christmas." Because her mother was getting old, Deborah felt this might be the last time they could all be together. Within a few days of her brother's rebuff, Deborah's sister stated that she had no interest in posing for a family portrait, which would be painted on the day after Christmas. My patient could think of nothing else. Angry and rejected feelings dominated her as the holidays approached.

Irvin Yalom (1989), in his moving collection of stories of psychotherapy, described the therapist as "love's executioner." He believes that one of the therapist's duties is to elicit the patient's irrational loves and hates so that they can be understood and reduced in power. Asking questions about childhood and youth can cut deeply into the emotional underpinnings of one's self-image and of one's cherished beliefs about family.

> One day I could see that Deborah was on the brink of tears as she recognized that she had always thought of her family as happy and that she couldn't understand why, now, people were pulling away. Once more I asked the open-ended question that facilitated the powerful linkage of past and present: "Was anyone, was everyone, in your family all there for you as you grew up? Are you sure they were ever *all* there for you?"
>
> As tears and angry words were expressed, Deborah described what it was like to be the youngest of three children: Helen was 3 years older, and Mark was 5 years older. Helen and Mark were an inseparable and exclusive twosome, whose activities rarely included little Debbie. Helen and Mark's bedrooms were on the second floor, with the parents; Deborah had a bigger bedroom, but it was on the first floor, "miles away from where the real action was." Deborah recalled always wanting to be "in" and always feeling "out," yet she idolized her older siblings and felt attached to them, even though they were evidently not attached to her. As she described her childhood, images of closed doors, of children running

off to play with their friends, of being excluded, came back to her. These were feelings she had never consciously thought about during her adult life. She experienced them now, again, intensely and vividly.

Why would such exclusion have such an impact? Why did it bother her, now, and what lay behind these feelings? Many people are excluded by their siblings and get angry about it, but they find playmates who provide contact, and the rejection by siblings loses its "sting."

Deborah told me that she hardly knew her father, who worked long hours, and who, when he did come home, spent most of his time sleeping or coughing with emphysema; around him she could never shout or laugh loudly, as her mother admonished her that Daddy was tired and sick, and might get sicker. In contrast with her ready access to dozens of memories about her brother and sister, she had no images of her father, other than of a man who came home tired, had dinner after the kids were fed, and stumbled into bed. She remembered her mother as critical, biting, and rigid. "She wasn't a person who would hug you, but she would criticize you. She was a strict disciplinarian, like an Army sergeant." There were *no* warm memories of her parents. Nevertheless, until this moment, she had never acknowledged to anyone, including herself, that the feeling of being ignored had been a major undercurrent of her emotional life for as long as she could remember.

There is enormous power in asking people questions about their siblings. Siblings are rarely viewed by psychologists as major actors on the stage of human development, and the culture itself gives siblings short shrift. When a person, such as Deborah, is given 45 minutes to do nothing except remember and experience the history of emotion with a sibling in the safe harbor of a therapeutic relationship that allows recognition of the importance of siblings, something special can happen, linking the past with the present. Deborah cried throughout this conversation, she cried when she got home, and she cried frequently that week.

Insight involves strong emotion, and it involves understanding of the emotion. The ideal result is a change in attitude and behavior in one's important relationships, where change would previously have been too frightening.

Two weeks later, trembling with anger and fear of further rejection, Deborah told her older sister how she felt: "I hardly wanted to see you today, and I want to know why you keep rejecting me. I'm hurt, and I'm angry and I can't go on like this with you."

The confidence to do this, I believe, came from her preparation in therapy, because I had suggested to her that her sister's avoidance of family gatherings might have to do with having grown up in the same household, with the same dysfunctional parents.

Helen and Deborah spent an afternoon talking about their family, their child-hood, and their feelings about the emptiness that had enveloped everyone long ago. As she spoke to her sister in the voice of an equal adult instead of as a pleas-ing, pleading "baby sister," Deborah learned that she had always been viewed by the other children as Mother's good girl, as her favorite. The mother had always made Helen and Mark feel guilty for failing to measure up to Debbie. Deborah was astounded to learn this; she had never considered herself her mother's favorite child.

Deborah then invited Helen to come home for Christmas the following year. (Deborah and the mother lived in the same town; Helen lived 5 hours away.) "No," Helen said, "I don't want to come to this town; it's too depressing for me, but why don't we call each other every month?"

Although this episode could be counted as at least a short-term success, there were no Hollywood endings: There rarely are in the psychotherapy of sibling relationships. The sisters were still wary, but a start had been made, and De-borah was speaking in a new voice. Deborah even began talking to her brother, but with less encouraging results, because he was indifferent. Facing the emp-tiness of a sibling relationship is usually painful, and it was for Deborah. Once she admitted to herself that clinging to her siblings had been part of a rosy-colored picture that filtered out the sadness of growing up in a home with a sick father and a martinet of a mother, she grieved, and after grieving, she became more realistic and more confident in her other relationships.

Deborah's sadness, anger, and agitation over the perceived neglect by her older siblings has the distinct marks of sibling relationships in dysfunctional families. It has been my clinical experience that younger children are particu-larly vulnerable in sibling bonding because the direction of the attachment is often from younger to older. The depth of the bond of the younger to the older is often more intense than from the older to the younger. This idea is support-ed by a wealth of formal research. Buhrmester and Furman (1990) found that older children stop nurturing their younger brothers and sisters in the middle and later years of childhood. Other research projects, such as those of Koch (1960), Bigner (1974), and Bryant (1982), have reported that older children have more powerful effects on younger children than younger children have on their elder siblings. Many of the most gripping stories involving intense, ambivalent bonding heard in the psychotherapist's office are told by later-born children, who, like Deborah, feel powerless and depressed. This area offers fertile ground for anyone interested in studying the potentially traumatic ef-fects children can have on one another.

A THEORY OF SIBLING ATTACHMENT

We all know that emotional rawness, vividness, or intensity is not always found among siblings. How are such intense and sometimes ambivalent bonds formed?

What do we mean by a *sibling bond?* Who does and who does not have a sibling bond?

First, a sibling bond is not necessarily accompanied by a conscious positive emotion (Boer, 1990).[1] A sibling bond can be warm and clinging, or fearful and ambivalent, or violently negative, or marked by chronic yearning and disappointment. Among the thousands of patients I have interviewed, mention of a sibling often brings no emotional reaction. If I say, "Tell me about your brother," many people will give me a blank look and describe him demographically rather than emotionally. Other people, however, may react to the same question with strong emotions: warmth, disgust, anger, fear, sadness, and so on.

What kind of histories are linked to the presence or absence of these emotions? Clinically, two circumstances tend to be associated with intense feelings about siblings. The first of these conditions is *high access;* the second is called *the vacuum of parental care.* The co-occurrence of these conditions increases the opportunity for children to seek a variety of intense and disturbed relationships with each other: master and slave, mutually dependent, hostile and exploitative, sexual, or mutually protective. (These disturbed relationships are more likely when there are no other social resources outside the family.) In some cases, the loyalty and contact between siblings is life-saving or promotes hardiness and academic achievement. When parents are frightening, abandoning, or invisible, siblings are not minor players in the family drama; they are the stars: the villains and the heroes who play a significant role in the child's life-and-death struggles for attachment, separateness, and identity.

High access to one another can occur because the children are close in age. Several well-controlled research investigations (Abramovitch, Pepler, & Corter, 1982; Buhrmester & Furman, 1990) demonstrate that closely spaced children are more likely to battle each other than are siblings more disparate in age. When the children are very close in age, the older child more often gets his or her way with the younger one (Sutton-Smith & Rosenberg, 1970), and there may be less nurturance in childhood and adolescence than there is between children who are not so closely spaced. (The literature on age spacing in non-clinical situations is not consistent on this point, but in my clinical

---

[1]Frits Boer (1990) carefully examined whether *warm* sibling connections would flourish when parents were distant from children in the 6 to 12 age group. His study, conducted on a normal sample of families that had few, if any, acutely dysfunctional parents, suggested that closeness among siblings was related in a positive, rather than an inverse way, to the perceived quality of parental care.

However, when the parents argued with one another, sibling conflict arose.

This second finding fits with my definition of a *sibling bond.* The theory of sibling bonding suggests that it is *intensity of emotion in the relationship* that is related to parental dysfunction. Moderate closeness—which Boer found to be a result of caring parent–child relationships, comes as no surprise. What we would expect, in families where there was a poor quality of care is an intense relationship, compulsive in its clinging quality, or compulsive in other ways: erotic, exploitative, victimizing, or rigidly avoidant.

experience, closeness in age promotes emotional intensity.) This means that when there is high access, the children will collide more because they have to share territory more: a bathroom, a bedroom, or, in impoverished families, even the same bed. Closely spaced children will share the same toys, the same interests, and go to the same schools. Children who are of the same gender also have high access because they may share same-sex friends, interests, and clothing. They have more in common, so they may be more rivalrous, especially if they are boys. The ultimate example of high access is identical twins, whose legendary enmeshments and struggles to be different are well documented.

Children who are many years apart usually live at very different developmental and social levels and are never in the same school together at the same time, so their access to each other will generally be low. These children will tend, during their adult years, to report less intensity than high-access children. Because they never share the same developmental time periods, they are more like strangers than are siblings who are closely spaced.

However, high access is not always a function of age and gender. It can also emanate from peculiarities of the family's structure, economic needs, and the idiosyncratic relationship "chemistries" that spring up between children. Imagine two children born 8 years apart. Separated from one another by half a generation, they may still have high access if the older child is forced to stabilize the family by caring for the younger child. Feelings of closeness and ambivalence characterize both the older and the younger child. Because of the weakness of the adult caregivers, the children become a microcosmic imitation of the family: a miniature parent and a miniature child, who develop their own world in response to the impaired parents who cannot meet their needs.

Access, when accompanied by a vacuum of parental care, is the environment in which intense sibling bonds are formed. When there is a heart of darkness within the family, children will search for the faintest flickers of light, even if the light illuminates nothing, and even if it carries little warmth. The last 40 years of research on human attachment, from Bowlby and Spitz to Harlow and Ainsworth, from Winnicott to Kohut, from the laboratory to the psychoanalyst's consulting room, supports this notion: that as warmth-seeking mammals, children will attach themselves to any available object that offers solace, even if that solace is more imaginary than real, and even if the object is hostile or frustrating to them.

Judith Dunn's Cambridge studies (Dunn, 1985) address this subject very clearly and dovetail nicely with my own observations of what adults remember about their childhood. She found that when the mother spoke to the older child about the newborn in a personal way, helping the child to understand that this baby was not a "thing," an "it" or an extraterrestrial object, but a little person with feelings, the child later enjoyed a warmer relationship with the sibling than did children whose mothers did not use this "humanizing" way of speaking about the baby.

There can be no substitute for the presence of intelligent, available parents who can serve as gentle mirrors, who can model conflict resolution, and who can be available to each of their children when they are overwhelmed or distressed. Sibling bonding in the extreme, arid, angry, and terrifying climate of acutely dysfunctional families forces an ambivalent and immature relationship into the vacant, dangerous space created by parental weakness.

Lacking parents to help them reflect or use conversation as a way of understanding one another, siblings from dysfunctional backgrounds store emotional information about themselves and about intimate relationships. This stored information becomes what I have called a *secret inscription,* a *frozen image,* or a *template.* Like the hard disc on a computer, it contains memories filled with visual and visceral information. Words are often inaccessible because these images were acquired before the children had full command of language and thought. These templates become operative only under specific conditions that remind us of our old relationships. Like most unconscious processes, secret inscriptions dictate irrational behavior and ignite conflict until they are no longer secret.

REINTERPRETING THE MEMORIES

It is in the reinterpreting of memories that psychotherapy helps. The task of psychotherapy with adult siblings is to raise the sunken ship of childhood, find its treasures, and explore its deck, its hull, and its inside in order to help the patient have enough confidence to swim through its abandoned chambers. My clinical work with disturbed adults convinces me that we cannot change something of which we are not conscious. Thus, I try to bring the past as well as the present emotional reality of the siblings to the surface so that, together, we can unfreeze the images of childhood. The result of therapy should be greater flexibility, greater choice, and an ability to allow both the self and the relationship between the self and others to become more spontaneous, less compulsive, more open to new information, and more open to reinterpretation.

Insight should ideally involve strong emotion combined with cognitive reorganization. Therapeutic insight draws energy from emotional catharsis, and catharsis depends, in turn, on re-experiencing very strong, sometimes primal emotions. Therefore, I use certain ways of speaking, gathered from the hypnotic style of Milton Erickson, that seem to provide both the safety and the guidance necessary for people to remember everything that their unconscious mind can allow them to know. In speaking slowly and hypnotically (without formally inducing a trance), I help the patient to create a special state in which all present concerns are screened out, and the patient is able to go from room to room in his or her childhood home, remembering what it might have felt like to be that particular child with that particular brother or sister. For a moment, the patient, as an adult, develops a relationship with the child he or she once was, and re-enters the world of being a brother or a sister.

As I suggested earlier, you cannot underestimate the power of simply asking for a person's memories of siblings. The fact that the therapist is willing to take seriously the importance of that connection makes the moment unique in the patient's eyes. The fact that the therapist's tone and attitude communicate that the patient is allowed empathy for his or her experience of being a sibling, makes it easier for the patient to bring memories to the surface. The questions are kept open-ended, following closely upon the patient's exact words, intonations, and gestures.

In a rhythm that matches the patient's need for comfort, I say:

> Picture your brother or your sister, some picture in your mind of something that happened. Pick a scene from some time when you were little or when you were growing up. Picture it and remember it. It could be the two of you, in a certain place or maybe you were doing something. It could be something that was painful, or something that was upsetting, or something that was pleasant, something that you did or something that happened. Your unconscious mind can remember all that it needs to know to remember it and you can remember what happened. It could be something that happened outside, or it could be inside the house where you grew up: a certain room, or a certain time of day. You can remember only what your unconscious mind is ready to tell you and you can remember everything that is important about that scene. You can feel it without remembering: just the two of you. You might want to keep these images and these feelings all to yourself. You could remember this thing that happened and all of the feelings, privately recapturing the scene in ways that I will never know but which you could begin to feel, as if it were yesterday.[2]

This can be very vivid. In psychotherapy, caretakers remember how angry and alone they were, how fearful they were that they would fail to keep their little brothers and sisters under control, fearing that they would disappoint their parents. They remember their guilt and their righteous anger at their nasty siblings and how ungrateful these siblings were. Abused siblings remember the pain of being physically beaten and some actually develop bodily memories, and begin rubbing their arms in the very spot where they were beaten, or they will develop a stomachache of the kind they used to get when they were scared or angry. Lonely, disappointed siblings remember, with tears and angry sobs, their aloneness. These moments in psychotherapy are moving not only to the patient but to the therapist, too.

Now that the memories have been retrieved, I encourage the patient to make

---

[2]I am indebted to Dr. Warren Leib, of Wethersfield, Connecticut, for his ideas on how trance can be brought about during conversation, without resorting to formal methods of hypnotic induction.

connections, and to grieve for some of the last opportunities of childhood. One of the things Dunn's (1985) studies revealed is that children as young as 15 months are able to be empathic and tuned in to the feelings of a brother or a sister. Her findings indicate that an affectionate and positive feeling between siblings is more the rule than the exception. Some might consider having a reasonably good brother–sister tie as a birthright. As the individual re-experiences the old, frozen relationship, and takes conscious account of the disappointments that occurred, he or she can then raise questions about why they happened, and perhaps what might be done about them. This remembering is particularly meaningful because, until the moment of psychotherapeutic contact, there has never been any adult who was seriously interested in how it felt to be this person at that moment in time, with that particular brother or sister.

The understanding and reliving of the sibling connection is then placed in the context of understanding that both the patient and the sibling grew up in a distorted family context. The purpose of broadening the view of the sibling relationship to include the parental context is not to lay blame on parents, but to help the person see that the children were the unwitting participants in a powerful and unconscious family system (see Bank, 1988). An analogy I use (adapted from Minuchin, 1974) is the following:

> Two children are in Antarctica and driving their dog sled due south to the South Pole. After 2 hours they learn that they are 50 miles farther north than when they started! So, they start fighting with one another about the dogs, their instruments, and so on. Then a scientist (therapist) comes along and tells them that there is a good reason why they are, in fact, 50 miles farther north than when they started and it is no one's fault. All along they have been on a gigantic ice floe that had broken off from the mainland and was floating northward. Nobody told them this might happen, so why should they blame each other?

People grasp the analogy to their family right away.

Siblings, as adults, may realize that their brothers and sisters, too, suffered, and as self-empathy increases, so does true empathy and the willingness to understand the other sibling. The sibling is a piece of a larger puzzle, an emblem, a powerful symbol of family pain and family failure, but the sibling did not *cause* the failure.

One of the important facets of modern sibling relationships is the fact that we usually settle at a geographical distance from our brothers and sisters. This makes the sibling relationship a matter of choice rather than of imposed necessity. The choice to be involved or not, free of the baggage of the past, can be enhanced by psychotherapy.

The progress made in therapy is sometimes assisted by natural changes going on outside the therapy, forces that make it more likely for brothers and sisters to become more connected as they age. The first is that one's brother or sister, perhaps because of marrying into better life circumstances, because of education or increased self-esteem acquired through work, or because of greater personal security, or from learning acquired in psychotherapy, may become more communicative and more mature.

The second has to do with developmental crises. A dominant sibling can become more humble if his child has died in an accident, and he can appeal to the brother he enslaved to understand him differently. A younger sibling can demonstrate that she is not the baby any longer because she has learned to assert herself through becoming a mother or a corporate achiever. Old images die hard, but people do change, and they do develop. The key is to help our patients to see through their own blindspots, and to replace feelings of anger, shame, inadequacy, envy, or disappointment with insight and with constructive actions.

The third change has to do with the fact that parents grow old and become infirm. Parents die, and one's sibling is the only person who might remember what one's childhood was like, how the food tasted bad, what secrets were shared, what it felt like when Aunt Mary would make a fool out of herself at Thanksgiving, or what it was like to laugh together when the dog tore up Uncle Harry's pants.

The effort made by therapists to help adult patients revitalize sibling relationships is well worthwhile. And even if the relationship cannot be revitalized, the patient still benefits, by learning to understand and accept the reality of lost opportunities, and by being able to let go of relationships that have been chronically destructive. We know from the work of Bedford and Gold (1989) and Cicirelli (1982, 1988), that in early adulthood, at mid-life, and during old age, most siblings judge their brothers and sisters to be compatible, and important, and feel warmly connected to them. It is a challenge, and occasionally it is deeply rewarding, to help adults become aware of the silent inscriptions of childhood, and provide them with the opportunity to enrich, and to understand, life's longest lasting connection.

REFERENCES

Abramovitch, R., Pepler, D., & Corter, C. (1982). Patterns of sibling interaction among preschool-age children. In M. E. Lamb & B. Sutton-Smith (Eds.), *Sibling relationships: Their nature and significance across the lifespan* (pp. 61–86). Hillsdale, NJ: Lawrence Erlbaum Associates.

Bank, S. (1987). Favoritism. In F. F. Schachter & R. K. Stone (Eds.), *Practical concerns about siblings: Bridging the research–practice gap* (pp. 77–89). New York: Haworth.

Bank, S. (1988). The stolen birthright: The adult sibling in psychotherapy. In M. D. Kahn & K. G. Lewis (Eds.), *Siblings in therapy: Lifespan and clinical issues* (pp. 341–355). New York: W. W. Norton.

Bank, S. (1989). Sibling rivalry. In E. Bernstein (Ed.), *Encyclopedia Britannica medical and health annual* (pp. 423–426). Chicago, IL: The Encyclopedia Britannica.

Bank, S., & Kahn, M. D. (1975). Sisterhood-brotherhood is powerful: Sibling subsystems and family therapy. *Family Process, 14,* 311–337.

Bank, S., & Kahn, M. D. (1980-1981). Freudian siblings. *The Psychoanalytic Review, 6,* 493–504.

Bank, S., & Kahn, M. D. (1982a). Intense sibling loyalties. In M. E. Lamb & B. Sutton-Smith (Eds.), *Sibling relationships: Their nature and significance across the lifespan* (pp. 251–266). Hillsdale, NJ: Lawrence Erlbaum Associates.

Bank, S., & Kahn, M. D. (1982b). *The sibling bond.* New York: Basic Books.

Bedford, V. H., & Gold, D. T. (1989). Siblings in later life: A neglected family relationship [Special issue]. *American Behavioral Scientist, 33*(1), 3–126.

Bigner, J. A. (1974). A Wernerian developmental analysis of children's descriptions of siblings. *Child Development, 45,* 317–323.

Boer, F. (1990). *Sibling relationships in middle childhood: An empirical study.* Leiden, The Netherlands: DSWO Press, University of Leiden.

Bryant, B. (1982). Sibling relationships in middle childhood. In M. E. Lamb & B. Sutton-Smith (Eds.), *Sibling relationships: Their nature and significance across the lifespan* (pp. 87–121). Hillsdale, NJ: Lawrence Erlbaum Associates.

Buhrmester, D., & Furman, W. (1990). Perceptions of sibling relationships during middle childhood and adolescence. *Child Development, 61,* 1387–1398.

Cicirelli, V. G. (1982). Sibling influence throughout the lifespan. In M. E. Lamb & B. Sutton-Smith (Eds.), *Sibling relationships: Their nature and significance across the lifespan* (pp. 267–284). Hillsdale, NJ: Lawrence Erlbaum Associates.

Cicirelli, V. G. (1988). Interpersonal relationships among elderly siblings. In M. D. Kahn & K. G. Lewis (Eds.), *Siblings in therapy: Lifespan and clinical issues* (pp. 435–456). New York: W. W. Norton.

Dunn, J. (1985). *Brothers and sisters.* Cambridge, MA: Harvard University Press.

Kahn, M. D., & Bank, S. (1981). In pursuit of sisterhood: Adult siblings as a resource for combined individual and family therapy. *Family Process, 20,* 85–95.

Kahn, M. D., & Lewis, K. G. (Eds.). (1988). *Siblings in therapy: Lifespan and clinical issues.* New York: W. W. Norton.

Kihlstrom, J. F. (1987). The cognitive unconscious. *Science, 237,* 1445–1452.

Koch, H. (1960). The relation of certain formal attributes of siblings to attitudes held toward each other and toward their parents. *Monographs of the Society for Research in Child Development, 25*(4, Serial No. 78).

Minuchin, S. (1974). *Families and family therapy.* Cambridge, MA: Harvard University Press.

Neisser, U. (Ed.). (1982). *Memory observed: Remembering in natural contexts.* San Francisco: W. H. Freeman.

Rilke, R. M. (1962). *Letters to a young poet* (H. Norton, Trans.). New York: W. W. Norton. (Original work published 1934)

Salaman, E. (1982). A collection of moments. In U. Neisser (Ed.), *Memory observed: Remembering in natural contexts* (pp. 49–63). San Francisco: W. H. Freeman.

Sutton-Smith, B., & Rosenberg, B. G. (1970). *The sibling.* New York: Holt, Rinehart & Winston.

Yalom, I. (1989). *Love's executioner.* New York: Basic.

Epilogue

Frits Boer
University of Leiden

About two decades ago, *The Sibling,* by Sutton-Smith and Rosenberg (1970), was published. It provided an extensive review of contemporary sibling research in 1970. In the conclusion of the book we read:

> At base level, many sibling differences have been reliably established. While much of the literature makes contrasts only between the firstborn and the later born, either those contrasts or the more careful ones that take into account the position, sex and age spacing of the siblings yield many replicated differences in sibling status. (p. 156)

The Sibling was essentially a book about what it means *for an individual* to grow up in a certain position between brothers and sisters. In that sense it is a document of an approach that we now consider outdated, yet a reading of *The Sibling* shows that it was precisely this book that laid the groundwork for a new perspective on siblings.

About one decade ago, Sutton-Smith (with Lamb) edited the volume *Sibling Relationships: Their Nature and Significance Across the Lifespan* (1982). In the Epilogue to that book, Sutton-Smith wrote:

> Our intention here is to take a step beyond considering each individual only as he is characterized by a particular birth order or a particular sibling status in isolation from other relationships or as a product of the mother–child dyad alone. (p. 383)

153

As the titles of these two books clearly show, a shift in emphasis had taken place in the 1970s—from the *individual* to the *relationship*. Many of the contributors to the 1982 volume have shaped sibling research in the last decade and have contributed to what Dunn (this volume) can justifiably call a rapidly growing field.

Again one decade later, in the epilogue to *this* volume, it is possible to sum up many of the recent research findings by saying, "Things are not quite as simple as they appear to be." In almost every chapter of this book, the authors stress that what may be true sometimes is not necessarily true all the time. Perspectives drawn from family systems approaches and developmental theory show us the factors that are responsible for this approach. We are reminded of the influences of context, the interactions with other relationships, and the changes that result from children's development itself.

This awareness by researchers of the complexity of family interactions should appeal to clinicians, because it does justice to the reality of life as they meet it in the consulting room. On the other hand, it may come as a disappointment to clinicians that research does not provide them with more assistance in the categorization and treatment of sibling-related problems.

Another aspect of contemporary research, which should be of special interest to the clinician, is the emphasis on *meaning* (McHale & Harris, this volume). Whether it is referred to as "attribution," "perception," or "meaning," we notice a growing interest in the cognitive and emotional interpretation of reality by the child. Falbo (this volume) provides us with an illustration when she discusses the finding that although only children are not disadvantaged, many of them believe that their problems are caused by their lack of siblings. She proposes that the influence of certain beliefs (social norms, cultural wisdom) can override the influence of actual experience.

I wonder if the same does not apply to birth order in general. Even though there is very little empirical evidence of a strong effect of birth order on the adult personality (Ernst & Angst, 1983), the popular belief in its significance is as alive as ever. In fact, birth order could become a serious competitor of the horoscope. Could it be that the vague feeling that one's sibling relationship has been of emotional importance is expressed in terms of birth order? When people explain their experiences in terms of "because I was the youngest . . . ," the story they are telling is in fact an *individual*—not a birth order—story, but it is given meaning in family mythology by being attributed to birth order.

When clinicians deal with the meanings patients have attached to their experiences with siblings, it is often because these meanings have become a source of problems. For instance, when the meaning has become a stereotype, that can no longer be influenced by new experiences within the relationship, it is a "frozen image," to use Bank's term (this volume). It is the very essence of psychotherapy to reconnect these fossiled meanings to actual and/or past experience in order to allow them to become less distorted.

However, meaning is not just a matter of interest in the context of distortion and pathology. It can also be the factor that makes the difference between being vulnerable and being resilient in the face of stressful experiences. Werner and Smith's (1982) longitudinal study in Hawaii of children "at risk" showed that caretaking of siblings by teenage girls can contribute to their resilience when the need to take care of the siblings is felt as a responsibility in the positive sense of the word. Thus, if such an experience leads to a feeling of competence, it can have beneficial effects, whereas exactly the same experience with another meaning attached to it (e.g., "My youth was taken away from me"), may have a negative effect on future development.

Now that researchers are becoming more interested in the attributions and meanings children attach to their daily and intimate experiences, clinicians can be a source of help and inspiration in unraveling the dynamics of these processes. In addition, when clinicians start to bring siblings into the consulting room, either literally or metaphorically, this will not only do more justice to the experiential world of their clients, but it will also bring out new questions that will need to be dealt with in systematic research.

The aim of this book was to bring together clinicians and researchers who share an interest in siblings. It is obvious that they have a great deal to tell each other. Let us hope that the epilogue of a book that will appear a decade or so from now (perhaps in the year 2000) will show that the dialogue has continued.

REFERENCES

Ernst, C., & Angst, J. (1983). *Birth order.* New York: Springer.
Lamb, M. E., & Sutton-Smith, B. (Eds.). (1982). *Sibling relationships: Their nature and significance across the lifespan.* Hillsdale, NJ: Lawrence Erlbaum Associates.
Sutton-Smith, B., & Rosenberg, B. (1970). *The sibling.* New York: Holt, Rinehart & Winston.
Werner, E. E., & Smith, R. S. (1982). *Vulnerable, but invincible.* New York: McGraw-Hill.

Author Index

Numbers in *italics* denote pages with complete bibliographic information.

A

Ablard, K. E., 4, *16*
Aboud, F., 59, *69*
Abramovitch, R., 8, *14*, 22, *39*, 60, *69*, 145, *150*
Adler, T., 19, *39*, 43, *53*
American Psychiatric Association, 129, *138*
Angst, J., 74, *81*, 154, *155*
Ascherman, L. I., 115, *121*
Asher, S. R., 7, *14*, 22, *38*
Ausubel, D., 33, *38*
Azmitia, M., 11, *15*

B

Baker, L., 115, *122*
Baldwin, A. L., 44, *52*
Banister, J., 78, *81*
Bank, S., 5, *14*, 42, *52*, 61, *68*, 117, 118, *121*, 125, *138*, 140, 149, *150*, *151*, 154
Barbarin, O., 55, *68*
Barbour, L., 83, *99*
Barrett, M. J., 115, *123*
Barth, J. M., *16*

Bartko, W., 89, *99*
Beardsall, L., 9, 11, *14*
Becker, H., 111, *121*
Beckman, K. A., 115, *121*
Bedford, V. H., 13, *14*, 150, *151*
Begun, A., 90, 92, *98*
Beitel, A., *16*
Bell, N. W., 52, *54*
Belsky, J., 6, *17*, 22, *38*
Beresford, T. P., 115, *122*
Berndt, T. J., 8, *14*, 25, 32, *38*
Berry, C., 107, *107*
Beumont, P. J. V., 111, *123*
Bhavnagri, N., *16*
Biederman, J., *122*
Bigner, J. A., 21, *38*, 144, *151*
Billings, A. G., 12, *14*
Blake, J., 74, 75, 76, 77, 78, *81*
Blos, P., 27
Blyth, D. A., 28, *38*
Boeller, D., 118, *123*
Boer, F., 2, 3, 4, 5, 6, *14*, 43, 47, 48, *52*, *53*, 67, *69*, 145, *151*
Boll, E., 21, *38*, 41, *53*
Bond, L. A., 3, *16*
Bonenberger, R., 110, *121*
Bossard, J. H., 21, *38*, 41, *53*

Braiker, H. B., 33, *38*
Breese, F. H., 44, *52*
Brenner, A., 61, *69*
Breslau, N., 83, *98*
Bretherton, I., 7, *14*
Brody, G. H., 3, 4, 5, 9, *14, 16*, 21, *38*, 45, 50, 51, *53*, 87, *100*
Broman, S., 105, *107*
Bronfenbrenner, U., 57, *69*, 84, *98*
Brown, B. B., 22, *38*
Brown, G. W., 129, *138*
Brown, J., 2, 11, *14, 15*
Bruch, H., 110, *121*
Bryant, B. K., 5, *14*, 30, *38*, 42, 45, *53*, 55, 56, 57, 58, 60, 61, 62, 63, 64, *69*, 144, *151*
Buckley, S., 103, *107*
Buhrmester, D., 2, 3, *14*, 19, 20, 23, 24, 25, 26, 27, 29, 31, 34, 35, 37, *39, 40*, 43, 46, *53*, 90, *98*, 144, 145, *151*
Bulleit, T. N., 8, *14*
Burke, M., 3, *14*, 45, 50, *53*
Burks, V. M., *16*
Burns, G. L., 115, *121*
Burroughs, J., 112, 113, *123*
Byrne, E. A., 103, *107*

C

Cairns, N., 5, *14*
Caldwell, B., 89, *98*
Campbell, S., 117, *123*
Cantwell, D., 12, *15*
Carey, E. G., 71, *81*
Carson, J., *16*
Casper, R., 111, 112, 113, *121*
Caspi, A., 7, *14*
Chaloner, D. A., 115, *122*
Chesler, B. E., 111, *122*
Cicirelli, V. G., 36, *39*, 60, *69*, 150, *151*
Clark, G., 5, *14*
Clayton, B., 128, *138*
Cleveland, D., 87, 89, *98*
Cohen, J., 72, *81*
Cohen, S., 125, *138*
Coie, J. D., 7, *14*, 22, *38*
Collins, G. B., 113, *121*
Conners, C., 85, *99*
Cooper, C., 33, *39*
Cooper, C. R., 76, *81*

Corter, C., 8, *14*, 22, *39*, 60, *69*, 145, *150*
Crisp, A. H., 110, 111, *121, 122*
Crnic, K. A., 12, *14*
Crockenberg, S., 5, *14*, 42, 45, *53*, 56, 60, 61, 62, *69*
Crocker, A., 83, 94, *98*
Croll, E., 78, *81*
Cromer, C. C., 36, *39*
Cronbach, L. J., 129, *138*
Crouter, A., 84, 89, *98, 99*
Cummings, E. M., 136, *138*
Cunningham, C. C., 103, *107*

D

Dale, N., 11, *15*
Dally, P., 114, *121*
Daniels, D., 12, *14*, 43, 44, *53*
Davin, D., 78, *81*
Dawson, D. A., 75, 77, *81*
Delves, T., 128, *138*
DeMorris, K., 55, *69*
Devereux, E. C., 57, *69*
Dignon, A., 115, *122*
Dishion, T. J., 9, *14*
Doise, W., 10, *14*
Dolan, B. M., 110, 111, *122*
Dreikurs, R., 5, *14*
Dunn, J., 2, 3, 5, 6, 8, 9, 10, 11, *14, 15, 16*, 20, 30, *39, 40*, 42, 43, 44, 50, *53*, 56, 60, 61, *69*, 90, *98*, 146, 149, *151*, 154
Dunphy, D. C., 22, *39*
Dupont, A., 103, *107*
Dyson, L., 83, *98*

E

East, P. L., 8, *15*
Ebert, M., 110, 111, *123*
Edgerton, M., 85, 90, *99*
Eicher, S. A., 22, *38*
Elder, G. H., 7, *14*, 89, *98*
Elkind, D., 90, *98*
Ellis, S., 36, *39*
Engel, K., 114, *122*
Ernst, C., 74, *81*, 154, *155*
Evans, C., 110, *122*

F

Falbo, T., 72, 73, 74, 76, 79, 80, *81*, *82*, 154
Farber, B., 87, 89, 94, *98*
Feldman, R. A., 126, *138*
Feldman-Rotman, S., 117, *123*
Fenton, N., 71, *81*
Ferguson, T., 113, *121*
Fichter, M. M., 111, *122*
Fleeson, J., 7, *16*
Foa, E. B., 22, *39*
Foa, U., 22, *39*
Folkman, S., 64, *69*
Foster-Clark, F., 28, *38*
Freud, A., 33, *39*
Furman, W., 2, 3, *14*, 19, 20, 22, 23, 24, 26, 27, 29, 30, 31, 34, 35, 37, *39*, *40*, 43, 46, *53*, 90, *98*, 144, 145, *151*
Furstenberg, F., 43, *53*

G

Gamble, W. C., 5, 12, 13, *15*, 84, 85, 86, 88, 89, 90, 92, 93, 95, *98*, *99*
Garfinkel, P. E., 110, 111, *122*
Garmezy, N., 92, *99*
Garner, D. M., 110, 111, *122*
Gath, A., 83, 87, *99*, 102, 103, 104, 105, *108*
Gavin, L. A., 22, *39*
Gelles, R. J., 61, *69*
Gershoni, R., 28, *40*
Gibbs, E. D., 3, *16*
Gilbreth, F. B., 71, 76, *81*
Gilbreth, F. B., Jr., 71, 76, *81*
Gilbreth, L. M., 71, 76, *81*
Glass, G. V., 72, *81*
Gleser, G. C., 129, *138*
Goedhart, A. W., 4
Gold, D. T., 13, *14*, 150, *151*
Gottlieb, L. N., 10, *15*
Gottman, J. M., 28, *40*
Gowers, S., 110, *121*, *122*
Goyette, C., 85, *99*
Graham, P. J., 9, 10, *15*, *16*, 127, 128, 129, *138*
Grossman, F., 87, 89, *99*
Grotevant, H., 34, *39*
Gu, Q., *81*

Gumley, D., 103, 104, 105, *108*
Guze, S., 89, *98*

H

Hall, A., 110, 111, 112, 114, *122*
Hall, A. K., 115, *122*
Hall, G. S., 71, 74, 76, 79
Hall, L., 83, *99*
Hall, R. C. W., 115, *122*
Halmi, K., 110, *122*
Hardee-Cleveland, K., 78, *81*
Harding, B., 110, *121*
Harmatz, J. S., *122*
Harper, G. P., *122*
Harris, I. D., 43, *53*
Harris, V. S., 5, 13, 84, *99*, 154
Hart, R., 59, *69*
Harter, S., 85, *99*
Hartshorn, J., 110, *121*
Hartup, W. W., 10, *15*, 20, 22, 23, *39*
Hawker, F., 111, *122*
Hayes, A., 12, *16*
Herzog, D. B., 110, 111, *122*
Hesser, J., 11, *15*
Hetherington, E. M., 3, 5, *15*, 42, 45, 51, *53*, 126, 136, *138*
Hill, J. P., 33, 34, *39*
Hinde, R. A., 50, 51, *53*
Hoffman, J., 28, *40*
Höhne, D., 114, *122*
Holland, A. J., 111, *121*, *122*, *123*
Holmbeck, G. N., 33, 34, *39*
Holt, J., 59, *69*
Houseworth, S., *122*
Howard, K. J., 43, *53*
Howe, N., 6, 10, *15*
Howells, K., 115, *122*
Howes, C., 22, *39*
Hsu, L. K. G., 110, 111, *121*, *122*
Hunter, F. T., 32, *39*
Hunter, R., 118, *123*
Huston, T., 88, *99*

I

Ianotti, R. J., 136, *138*
Igoin-Apfelbaum, L., 110, *122*

J

Jacklin, C. N., 20, *40*
Jacobs, B. S., 44, *53*
Jacobs, C., 112, *123*
Janesz, J. W., 113, *121*
Jenkins, J. M., 3, 4, 10, *15*, 127, 130, 133, *138*
Jenne, W., 89, *98*
Ji, G., *81*
Jiao, S., *81*
Jing, Q., *81*
Johnson, C., 110, *122*
Jones, L., 19, *39*, 43, *53*
Jung, K. G., 126, *138*

K

Kadambari, S. R., 110, *122*
Kahn, M. D., 5, *14*, 42, *52*, 61, *68*, 117, 118, *121*, 125, *138*, 140, *151*
Kalhorn, J., 44, *52*
Kandel, D., 28, *39*
Kane, P., 78, *81*
Kelley, H. H., 22, 33, *38*, *40*
Kemper, K., *122*
Kendrick, C., 6, 10, *15*, 42, *53*, 60, 61, *69*
Kennedy, M., 111, *123*
Kennedy, W., 105, *107*
Kihlstrom, J. F., 141, *151*
Klosinski, G., 110, *121*
Koch, H., 144, *151*
Kog, E., 109, *123*
Kotz, M., 113, *121*
Kovacs, M., 85, *99*
Kramer, L., 8, 10, *15*

L

Lacey, J. H., 110, *122*
Lamb, M. E., 59, *69*, 153, *155*
Lampert, C., 112, *123*
Lansdown, R., 128, *138*
Lansky, S., 5, *14*
Lanthier, R., 59, *69*
Larson, R. W., 36, *40*
Lasko, J. K., 44, *53*
Lazarus, R., 64, *69*
Leconte, J. M., 12, *14*

Lesser, G., 28, *39*
Levine, M. P., 115, *123*
Levy, D. M., xiii, *xv*
Lewin, K., 97, *99*
Lewis, C., 110, *122*
Lewis, K. G., 116, *122*, 140, *151*
Lewis, L., 110, *122*
Lindon, J. A., 42, *53*
Litman, C., 60, *69*
Liu, Y., *81*
Lobato, D., 83, 84, *99*
Love, S., 110, *122*

M

Maccoby, E. E., 20, 38, *40*
MacDonald, K. B., *16*
MacKinnon, C. E., 3, *15*, *16*, 21, *38*, 126, *138*
MacKinnon, R., 21, *38*
Maloney, M. J., 112, *122*
Marquis, R., 117, *123*
McGaw, B., 72, *81*
McHale, S. M., 5, 12, 13, *15*, 84, 85, 86, 88, 89, 90, 92, 93, 94, 95, 96, *99*, *100*, 154
Mendelson, M. J., 10, *15*, 59, *69*
Messenger, K., 83, *98*
Mester, H., 110, *122*
Milgram, J. I., 43, *53*
Miller, C., 83, *99*
Miller, J. J., 12, *14*
Miller, N., 87, 89, *98*
Miller, N. B., 12, *15*
Minnett, A. M., 2, 8, *17*
Minuchin, P., xiii, *xvi*, 41, *53*
Minuchin, S., 21, *40*, 58, *69*, *122*, 149, *151*
Mobley, L. A., 10, *16*
Moldofsky, H., 111, *122*
Montemayor, R., 33, *38*, *40*
Moos, R. H., 12, *14*
Morgan, H. G., 114, *122*
Morrell, W., 112, 113, *123*
Moss, H. A., 44, *53*
Mugny, G., 10, *14*
Munn, P., 2, 3, 5, 9, 11, *15*, 57, *69*
Murray, R., 111, *122*
Mutcher, D., 89, *99*

N

Nanda, H., 129, *138*
Neisser, U., 141, *151*

Nettles, M., 44, *53*
Nezlek, J., 25, *40*
Nichols, P. L., 105, *107*
Noegel, R., 111, *122*

O

Ogle, P. A., 12, *16*, 83, 84, 90, *99*
Olson, D. H., 25, *40*
Oppenheimer, R., 115, *122*

P

Palmer, R. L., 115, *122*
Parke, R. D., 7, *16*
Parker, J., 28, *40*
Patterson, G. R., 9, *16*, 55, *69*
Pawletko, T., 84, 94, 95, 96, *99*
Peplau, A., 33, *40*
Pepler, D. J., 8, *14*, 22, 32, *38*, *39*, 60, *69*, 145, *150*
Perry, T. B., 32, *38*
Perry-Jenkins, M., 89, *99*
Petrie, S., 22, *38*
Petty, T. A., xiii, *xvi*
Piaget, J., 10, *16*, 23, *40*
Pierloot, R., 111, *123*
Plomin, R., 2, 3, 5, 9, *15*, *16*, 20, *40*, 43, 44, 50, *53*
Polit, D., 72, 73, 74, 76, 77, 80, *81*, *82*
Poston, D. L., 79, 80, *81*, *82*
Powell, T. P., 12, *16*, 83, 94, *99*
Purgold, J., 114, *122*
Putallaz, M., 7, *16*

Q

Quinton, D., 127, 129, *138*

R

Raffaelli, M., 7, *16*, 36, *40*
Rajaratnam, N., 129, *138*
Reis, H. T., 25, 28, *40*
Reynolds, C., 85, *99*
Richards, H. C., 114, *123*
Richman, N., 9, *16*, 127, 129, *138*
Richmond, B., 85, *99*

Rilke, R. M., 139, *151*
Ritvo, S., 42
Rivinus, T. M., 113, *122*
Robb, M. D., 44, *54*
Roberto, L. G., 115, *123*
Rodgers, R. R., 57, *69*
Rogoff, B., 36, *39*
Rosenberg, B. G., 145, *151*, 153, *155*
Rosenthal, R., 74, *82*
Rosman, B. L., 115, *122*
Ross, H. G., 43, *53*
Ross, H. S., 6, 10, *15*
Rowlands, O., 127, *138*
Rubin, D. B., 74, *82*
Russell, G. F. M., 111, *122*
Rutter, M., 92, *99*, 127, 129, *138*

S

Saba, G., 115, *123*
Sacks, B., 103, *107*
Safier, E. J., 115, *121*
Salaman, E., 142, *151*
Salkin, B., 112, 113, *123*
Salmond, C., 111, *122*
Salvador, M. A., 10, *16*
Samuels, H. R., 60, *69*
Sandler, I., 126, *138*
Santhouse, R., 111, *122*
Santrock, J. W., 2, 8, *17*
Savin-Williams, R. C., 22, *40*
Schachter, F. F., 5, 12, *16*, 117, *123*
Schaefer, E. S., 47, *53*, 85, 90, *99*
Schwartz, R. C., 115, *123*
Seligman, M., 93, *100*
Selvini Palazolli, M., 117, *123*
Senapati, R., 12, *16*
Sharabany, R., 28, *40*
Shatz, M., 2, *15*
Shaughnessy, P., 105, *107*
Shaver, P., 33, *40*
Shepard-Spiro, P., 112, *122*
Shepperdson, B., 103, *108*
Shore, E., 117, *123*
Sicotte, N., 111, *122*
Sights, J. R., 114, *123*
Simeonsson, R., 84, 90, *99*, *100*
Slim, E., 111, *122*
Sloan, J., 84, 90, *99*
Slomkowski, C., 6, 11, *15*, *16*

Sloper, P., 103, *107*
Smith, M. A., 4, 10, *15*, 127, 128, 130, 133, *138*
Smith, M. L., 72, *81*
Smith, R. S., 126, *138*, 155, *155*
Smith, S., 5, *14*
Smith, T. L., 71, *82*
Smolak, L., 115, *123*
Smollar, J., 23, 28, 33, *40*
Sourkes, B. M., 12, 13, *16*
Speckens, A., 43, *52*
Sroufe, L. A., 7, *16*
Stanhope, L., 8, *14*
Steinberg, L., 33, *40*
Steinmetz, S. K., 61, *69*, 94, *100*
Stevenson-Hinde, J., 50, 51, *53*
Stevenson, J. E., 9, *16*, 127, *138*
Stewart, R. B., 10, *16*, 60, *69*
Stierlin, H., 110, 114, 115, *123*
Stiffman, A. R., 126, *138*
Stocker, C., 2, 3, 5, 8, 9, *15*, *16*, 20, 31, *40*, 50, 51, *53*
Stone, R. K., 5, 12, *16*
Stoneman, Z., 3, 4, 5, *14*, *16*, 21, *38*, 45, 50, *53*, 87, *100*
Straus, M. A., 61, *69*
Strober, M., 112, 113, *123*
Stuckey, M., 110, *122*
Sullins, E., 115, *123*
Sullivan, H. S., 10, *16*, 23, 24, 28, *40*
Sutton-Smith, B., 145, *151*, 153, *155*
Svajian, N., 33, *38*

T

Tesla, C., 11, *15*
Tesser, A., 77, *82*
Teti, D. M., 3, 4, 10, *16*
Theander, S., 110, 112, *123*
Tice, L., 115, *122*
Tizard, J., 129, *138*
Tooley, K. M., 52, *54*, 61, *69*
Touyz, S., 111, *123*
Treasure, J., 111, *122*, *123*
Treffers, P. D. A., 4

U

U. S. Bureau of the Census, 77, *82*

Ulrich, R., 85, *99*

V

van Diest, C., 43, *52*
Van Tuyl, S. S., 10, *16*
Van Vreckem, E., 10, 11, 12
Van Krevelen, D. A. 72, *82*
Vandell, D. L., 2, 8, 10, *16*, *17*
Vandereycken, W., 10, 11, 12, 109, 111, 115, 116, *123*
Vanderlinden, J., 109, *123*
Vaugh, B. E., 44, *54*
Vauhkonen, K., 43, *54*
Veenhoven, R., 56, *69*
Verkuyten, M., 56, *69*
Vogel, E. F., 52, *54*
Volling, B., 6, *17*

W

Wagner, V. S., 118, *123*
Wang, S., *81*
Ward, M. J., 44, *54*
Waters, B. G. H., 111, 114, *123*
Weber, G., 110, 114, 115, *123*
Weiss, R. S., 23, 24, *40*
Weiss, S., 110, 111, *123*
Weitzman, M., 83, *98*
Welbourne, J., 114, *122*
Werner, E. E., 126, *138*, 155, *155*
Wheeler, L., 25, *40*
Whitmore, K., 129, *138*
Wills, T. A., 125, *138*
Winnicott, D. W., xiii, *xvi*
Wishart, J. G., 11, *17*
Wooley, B., 115, *122*

Y

Yalom, I., 142, *151*
Yin, H., *81*
Youngblade, L., 11, *15*
Youniss, J., 23, 28, 32, 33, *39*, *40*

Z

Zahn-Waxler, C., 136, *138*

Subject Index

A

Access, Sibling-, 145
Achievement motivation, 74
Adolescence, 24-37
Adult sibling relationship, 36, 150
Affective disorders. *See* Mood disorders
Age gap. *See* Age interval
Age interval, 3, 20
Aggression between siblings. *See* Sibling conflict
Anorexia nervosa. *See* Eating disorders
Anxiety of children with disabled siblings, 90
Attachment, 4, 7, 44
  theory of sibling-, 144-47
Attributions, 6, 13, 76-78, 95-97, 154-55

B

Beijing survey, 79
Birth of sibling, 6, 10
Birth order, 3, 20, 25, 29, 31, 34, 71, 73, 110, 153, 154
  and personality traits, 73
  and social traits, 73
Bulimia nervosa. *See* Eating disorders

C

California Psychological Inventory (CPI), 113
Cambridge study, 2, 42, 61, 146
Caregiving. *See* Sibling caretaking
Child's Report of Parental Behavior Inventory (CRPBI), 47
Childhood Depression Inventory, 85
Compensatory function of siblings, 5, 6, 41-43, 50-51, 61, 67, 125, 137
Competition. *See* Sibling rivalry
Conflict. *See* Sibling conflict
Conners' Parent Rating Scale, 85
Coping with stress, 64, 92, 125, 155
  strategies used, 64, 93
Cornell Parent Behavior Inventory, 57

D

Daily activities of siblings, 86-90
Deidentification, 117, 118
Depression. *See* Mood disorders
Developmental course of sibling relationship, 1-3, 27
Differential treatment, 5, 9, 43, 45-46, 52, 84
  dimensions of, 94

163

Differential treatment *(Continued)*
  meanings attributed to, 95–96, 97
  of disabled and nondisabled children,
    93–96
Disabled siblings, 5, 11–13, 83–98. *See also*
    Mentally retarded siblings
  and differential treatment, 93–96
Disengaged family systems, 58
Disharmonious homes. *See* Marital conflict
Divorce, 3, 5, 126, 136
Down Syndrome, 101, 102, 104, 105

E

Eating disorders, 10, 109–121
  and behavioral and mental disorders of
    siblings, 112–13
  and personality of siblings, 113–14
  siblings of patients with, 111–12
Eating Attitudes Test, 112
Eating Disorder Inventory, 112
Egalitarianism, 2, 23, 89
Enmeshed family systems, 58

F

Family size, 71, 73, 110
  and educational attainment, 75
  and personality traits, 73
  and social traits, 73
Family systems theory. *See* Systems theory
Fathers, 22, 48, 55, 66, 67, 133
Favoritism. *See* Parental favoritism
Fels Parent Behavior Rating Scales, 44
Fragile X Syndrome, 105
Friends, 7–8. *See also* Peer relationships

G

Gender of siblings, 3, 20, 25, 28, 29, 31,
    33, 88, 89
Genetic counseling of siblings, 106–7

I

Intimate conversations of children, 62, 64

L

Large families, 21
Leiden Parental Care Questionnaire (LPCQ), 47
*Leiden Sibling Relationship Questionnaire
    (LSRQ)*, 46, 51
Life events, 3

M

Marital conflict and sibling relationship, 4,
    10, 127, 129–33
Meanings. *See* Attributions
Mentally retarded siblings, 101–7
Meta-analysis of only child studies, 72, 74
Middle childhood, 2, 46, 55–68, 85, 128
Mood disorders
  siblings of patients with eating disorders,
    113
*Multidimensional Personality Questionnaire,
    (MPQ)*, 113

N

Neglect. *See* Parent–child relationship, quali-
    ty of
Neighborhood walk, 64
Network of Relationships Inventory (NRI), 24, 31

O

One-child family. *See* Only child
Only child, 71–81, 110, 154
  parent–child relationships, 75–76
  social beliefs, 76–78
  China's policy, 78–81
  rural or urban environment, 80–81

P

Parent–child relationship
  and sibling relationship, 4, 6, 41–52, 48,
    57–68, 129–33
  only child, 75–76
  quality of, 42, 49, 60, 66, 141, 144–47
Parental favoritism, 41, 43, 47, 48, 49–50,
    51–52, 136. *See also* Differential
    treatment

Parental neglect. *See* Parent–child relationship, quality of
Parental partiality. *See* Parental favoritism
Parental quarreling and siblings, 133
Parental unavailability. *See* Parent–child relationship, quality of
Parentified sibling, 117
Parenting. *See* Parent–child relationship
Parenting style, 49
Peer relationships, 7–8, 19–38
Perceived Competence Scale, 85
Perception
    of parental care, 48, 49
    of sibling relationship, 48, 49
Perspective taking, 11
Phone interviews. *See* Telephone interviews
Placement away from home, 105
Power in sibling relationship, 2, 23
Preferential treatment. *See* Differential treatment
Presence of family member affecting sibling interaction, 22, 60
Private discussions. *See* Intimate conversations
Protective influence of siblings, 125–37. *See also* Coping with stress; Compensatory function of siblings
Psychotherapy of sibling relationships, 144, 147–50, 154. *See also* Therapist, sibling as

R

Relationship structure, 19–23
Relationship Satisfaction Questionnaire, 85
Rett Syndrome, 102
Revised Children's Manifest Anxiety Scale, 85
Rivalry. *See* Sibling rivalry

S

Scapegoating, 52
Self-esteem, 9, 74, 77
    of children with disabled siblings, 90
Separation and individuation process in adolescence, 27, 34
Sex of siblings. *See* Gender of siblings
Sibling abuse, 61, 141
Sibling access, 145
Sibling caregiving. *See* Sibling caretaking
Sibling caretaking, 36, 55–68, 87, 89
Sibling conflict, 8, 9, 11, 34, 36, 90–93
    and friends, 7
    parental involvement, 5

Sibling incest, 115
Sibling relationship
    and friendship, 7–8, 19–38
    and marital conflict, 4, 10, 129–33
    and parent–child relationship, 4, 6, 41–52, 48, 57–68, 129–33
    and parental quarreling, 133
    and peer relationships, 7–8, 19–38
    children's and mother's ratings of, 90–92
    individual differences, 3
Sibling rivalry, 47
    and eating disorders, 114, 117
    mentally retarded child and normal child, 103–4
Sibling Inventory of Behavior, 85, 91
Sibling Relationship Questionnaire (SRQ), 30, 34, 46, 90
Social address variables, 84
Social comparison, 9–10
Social provisions and needs, taxonomy of, 24
Sociocognitive development
    siblings and, 10–11
Socioemotional need fulfillment, 23–29
Stability in development, 2
Stress. *See* Coping with stress
Support, sibling as source of, 10, 11
Systems theory, 21, 58

T

Telephone interviews, 85–86
Temperament, 3, 4, 31, 51
Therapist, sibling as, 10, 12, 61, 115–21
Triangular dynamics, 119–21
Twin studies of eating disorders, 111
Twinning, 118

U

Unconscious memory, 141, 142
Unique perception of relationship, 49

V

Vacuum of parental care, 141, 145, 146. *See also* Parent–child relationship, quality of

W

Within-family differences, 9

DATE DUE

OCT 4 '97		
OCT 2 8 1998		
MR 19 '99		
APR 3 2002		
AG 21 '03		
OC 24 '05		
AP 27 '08		